James Phillip Lilley

The Principles of Protestantism

An Examination of the Doctrinal Differences between the Protestant Churches and

the Church of Rome

James Phillip Lilley

The Principles of Protestantism
An Examination of the Doctrinal Differences between the Protestant Churches and the Church of Rome

ISBN/EAN: 9783744778107

Printed in Europe, USA, Canada, Australia, Japan

Cover: Foto ©Lupo / pixelio.de

More available books at **www.hansebooks.com**

OF

PROTESTANTISM

*AN EXAMINATION OF THE DOCTRINAL
DIFFERENCES BETWEEN THE PROTESTANT
CHURCHES AND THE CHURCH OF ROME*

BY

REV. J. P. LILLEY, M.A.
ARBROATH

EDINBURGH
T. & T. CLARK, 38 GEORGE STREET
1898

PRINTED BY MORRISON AND GIBB LIMITED,

FOR

T. & T. CLARK, EDINBURGH.

LONDON : SIMPKIN, MARSHALL, HAMILTON, KENT, AND CO. LIMITED.
NEW YORK : CHARLES SCRIBNER'S SONS.
TORONTO : FLEMING H. REVELL COMPANY.

PREFACE

THIS handbook has been prepared as a companion to Dr. T. M. Lindsay's on *The Reformation*. The aim of that volume was to set forth the historic origin of Protestantism in Europe: the present is designed to exhibit its leading doctrines as they took shape in the Reformed Churches in opposition to those of the Church of Rome.

Strictly speaking, Protestantism has but one great principle, namely, the right of direct access to God through Christ His Son. This is its ultimate idea. But when it came into conflict with the views of the Roman theologians, like all fundamental ideas, it threw out branches in various directions; so that, as I have tried to show in the Introduction, it may now be said with truth that Protestantism has three master principles, leading to differences from the Church of Rome on the whole evangelic method of salvation, the word of God and the fellowship of believers.

In endeavouring to expound and illustrate these contrasts, I have, of course, used the authoritative sources of information on both sides.

The Decrees and Canons of the Council of Trent, its Catechism and the Creed of Pope Pius IV. are still acknowledged by the Church of Rome as her leading statements of doctrine. Constant reference has been made to these authorities. But it has also been found necessary for a complete view of her teaching to show how these are reflected in the expositions of eminent divines, like Bellarmin, Möhler, Perrone, and Newman. For this same purpose, frequent use has been made of one of the most recent and candid expositions of Roman Catholic doctrine issued in this country, namely, *The Outlines of Dogmatic Theology*, by Father S. J. Hunter, the present Professor of Theology in Stonyhurst College (Stonyhurst Series, 3 vols., Longmans & Co., 1895-96).

The chief authorities on the Protestant side are the Confessions of the Reformed Churches; and of these, the Augsburg Confession, the Westminster Standards, and the Articles of the Church of England, have been most frequently referred to. But particular doctrines have been illustrated from the writings, not only of the Reformers, Luther, Melanchthon, Zwingli and Calvin, but also of prominent theologians of modern times. As a former student of the New College, Edinburgh, I could not avoid attaching great weight to the discussions of Protestant doctrine found in the works of Principal W. Cunningham. He is, perhaps, the only Scottish theologian that ever thoroughly mastered this field. I can conceive nothing more helpful to students than a thorough acquaintance with his supremely able lectures.

The limits of a handbook did not permit me to give all the references to other literature I have used. Special acknowledgment will be found in connection with quotations. For knowledge of the most recent German literature on Protestantism I have to express my indebtedness to Professor Carl Mirbt of Marburg. His own *Quellen zur Geschichte des Papsttums* (Leipzig, 1895) has been constantly in my hands. It gives the original form of the Decrees and Canons of Trent, with much additional matter, and is invaluable to every student of the subject.

The method and spirit of the exposition will, I trust, be beneficial to teachers and students. It cannot be said that there is any lack of manuals on the Protestant controversy. The chief defect in them, so far as my judgment goes, is that they are for the most part merely negative or destructive in their aim. The majority of them seem designed simply to "expose" the errors of Romanism without exhibiting in any adequate fashion the corresponding truth. It is an additional fault that this work is often done in a spirit of narrowness and bitterness that does not appear perfectly consistent with the ends of Christian controversy. In the present manual, I have sought to avoid these snares. While indicating plainly enough the origin and progress of what we believe to be the errors of the Church of Rome, I have endeavoured to make these the starting-point of a careful and complete statement of the evangelical Protestant position and the grounds on which it is based. I have also tried to couch the exposition in language that shall approve itself as alike accurate, impartial and temperate. If this method does not actually convert our opponents, it may at least conciliate them to give our Protestant Evangel a more patient and charitable hearing. With this result at the outset we may well be content. The truth will do the rest.

J. P. L.

ARBROATH, *June* 1898.

CONTENTS

INTRODUCTION

THE ORIGIN AND NATURE OF PROTESTANTISM . . . 1

PART I

THE GOSPEL OF PROTESTANTISM

DIFFERENCES CONCERNING THE EVANGELIC APPLICATION OF THE TRUTH—THE MATERIAL PRINCIPLE

CHAP.
I. THE STATE OF MAN AS CREATED . . . 11
II. THE CONDITION OF MAN AS FALLEN—ORIGINAL SIN . 17
III. THE INABILITY OF MAN THROUGH SIN—THE STATE OF THE UNREGENERATE 24
IV. SIN IN RELATION TO DIVINE PROVIDENCE . 32
V. THE METHOD OF CHRISTIANITY—REPENTANCE AND FAITH 38
VI. THE PRIMARY BLESSINGS OF THE GOSPEL—FORGIVENESS—JUSTIFICATION 45
VII. REGENERATION—THE STATE OF THE REGENERATE—POST-BAPTISMAL SIN 57
VIII. THE HIGHER BLESSINGS OF THE GOSPEL . 67
IX. GOOD WORKS 74
X. THE STATE AFTER DEATH—PURGATORY . 84

PART II

THE CHARTER OF PROTESTANTISM

DIFFERENCES CONCERNING THE SOURCE OF TRUTH—THE FORMAL PRINCIPLE

CHAP.		PAGE
I.	THE CONTENTS AND USE OF THE SCRIPTURES	95
II.	THE RESPONSIBILITY OF THE INDIVIDUAL CHRISTIAN TOWARDS THE SCRIPTURES	102
III.	THE SOURCE OF CERTAINTY RESPECTING THE AUTHORITY OF THE SCRIPTURES	111
IV.	THE PERSPICUITY OF SCRIPTURE	119
V.	THE PERFECTION OF SCRIPTURE	127
VI.	THE PERFECTION OF SCRIPTURE—TRADITION (*continuation*)	138
VII.	THE DOCTRINAL STUDY OF SCRIPTURE—THE THEORY OF DEVELOPMENT	145

PART III

THE POLITY OF PROTESTANTISM

DIFFERENCES CONCERNING THE ECCLESIASTICAL EMBODIMENT OF THE TRUTH—THE SOCIAL PRINCIPLE

I.	THE NATURE OF THE CHURCH	159
II.	THE MINISTRY OF THE CHURCH	170
III.	THE WORSHIP OF THE CHURCH	178
IV.	THE SACRAMENTS OF THE CHURCH—THEIR NATURE AND NUMBER	187
V.	THE SACRAMENTS OF THE CHURCH—BAPTISM	195
VI.	THE SACRAMENTS OF THE CHURCH—THE LORD'S SUPPER—THE MASS	200
VII.	THE CONSTITUTION OF THE CHURCH—THE ROMAN PRIMACY	210
VIII.	THE TEACHING OF THE CHURCH—PAPAL INFALLIBILITY	219
IX.	THE AUTHORITY OF THE CHURCH—PAPAL SUPREMACY	228
X.	THE CHURCH IN RELATION TO THE UNSEEN WORLD	237

THE
PRINCIPLES OF PROTESTANTISM

INTRODUCTION

THE ORIGIN AND NATURE OF PROTESTANTISM

IT would be going in the face of historic fact to deny in any way the strong influence exercised on the Reformation of the sixteenth century by the intellectual and social forces of the time. There was then a great awakening in the mental life and political activity of Europe; and the movement initiated by Luther was largely moulded by it. But however much the Reformation may have been aided by these factors, its primary and dominant cause is to be found in the new religious convictions which then began to take such deep root in the hearts of men. It was above all a revival of spiritual life. The longing for a closer fellowship with God and a more assured peace that manifested itself with such intensity in the spiritual conflicts of Luther was present to a greater or less degree in thousands of souls all around him. Men began to see that the essence of religion lay in the soul's sense of obligation to God, not in mere compliance with the institutions of the Church. This feeling in turn brought upon the conscience a deeper conviction of the guilt and bondage of sin. Luther and his friends discovered what they believed to be the divinely-ordained method of becoming free from this awful burden, and embracing it themselves, they proclaimed it far and wide. By the practice of the mediæval Church, Christianity had been reduced to the level of a barren law which left the soul under the yoke of a routine of external duties and thereby in bondage to the priesthood. Against this subjection Luther protested as an unjustifiable "Babylonish captivity." To him, as to its first preachers, Christianity was essentially a manifestation of the sovereign grace of God, drawing sinners into direct communion with Him; and the Christian life was a life not of servitude but of freedom, not of gloom but of gladness, not of weakness but of power. It was the cordial acceptance of this new way of entering into close and loving fellowship with God that gave rise to the outburst of spiritual energy that carried forward the Reformation. Amid all the moral and political forces that came to its aid, it was a movement religious alike in its essence, its operation and its ultimate fruits. Even a historian so unsympathetic as Hallam is forced to make this admission : " Every solution of the conduct of the Reformers is nugatory except one, that they were absorbed by the conviction that they were fighting the battle of God." [1]

If religious conviction was the distinctive feature of the Reformation in its origin, it was no less manifestly the supreme characteristic of all its subsequent course. Throughout the whole conflict, it was the sense of obligation to God as the only source of salvation that enabled the Reformers to withstand the temptations and threats of the Church of Rome. To see how the Reformation assumed the character of Protestantism, however, as well as to understand the real nature of Protestantism itself, it is necessary for us to recall the first occasions on which the adherents of the new revival came into direct contact with the Papacy and the Empire.

The first of these was the Diet of Worms held in 1521. Here it was Luther alone that was the spokesman of the Reformation, though he had the manifest sympathy and protection of not a few of the princes. The attitude he took up and maintained so bravely is familiar to all. The direct obligation of man to God constrained him to appeal to the Scriptures as the only source of a decisive judgment on the question he had raised. "Unless therefore I am convinced by the testimony of Scripture or by the clearest reasoning, —unless I am persuaded by means of the passages I have quoted,— and unless they thus render my conscience bound by the word of God, I cannot and I will not retract, for it is unsafe for a Christian to speak against his conscience. Here I stand, I can do no other : May God help me. Amen." [2] The edict which the Emperor signed and caused to be promulgated is also well known. "We have therefore dismissed from our presence this Luther whom all pious and sensible men deem a madman or one possessed by the devil ; and we enjoin that, on the expiration of his safe conduct, immediate recourse be had to effectual measures to check his furious rage. . . . And if any person, whatever be his dignity, should dare to act in contradiction to the decree of our imperial majesty, we order him to be placed under the ban of the Empire." [3] A decree like this plainly meant that the adherents of the Reformation were either to submit to the Pope or suffer the extreme form of persecution.

The next occasion was the Diet of Speier held in 1526. The professed intention of this meeting was to take steps for executing the Edict of Worms, which had been nullified by the protection

---

[1] *Literature of Europe*, etc. vol. ii. p. 419.
[2] D'Aubigné, vol. ii. p. 249.   [3] D'Aubigné, *ut sup.* p. 274.

extended to Luther in the Wartburg. Ferdinand of Austria, the brother of the Emperor Charles, then on his way to Rome to confer with Pope Clement VII., brought with him to the Diet imperial instructions reaffirming the Edict of Worms and ordering all the subjects of the Empire to carry it out. The knowledge of this fact imparted great boldness to the Papists and caused dismay to the princes and other adherents of the evangelical party. The political complications of the period, however, turned to their deliverance. Forming an alliance with France, Clement opposed the Emperor and took the field against him This convinced Charles that he might yet need the help of the evangelical princes and led him to relax his severity against the cause they represented. The result was that instead of being repressed, as the priests so earnestly desired, liberty of conscience was allowed in all the States that had already become favourable to the Reformation. Each State was to behave within its own domain so as to be able to render an account to God and the Emperor. Luther thought little of this issue ; but the historians of the Reformation all magnify it as a turning-point in the movement. "The Diet of 1526," says d'Aubigné, "forms an important epoch of history. . . . In this single step there is a complete victory : the cause of the reform is won."

After a peaceful period of three years, during which the evangelical movement strengthened and extended its grasp of Germany and neighbouring countries, the Reformers were called on to face another Diet which was convened again at Speier in 1529. It was a time of great anxiety for the Lutheran princes and their friends. For the Emperor and the Pope had once more joined hands in friendship and the supreme condition of its maintenance was that the Reformation in Germany should be suppressed without delay. To this aim, Ferdinand, who once more presided at the Diet, addressed himself at once. At an early meeting, the imperial commissioners announced that the last Edict of Speier having been the cause of much disorder, the Emperor had in the exercise of his sovereign authority resolved to annul it. This decree set the Papists free to demand the execution of the Edict of Worms. The evangelical members of the Diet on the other hand declared for the maintenance of the last Edict of Speier. It had been legally established in the country and not even the Emperor had the power to set it aside. Feeling the force of this contention, a majority of the Diet passed a resolution declaring that, while those who had embraced the Reformation might continue in the exercise of their freedom, no further attempts at extending the movement should be made either in those States where it had not been already introduced or in other places where it had already taken root. It was also stipulated that the jurisdiction of the Romish hierarchy was still everywhere to be acknowledged.

If the evangelical princes and other deputies had been in any degree under the influence of merely selfish motives, this compromise might have satisfied them. As it was, they were too loyal to the principles of civil and religious liberty they had espoused, ever to dream of submitting to it. They clearly foresaw that the only issue of such an agreement would be to put an effectual arrest on the whole work of Reformation and subject all its adherents to trouble and defeat. After various attempts at negotiation had proved fruitless, these deputies resolved to lay on the table of the Diet an appeal from the Emperor and the papal authorities to the heavenly jurisdiction of the Lord Jesus Christ.

Of this memorable Protest, the following are the essential statements :—

"We have heard and learnt that the decisions of the last Diet concerning our holy Christian faith are to be repealed, and that it is proposed to substitute for them certain restrictive and onerous resolutions. . . . We cannot consent to its repeal. . . . Because it concerns the glory of God and the salvation of our souls, and that in such matters we ought to have regard above all, to the commandment of God who is King of kings and Lord of lords ; each of us rendering Him account for himself, without caring the least in the world about majority or minority.

"What ! we ratify this edict ! We assert that when Almighty God calls a man to His knowledge, this man cannot, however, receive the knowledge of God ! Oh, of what deadly backslidings should we not thus become the accomplices, not only among our own subjects, but also among yours.

"Moreover the new edict declaring the ministers shall preach the gospel, explaining it according to the writings accepted by the holy Christian Church, we think that for this regulation to have any value, we should first agree on what is meant by the true and holy Church. Now, seeing that there is great diversity of opinion in this respect ; that there is no sure doctrine but such as is conformable to the word of God ; that the Lord forbids the teaching of any other doctrine ; that each text of the Holy Scriptures ought to be explained by other and clearer texts ; that this holy Book is in all things necessary for the Christian, easy of understanding and calculated to scatter the darkness : we are resolved, with the grace of God, to maintain the pure and exclusive preaching of His only word, such as it is contained in the Biblical books of the Old and New Testament, without adding anything thereto that may be contrary to it. This word is the only truth ; it is the sure rule of all doctrine and of all life and can never fail or deceive us. He who builds on this foundation shall stand against all the powers of hell, whilst all the human vanities that are set up against it shall fall before the face of God.

"For these reasons, we earnestly entreat you to weigh carefully our grievances and our motives. If you do not yield to our request, we PROTEST by these presents before God, our only Creator, Preserver, Redeemer, and Saviour, who will one day be our Judge, as well as before all men and all creatures, that we, for us and for our people, neither consent nor adhere in any manner whatsoever to the proposed decree in anything that is contrary to God, to His holy word, to our right conscience, to the salvation of our souls, and to the last decree of Speier."[1]

After formally presenting this declaration and appeal, the evangelical princes and their adherents had it recorded in strictly legal form. The following significant explanation of their action was also then given: "Since there is a natural communion between all men, and since even persons condemned to death are permitted to unite and appeal against their condemnation; how much more are we, who are members of the same spiritual body, the Church of the Son of God, children of the same heavenly Father, and consequently brothers in the Spirit, authorised to unite, when our salvation and eternal condemnation are concerned."[2]

It is well-nigh impossible to overrate the importance of this action on the part of the princes and the deputies of the fourteen evangelical cities that joined their side. The fact in connection with it best remembered by the ordinary student of history is that it gave to the Reformers the new name of Protestants, by which they were thenceforth to be known. In reality, this is the most superficial result of their procedure. The event itself was one of momentous interest and was fraught with issues of more transcendent importance than any of the actors in it or their friends could possibly see at the time. Melanchthon indeed said: "It is a great event that has just taken place at Speier"; but this was chiefly because it seemed to him fraught with "dangers, not only to the Empire, but to religion itself." Luther on the other hand fairly underestimated it. "The Diet," said he, "has come to an end almost without results." Modern historians have taken a quite different view, and one that is based on fact. The presentation of this noble document at Speier was nothing short of the formal establishment of Protestantism in Germany. Up to that crisis, the Reformation was largely the expression of the convictions of individuals, especially Luther. But at Speier, even in Luther's absence, there is seen a body of believing men united in cherishing the same evangelical truths and enabled to publish them in a definite form in the face of all Christendom. They are not the representatives of a political party battling for a new policy, but living members of the Church of Christ cleaving to and contending for the faith once delivered to the saints. Who shall count it an exaggeration to say that the statement drawn up in the little room of the humble pastor of St. John's at Speier is but a reproduction, in a form demanded by the sixteenth century, of the very convictions that had been burned into the heart of the apostles by the Spirit of God in the upper chamber at Jerusalem? The very life and progress of Christianity at that time depended on the action of the evangelical princes and their friends. It stands to their everlasting honour that they listened to the voice of God and their own conscience and defied the threats of men.

[1] D'Aubigné, vol. iv. pp. 58-60.   [2] D'Aubigné, *ut sup.* p. 65.

In this way also we are now in a position to appreciate the real nature of Protestantism. A historian of the Romish Church has no better description of Protestants than, "enemies of the Pope and Cæsar."[1] Some modern writers are perhaps less disrespectful but hardly more judicious when they represent Protestantism as essentially a negation, or as the mere watchword of a sect. Such a view rests on the mere literal significance of the word itself and takes no account of the richer meaning breathed into it by the principles of the document in which it is found and the whole attitude it exhibits. The description is utterly inadequate. The Protestant Reformers had indeed to face the task of combating the errors of the Papacy. But this was only a part, and by no means the largest part of their conflict. The heaviest side of their responsibility lay behind and beneath all controversy, in the appropriation of the saving truth of the Scriptures. They would never have been able to undertake the work of refuting error, and far less have been sustained in the performance of it, if they had not entered on the possession of a new heritage of positive truth drawn from the word of God. The essence of Protestantism therefore lies in the fact that it is a reaffirmation in forms called forth by the errors of the Romish Church of all the great evangelical principles set forth by Christ and His apostles. The burden of its message is the sovereign grace of God. Viewed in its fulness, Protestantism is the reassertion of the power of apostolic Christianity, the formative principle of evangelical religion acting on the conscience, and mind and heart of men. It is the saving method of the Spirit of God, exhibited gradually from the beginning of redemption, manifested in the life and teaching of Christ, elaborated by Him more fully in the work of His apostles and now by their writings committed to the Church to be maintained by her ministers and members in every age, in conflict with the spirit of the world.

Accordingly no greater mistake could be made than to suppose that the advent of Protestantism was coincident with the use of the name. As there were reformers before the Reformation, so there were Christian Protestants in the Church many centuries before the Diet of Speier. That famous meeting was only a vantage ground on which was displayed the effulgence of a light that had been burning more or less brightly in Christendom ever since the close of the apostolic age. Hence also Protestantism is a principle that has yet a great future before it. Bound up with the very life of the Church, itself constituting the very element of the whole Christian enterprise in the world, Protestantism must abide and grow in the world till the consummation of all things under the sway of Christ. The Reformation of the Church is not yet completed; and evangelical Protestantism is yet to exhibit grander issues than the Christian society or the nations of the world have ever seen.

If this goal is to be obtained, however, it will only be by a wider

[1] Cardinal Pallavicini.

diffusion of the great principles which this movement involves. Moreover these truths must be still more carefully discriminated from the errors of the Papacy. Much help was afforded by the controversies into which the Reformers were drawn by the antagonism of Rome and the efforts frequently made for conciliation as well as by the doctrinal discussions amongst themselves conducted by Protestant theologians in different countries. The Confessions of the Reformation are an invaluable repository of evangelic truth for the Church in all time. But the "Decrees" put forth by the Council of Trent have long shown that all hope of reunion on the basis of doctrine must be for ever abandoned. The fact that this Symbol, with its Catechism and Creed, is not only adhered to without change to the present day but has been actually developed in directions still more characteristic of the peculiar system of the Papacy, lays upon the Protestant Churches the necessity of continually instructing the people of their communion in the great truths which Rome ignores and the errors she never ceases to propagate.

It is to this task that the following chapters are to be devoted. Examining carefully the terms of the Protest handed in at Speier, we find three main elements in its doctrinal position. There is a new recognition of the way in which men are to enter on the blessings of the gospel; a new conception of the Scriptures as the source of divine teaching; and a new view of the life and polity of the society of believers. We propose giving an exposition of the main differences betwixt the leading Protestant Churches and the Church of Rome on these lines. In which order we take these divisions is not of so much consequence. Some theologians prefer to start with the convictions entertained on the Scriptures, as Neander has done: others, like Hase, with the views held on the Church: others, like Nitzsch and F. C. Baur, with the truths that directly affect Christian experience, in this following the example of their great opponent J. A. Möhler. We prefer the last method as the most suitable for a systematic exposition and best fitted to exhibit the cumulative force of the Protestant argument.

Beginning then with the differences connected with the evangelic application of the truth,—the Gospel of Protestantism,—we shall compare in detail the teaching of the Churches on such points as the primitive state of man, the effects of the Fall, and then the requisitions and blessings of the gospel from repentance and faith to justification sanctification and entrance into heaven. In this way we shall see the operation of what has been called the *material* or *life* principle of Protestantism (*principium essendi*) from the fact that it asserts and vindicates the right of direct access to the grace of God in His Son Jesus Christ.

Taking next the differences on the Scriptures,—the source of truth, the charter of Protestantism,—we shall study the antagonistic views held of the contents and use of the Bible, the right of private judgment, the perspicuity, authority, and sufficiency of Scripture, and the Romish theory of the development of doctrine. This course will bring before us the *formal* or *knowledge* principle of Protestantism (*principium cognoscendi*) which derives its name from the fact that it directs us to the written word of God as the only source and standard of all saving truth.

Last of all, we shall take up the differences connected with the social and ecclesiastical embodiment of the truth—the Polity of Protestantism. Here the main facts concerning the nature of the Church, the origin and functions of the ministry, the methods of worship, the constitution, authority, and heavenly relations of the Church will find a fitting place and close our study of the radical divergence of the two systems.

The dominant feature of this last section may be called the *social* principle of Protestantism.[1] Though the leading truths that give expression to it have always been more or less insisted on, it has, unhappily, never received the full recognition it demands. Even so eminent a defender of Protestantism as Dorner has not exhibited the immense influence wielded by the idea of the new Christian fellowship which the Protestant evangel disseminated amongst the people. In the section of his great work on the *History of Protestant Theology*, where, if anywhere, this truth should have been presented, —namely, "*The exhibition of the Evangelical principle in the formation of the Church*,"[2]—it is only barely alluded to. Some recent theologians, however, have begun to see that the first two principles are really stript of their force unless they are placed in vital union with the new social life in the Church to which they give rise. Amongst these, Schaff[3] and Ritschl deserve special mention. The latter truly says: "It is perfectly unintelligible to me how a theologian, who is avowedly defending Church Protestantism and striving against any degradation of the Church to the level of a school, such as is carried out by the extreme left and the extreme right, can fail to comprehend, in his view of the leading principles of the Reformation, the evangelical idea of the Church. For that which is to be the chief thing in the final result must also be thought of in the first principle; otherwise it cannot be recognised as an end, but, at most, as only an incidental phenomenon."[4] It is hoped that the following pages may be helpful in furthering this view. By showing how its gospel led to the recognition of the supreme authority of Scripture and the word of God received in its fulness influenced in turn the whole life and worship and activity of the Church, Protestantism must commend itself as characterised at once by simplicity, unity, and power.

---

[1] Shall we call it *principium communicandi*?
[2] Bk. I. div. ii. ch. iv. (Clark) p. 220.
[3] Schaff, Herzog's *Encyclopædia*, art. "Protestantism."
[4] *History of the Christian Doctrine of Justification*, etc. (Edin.) p. 158.

PART I

THE GOSPEL OF PROTESTANTISM

DIFFERENCES CONCERNING THE EVANGELIC APPLI-
CATION OF THE TRUTH — THE MATERIAL
PRINCIPLE

CHAP.		PAGE
I.	The State of Man as Created	11
II.	The Condition of Man as Fallen—Original Sin	17
III.	The Inability of Man through Sin—The State of the Unregenerate	24
IV.	Sin in Relation to Divine Providence	32
V.	The Method of Christianity—Repentance and Faith	38
VI.	The Primary Blessings of the Gospel—Forgiveness—Justification	45
VII.	Regeneration—The State of the Regenerate—Post-Baptismal Sin	57
VIII.	The Higher Blessings of the Gospel	67
IX.	Good Works	74
X.	The State after Death—Purgatory	84

CHAPTER I

THE STATE OF MAN AS CREATED

AT first sight it may appear strange that we should begin our exposition of the differences betwixt Romanism and Protestantism with such a topic as the primitive condition of man. This, it may be said, is a point that lies quite beyond the sphere of our present experience. Any differences of opinion upon it must be largely matter of theory. Why not proceed at once to deal with those subjects that lie at the heart of the conflict?

Such an objection as this is due to a superficial estimate of the two systems and the radical character of the points at issue betwixt them. As we have already seen, the main questions round which the contest with Rome began were those that concerned the way in which salvation was to be obtained and the effects it exercised on the spiritual life and experience. On some grounds it would be natural enough to enter at once on the discussion of these themes. Yet not even thus could we escape the necessity of dealing with such points as the original condition of man. For, as an eminent expositor of the Romish doctrines has said, " The great controversy that now occupies us had rather its starting-point in the inmost and deepest centre of human history, since it was concerned with the manner and way in which fallen man is established in fellowship with Christ and becomes partaker of the fruits of redemption. But from this centre the opposition soon necessarily extended forwards and backwards and stretched to the two poles of the history of mankind, which had then to be regarded in accordance with the changes introduced into the central point. The more consistently a system is developed, the more harmoniously it is carried out, the more does any modification in its fundamental idea affect all its parts. The doctrines of Catholicism are altogether most intimately intertwined. Whoever therefore attacked it in its centre was at the same time constrained to combat in succession many other tenets the connection of which with that first controverted was at the outset hardly anticipated." [1] This witness is true. The difference between the Reformers and their opponents on the subject of justification and entrance into peace with God was so fundamental and pervasive that in the long-

[1] Möhler, *Symbolik*, s. 26.

run they found themselves at variance on the condition of man as created by God. To this day, our view of the Christian redemption alike affects the position we take up on this topic and is affected by it. Since therefore the point must come up for discussion at one stage or other, it seems the most advantageous order to take it at the beginning. For in this way we shall best understand both the effects of sin and the way in which they are overcome in Christ Jesus.

There is no difficulty in ascertaining the real drift of the Romanist doctrine on the primitive condition of man. In the decrees of the Council of Trent indeed we have only the barest allusion to this point and that of a very ambiguous kind. It simply states that man was "constituted" in holiness and righteousness.[1] But the lack is supplied in the Catechism drawn up under the auspices of the Council and in the exposition of the most learned divines.

The statement of the Catechism is to this effect: "Lastly, God fashioned man out of the clay of the earth, so made and constituted in body, that he was immortal and impassible, not indeed by the force of nature itself, but by the divine favour. But as to his soul, He formed him after His own image and likeness, endowed him with free will and besides so tempered within him all motions as well as appetite of mind that they should never disobey the rule of reason. Then He added the admirable gift of original righteousness and thereupon decreed that he should have superiority over all other animals."[2]

In order to bring out the full force of this last statement, it will be helpful to have before us the meaning attached to it by a theologian whose opinion is still of great authority in the Church of Rome. "That integrity," says Cardinal Bellarmin, "with which the first man was furnished and without which all men are born since his fall, was not his natural condition but a supernatural elevation. . . . It is to be observed in the first place that man naturally consists of flesh and spirit and thereby shares his nature partly with the lower animals and partly with the angels; and indeed in virtue of the flesh and his community with the lower animals man has a certain propensity to physical and sensible good towards which he is borne by sense and appetite; while in virtue of the spirit and his community with the angels he has a certain propensity to spiritual and intellectual good towards which he is borne by intelligence and will; but out of these diverse or contrary propensities there arises in one and the same man a certain conflict and out of that conflict an enormous difficulty of acting rightly, since one propensity hinders the other.

"It is to be observed, in the second place, that in order to apply a remedy to this disease or languor of human nature, which arose from the condition of its material element, divine providence in the beginning of creation added to man a certain distinguished gift, namely, original righteousness by which as by a kind of golden curb the inferior part might be easily held subject to the superior and the

---

[1] Sess. v. i.   [2] Ch. ii. q. xix.

superior to God; but the flesh was so subjected to the spirit that it could not be excited while the spirit was unwilling, nor would it become rebellious against the spirit unless the spirit itself became rebellious against God, while yet it was in the power of the spirit to become or not to become rebellious against God. We think that that rectitude of the inferior part was a supernatural gift and that too in itself and not by accident, so that it neither flowed nor could have flowed from the principles of nature. And because that gift was supernatural, as soon as it was removed, human nature left to itself began to experience that conflict of the inferior part with the higher, which would have been natural, that is, would have followed from the condition of its material element, if God had not added to man the gift of righteousness." [1]

Essentially the same account of the Romish doctrine is given by more recent writers. Some, it is true, lay greater stress on the motions of the mind than on the propensities of the body as the source of man's instability. Yet when they have to deal with the objections of Protestantism, they fall back on what is practically the same opinion as that of Bellarmin.

The Romish doctrine on the primitive condition of man, therefore, is seen to have diverged from the main stream of the teaching of the Western Church as represented by Augustine and Anselm. According to these theologians, man as he came from the hands of the Creator could not have any inherent source of weakness. Human nature is not a composite product, the elements of which are lacking in natural affinity for each other. It is a unity whose parts were made to exist and act in harmony. Hence there was no need for any special force to be superadded to human nature to maintain its varied faculties in concord. It was created by God with a positive preparation and predisposition towards that which is good. The will of man was fitted to move in the line of God's holy will, and he had only to be left to go forward in this pathway, unhindered by external obstacles or seductions, to reap all the benefits of growing communion with his Creator.

The doctrine of the Church of Rome, on the other hand, followed the tendencies of the schoolmen that favoured the views of Pelagius rather than those of Augustine. Looked at solely in respect of his original moral constitution, man was not without fault or flaw. In the inherent antagonism betwixt the rational and sensuous elements of which human nature was held to consist, the seeds of latent disunion were already sown and there was only wanting an opportunity of temptation that in the nature of the case could never be very remote, to bring them out in sinful action. This, as Bellarmin acknowledges, is tantamount to an admission that humanity, as it came forth from the hands of God, is infected with an essential disease or languor (*morbus, languor*). The nature of man as created by God was not bent and actively predisposed towards that which is

[1] *Gratia Primi Hom.* 2. Winer, p. 79 (Clark).

good. It was brought into being with an element of imperfection cleaving to it, which could be overborne and kept from developing into evil only by the presence and operation of supernatural grace in the shape of original righteousness.

What attitude did the Reformers take up towards this representation? At the outset they could not fail to be influenced by several strong preliminary objections to which it is exposed.

For, in the first place, this view does not fall in well with what we might expect from the origin of human nature. Creaturehood carries with it the idea of perfection according to its kind. As coming from the only wise God, it must be able to realise the idea it suggests. Moreover this perfectness must spring from the inherent capacities of the creature and their harmonious adjustment. But, according to the Romish view, man as God's creature is imperfect. His natural faculties of soul and body can be preserved in a right moral condition only by the added gift of a force beyond his creaturely attainments, namely, the gift of original righteousness. This is a conception that really does injustice to the beneficent intentions and perfect omnipotence of the Creator.

Moreover, it is certainly not an ennobling view of human nature that is here presented. Man feels that it is in the soul, the indestructible spirit, that the kernel and the glory of his humanity lies. It is in its essential qualities so far exalted above the body that he is instinctively persuaded it ought to have the unlimited government of the body and all its propensities. At the same time the soul is united to the body and animates it; and it seems but fitting that at the outset the soul should not have any antagonism to its claims to encounter. But, according to the Romish view, this is inevitable. The body as to its material organisation has an element of weakness attaching to it and the soul is hampered in its action from the beginning of its created life. This, as one has said, is a degrading view of the original constitution of human nature. It is, in fact, a relic of the old Manichæan principle of the inherent evil of matter.

The great duty, therefore, to which the Reformers addressed themselves was to study carefully the utterances of the word of God on the subject. When they did this with the simple desire to ascertain the truth, they found evidence ample enough to set it beyond doubt that man was originally created by God in a state of perfect uprightness before Him.

Was there not, for example, the divine verdict on the perfection of creation: "And God saw all that He had created and made, and, behold, it was very good"?[1]

Was there not also the express statement on the close affinity betwixt the nature of God and man? God is everywhere represented as the divine Parent of mankind. Paul quoted with approval the saying of the heathen poet, Aratus of Soli: "For we are also His

[1] Gen. i. 31.

THE STATE OF MAN AS CREATED

offspring"[1]—children of the race of God. The evangelist calls Adam the son of God.[2] In actual consciousness man may have been only the creation or offspring or servant of God; but potentially and in the light of the ideal he might yet reach he was His "son." This gives a deep significance to the statement that God made man "in His own image and likeness."[3] The Romanist theologians following some of the earlier schoolmen would have a distinction drawn betwixt the reference of these two phrases. According to Bellarmin, "the image of God" refers simply to man's natural powers of intellect and will. The "likeness" refers to his moral character as constituted in original righteousness by special divine grace. It is probably in this distinction indeed that the root of the Romish error on this subject is to be found. The distinction itself is not founded on fact. As Calvin pointed out long ago, "image" and "likeness" are really one and the same, the latter being only the interpretation of the former: God created man in His own image, so as to be like Himself. But this involves the truth that man was morally like God. If the Creator be perfectly righteous, man must have been made upright.

Yet again: there is the description given of the nature of man, as it is found in Jesus Christ, the Son of God. He was "the Son of Man," the type as well as the Saviour of humanity.[4] Since Jesus came not merely to restore but to develop the life man had at the beginning, the inference is undeniable that the first man as he came forth from the hands of God must have been endowed with a soul free from every taint of sin and filled with the germs of all that was pure and just and good.

Last of all, there are the distinct testimonies of the New Testament as to the qualities that are to characterise man as included in the new creation of grace.[5] Since, according to the New Testament, redemption is to be not merely a liberation but a growth, no stronger proof could be given that the elements of these perfect moral qualities found place in man in his primitive unfallen state.

Putting all the facts together, the Reformers felt themselves fully equipped for combating the doctrine of the Church of Rome. Even if they did not claim the familiar statement of Ecclesiastes[6] as a proof text, they still felt that it was only the expression of the truth. So sure of their ground on this point were they indeed that they were often tempted to depict the primitive condition of man in more definite terms than the simple statements of Scripture always warrant. It cannot be said with truth that the Reformed theologians always escaped the snare of unconscious exaggeration. For some of them depicted man as possessed from the beginning with knowledge, righteousness and holiness in the fully developed forms suggested by the new creation of grace. This is a point at which Protestant theology ought to be on its guard. No greater mistake or

[1] Acts xvii. 28.
[2] Luke iii. 38.
[3] Gen. i. 26.
[4] 1 Cor. xv. 45, 47; Luke i. 35.
[5] Eph. iv. 24; Col. iii. 10.
[6] Ch. vii. 9.

one more likely to provoke recoil can be made than to describe unfallen man wholly from the platform to which he is raised by the Christian redemption. Salvation is never represented in Scripture as a mere restoration of the paradisaic condition. Rather is it constantly set before us as an entrance on a higher and more abundant life. In point of fact the Biblical account of the creation of man is very simple and reserved. Beyond the facts that man was made good and in the divine image and therefore in the line of the human nature of Christ and of man as redeemed—evidence ample enough to establish the Protestant general position—the Bible does not go. It certainly does not tell us in express terms what man's actual attainments were. As an eminent teacher has said, " Man, standing in the image of God certainly had (according to the Scripture indication) in his intelligent nature, his unperverted affections, his unpolluted conscience, the germs of and the preparation for, glorious attainments in knowledge, as he should walk with God and as he should survey the world in which God's goodness placed him."[1] So also, we must add, he had the basis of growth in righteousness and holiness. But what at that time he had actually attained in these directions is a matter on which we have no definite information. On many grounds it is safer to hold that man had simply the principles of these attainments implanted in his nature. Had he continued under the guidance of the light that filled his mind, the gratitude that flowed from his soul and the peace that possessed his conscience, his progress towards the lofty moral ideal set before him must have been both rapid and stable.

With these explanations, we are now able to discriminate and sum up the leading features of the Protestant position.

1. As regards the constitution of his nature as a whole, man was brought into being with all his faculties in harmonious operation. The body with all its propensities was under the dominion of the soul. In the soul, the inclinations and affections were subject to the will, the will to conscience and judgment, while these in turn reflected perfectly the mind and will of the Creator.

2. The moral nature of man therefore was created with inherent moral integrity. He had the power of choosing good or evil ; but as created by God, he was freely and fully disposed towards good. The whole bent of his original nature was towards that which was right.

3. Man was thus from the beginning capable of knowing and loving God. His desire was towards God as the source of his life. As the Swiss Reformer Zwingli asserted so strongly, this is a necessary consequence of his being made in the image of God. In this fact is found the basis of all divine revelation.

4. As thus fully conformed to the mind and will of God at the stage he had reached, man was in spiritual communion with God. Within his own nature he had everything needful for abiding happiness on earth and higher fellowship in heaven.

[1] Rainy, *The Development of Doctrine*, p. 41.

CHAPTER II

THE CONDITION OF MAN AS FALLEN—ORIGINAL SIN

IF the views we have taken of the Church of Rome's teaching on the state of man as created are correct, it is evident that her theologians are not prepared to take a very unfavourable view of human nature in its present condition. Since they hold that original righteousness is not an inherent quality of the soul, but only a supernatural gift, the inference seems justified that a basis is laid for a representation of the results of sin that shall make it out to be not a very radical or inveterate defect. This anticipation is confirmed by a closer scrutiny of the views that prevailed before the Reformation, and of the way in which these were reflected in the statements of the Council of Trent.

The doctrine concerning the state of man as fallen which prevailed in the early Latin Church was that of Augustine. He taught that man was created by God in His likeness, and therefore with inherent moral integrity. When he sinned, he not only lost this original righteousness, but thereby also corrupted his whole moral nature, and so became subject to physical death and all the other miseries that accompany it. The consequences that he thus brought upon himself, he, as the representative of the whole race, also entailed on his posterity. Every human being is at once born without original integrity and with a disordered moral nature. This native corruption is itself sinful; it has the nature of sin in itself, even before it be manifested in conscious voluntary sinful deeds.

These views of Augustine were accepted by the Latin Church of his day as expressing the only orthodox doctrine on this subject. Yet no long time elapsed ere opposition to them began to find voice in different quarters. A school of divines, of whom Vincent of Lerinum is perhaps the best known, began to teach that the true doctrine was to be found, not in Pelagianism or in Augustinianism, but in a view that lay betwixt these two extremes. This Semi-Pelagian doctrine, as it has come to be called, was to the effect that Adam's sin did exercise a directly injurious effect on his posterity, by entailing physical death and a certain moral deterioration in his whole nature. From these effects, moreover, man was unable wholly to deliver himself. Yet neither the disorder nor the weakness were such as to prevent man's taking the initiative in his redemption and co-operating with the grace of God till it was finally achieved.

In spite of condemnation passed on their doctrine by successive councils of the Church, the Semi-Pelagian party continued to grow in numbers and activity up to the time of the Reformation.

The adherents of the Augustinian school, however, were no less earnest in the endeavour to maintain their views. Encouraged by the fact that it was really the teaching of Augustine that had been embodied in the doctrines of the Church, they strenuously maintained the leading features of his conclusions on the nature and results of sin.

Embracing as it did resolute adherents of these two opposing parties, the Council of Trent, it is easy to see, found it very difficult to formulate views on the condition of man as fallen that might be acceptable to all its members. This fact has been expressly noted by the historians of the council. The Romanist theologians would have been very glad to condemn the Protestant doctrine, and actually had a list of the main points in it drawn up for the purpose of expressly repudiating them. But after discussion they could not deny that the Reformers only adhered to the views of Augustine; and since they had many amongst themselves who maintained essentially the same convictions, they agreed, at the urgent request of the papal legates, to forego attempting to make any very explicit statements of the truth on the subject, and to content themselves with condemning again the views of Pelagius that had been adjudged to be heretical long centuries before.

The fact of this compromise is seen to be stamped on the decrees themselves. The first three sections, so far as we are concerned with them at this stage, are expressed in these terms :—

"1. If anyone does not confess that the first man Adam when he had transgressed the commandment of God in Paradise immediately lost the holiness and righteousness in which he had been constituted, and that he incurred by the offence of that prevarication the wrath and indignation of God and therefore death with which God had previously threatened him, and along with death captivity under the power of him who thenceforth had the dominion of death, that is, the devil, and that the whole Adam through that offence of prevarication was changed for the worse in body and soul : let him be anathema.

"2. If anyone asserts that the prevarication of Adam injured himself alone and not his posterity ; and that the holiness and righteousness received from God which he lost, he lost for himself alone and not for us also ; or that he being defiled through the sin of disobedience has transfused death and physical punishment only into the whole human race but not also sin, which is the death of the soul : let him, etc.

"3. If anyone asserts that this sin of Adam, which in its origin is one, and being transfused into all by propagation, not by imitation, is in each individual as his own, is taken away either by the powers of human nature or by any other remedy than the merit of the one mediator our Lord Jesus Christ . . . let him," etc.[1]

With the exception of the points adverted to in the preceding chapter, this is a representation that, so far as it goes, cannot be said to be other than strictly scriptural. The effects of Adam's sin on himself and his posterity are clearly recognised and stated in unimpeachable language.

Moreover what is thus found in the decisions of Trent is confirmed by some of the foremost Romish divines. Even Bellarmin admits in one passage of his writings that the loss of original righteousness carries with it the idea of a sinful nature. So also J. A. Möhler takes the view of the Council's decree which would naturally be adopted by the Augustinian party. For he quotes with approval the statement of Bonaventura in these terms : " The force of evil desire and the law of the members which everyone has from birth takes the spirit captive and rules over it. It is thus indisputable that the soul of every man is perverted from birth. If the right condition of the soul is righteousness, the perverted condition is guilt ; and since we are perverted from birth, we have from birth onwards a guilt resting upon us. Of this no one doubts except him who does not recognise the force of evil desire and does not know in what way the rational spirit is to be obedient to God."[2]

While not a few Protestant theologians are willing to take such statements as truly representing the doctrines of the Church of Rome, there are others who hold that they do not truly exhibit either the real spirit of the decisions of Trent or the main drift of Romish theological teaching. For this contention they are able to adduce very cogent reasons. In declining to give any decisive utterance on the different elements of man's present sinful condition and thereby confining themselves to statements of a very general character, the Fathers left open a loophole for the entrance of views very different from those which had received the sanction of earlier Councils. Of this vagueness many Romish theologians, from the Reformation to our own day, have not scrupled to take fullest advantage.

Bellarmin, for example, did not hesitate to throw the whole weight of his authority on the side of those who adhered to the Semi-Pelagian opinions of Abelard and Duns Scotus. " The state of man since the fall of Adam," he says, "does not differ from the state of Adam in its original natural elements more than one who has been stripped of clothing differs from one that is naked : nor, if you except the original fault, is human nature worse than it was, when fashioned in its primitive condition : nor does it labour more under ignorance and infirmity than it originally did. Hence the corruption of human nature proceeds, not from the lack of any natural gift or from the addition of any evil quality, but only

[1] Sess. v. Mirbt, p. 128.   [2] *Symbolik*, s. 59.

from the loss of the supernatural gift on account of the sin of Adam."[1] Substantially the same views are repeated by Perrone.

That the Church of Rome has not changed her views on this point is plain from the statements made by one of her living teachers. "Besides being born without the supernatural gift of sanctifying grace, man is also born without the preternatural gifts of integrity and the rest, the absence of which constitutes a privation, no less than the absence of grace. This privation, however, is something different from the privation of grace, and is a punishment of original sin, rather than itself original sin. . . . Had God so pleased, He might have created us in the State of Pure Nature, without interfering with any of His Attributes. The state in which we actually are born does not differ from the state of Pure Nature, except in the train of circumstances that led up to it and in the prospect of restoration."[2]

From this review of the Romanists' position, it will now be abundantly plain at what precise points we as Protestants diverge from them. We have happily no controversy with them, for example, as to the reality or origin of sin, as we have with Pelagians, Socinians, and Rationalists. The theologians of Trent were still so much under the influence of the anthropology of Augustine, that, equally with the Reformers, they felt themselves bound to dissent from such opinions. Neither have we any controversy with them as to the present and final results of sin when it is left to bring forth all its bitter fruits. On the consequences of sin itself we are at one. No Romanist could refuse to subscribe to the answer given in the Westminster Catechism to the question: "What is the misery of that estate whereinto man fell? All mankind by their fall lost communion with God, are under His wrath and curse, and so made liable to all miseries in this life, to death itself, and to the pains of hell for ever." Our sole differences from them—though these are grave enough—turn upon "the sinfulness of that estate whereinto man fell":[3] that is, the elements of man's present condition as a sinner and the extent to which they have affected his whole moral and spiritual nature.

As to the first of these points, the Protestant views may now be very simply stated. Holding as they did that man when he came from the hand of God had in him an inherent moral integrity, the Reformers after Augustine taught that the primary element of man's sinfulness lies in his lack of this native quality. By his disobedience to the command of God, man broke up that conformity to His mind and will which he had as a feature of his whole moral life. That the image or likeness of God was wholly obliterated in man by sin, Reformed theologians have never held. In the fact that man has still a self-conscious personal spirit, endowed with reason

[1] *Apud* Perrone, *Prælectiones Theologicæ*, iii. p. 220.
[2] S. J. Hunter, *Outlines of Dogmatic Theology*, vol. ii. pp. 413, 414.
[3] Q. 18.

and capable of longing after God, we have enough to justify us in contending that thus far the image of God is "the inalienable possession of the race." Yet of his moral likeness to the Creator man has lost the predominant feature. He has lost the moral uprightness in which he was created and which he was bound over to preserve: and thus far the glory of the divine similitude in him has been lost. The stern picture of the moral condition of the race drawn by one of the psalmists and reproduced by Paul has this statement in the foreground: "There is none righteous: no, not one."[1]

But if man has lost the integrity in which he was created, what must now be the present condition of his moral nature? It can only be in a state of disorder or corruption. Since the integrity which was native to him has been lost, there must now be inherent in him a depravity of that nature. Hence, in the Augsburg Confession presented to the Emperor Charles V. so early as 1530, the Reformers said: "They (the Churches) also teach that, after Adam's fall, all men begotten according to nature are born with sin: that is, without the fear of God, without trust in Him and with evil desire; and that this disease or depravity of birth is truly sin."[2]

This is a position fully borne out by the testimonies of Scripture. The writer of Genesis, while telling us that the Lord saw the greatness of man's wickedness on the earth also at the same time indicates the divine conviction, "that every imagination of the thoughts of his heart was only evil continually": a verdict that is explained by a later statement to the effect that "the imagination of man's heart is evil from his youth." The devotional utterances of the Old Testament are full of the same feeling.[3] The more didactic statements of the New Testament are quite in harmony: "That which is born of the flesh is flesh."[4] "The mind of the flesh is enmity against God: for it is not subject to the law of God, neither indeed can be."[5] This is the decisive test. The law demands perfection in created life, because it is the reflection of the nature of God. Whatsoever is not in conformity to the divine mind, in feeling or disposition as well as in action, must have the nature of sin.

On the extent to which man's moral nature has been corrupted by sin, the Protestant testimony is equally decisive. The terms in which it is stated, however, have been so frequently misunderstood that it is necessary to use the utmost precision. The form of expression commonly adopted is that man's nature has become "totally depraved." But what does this phrase mean? An American commentator has defined it thus: "It is a term of *extensity*, rather than of intensity. It is opposed to *partial*, to the idea that man is sinful in one moment and innocent or sinless in another or sinful in

[1] Ps. xiv. 3; Rom. iii. 10.
[2] Schaff, *Creeds of Christendom*, vol. iii. p. 8.
[3] Job xiv. 4, xv. 14; Ps. li. 5.   [4] John iii. 6.   [5] Rom. viii. 7.

some acts and pure in others. It affirms that he is wrong in all things, and all the time. It does not mean that man is as bad as the devils or that every man is as bad as every other or that any man is as bad as he possibly may be or may become. That is, there are degrees of intensity, but no limit to the universality or extent of the evil in the soul."[1]

This explanation is confirmed, first of all, by the voice of conscience as well as by experience and observation. The chief faculties of the human spirit in this connection may be set down as conscience, heart, mind and will. But every awakened soul is convinced that sin has affected and depraved his nature on all these sides. How often does conscience fail to discern betwixt good and evil, or, if it does indicate the choice to be made, how often does it not deter from evil with the force it should wield. With what an inveterate bias also does the heart cleave to that which is evil or to that which has been expressly forbidden. So the mind is felt to be darkened and the will weakened or inert. In short, human nature is a moral unity, and all its faculties so interact that it is impossible one should be injured by sin and the others go unscathed.

This view is also in full accord with the statements of Scripture. There is not a single faculty of man's nature that is not directly or indirectly mentioned in Scripture as having been tainted with sin. Ordinarily it is the heart alone that is referred to as the source of corruption, as when Jeremiah says: "The heart is deceitful above all things, and desperately sick: who can know it?"[2] But even in the statement quoted from Genesis, we see how from the heart sin rises into the mind and thence into the imagination, influencing thus not only the feeling but the thoughts and the specific purposes which the mind shapes. So the Lord Jesus said: "Out of the heart proceed evil thoughts."[3] By the apostles stress is laid on the effect sin has on the reason and intellect, as when Paul testifies: "that ye no longer walk as the Gentiles also walk in the vanity of their mind, being darkened in their understanding, alienated from the life of God because of the ignorance that is in them, because of the hardening of the heart";[4] where, if we read the passage backwards, we shall see the same process of sin's corrupting the heart, and thence affecting the intellect and higher reason. Elsewhere in Scripture, conscience or the faculty of self-knowledge is coupled with the mind as injured by sin, as when Paul says: "To them that are defiled and unbelieving, nothing is pure, but both their mind and their conscience are defiled."[5] It was doubtless certain extreme instances of corruption the apostle had in view, but the statement on the operation of sin here is true for humanity as a whole.

If the heart and mind and conscience are thus corrupted by sin, it is impossible that the will also should not be weakened and perverted. This faculty of the human spirit is not indeed expressly

---

[1] Taylor Lewis in Lange's *Genesis* (Clark), p. 287.   [2] Jer. xvii. 9.
[3] Matt. xv. 19.   [4] Eph. iv. 17–19.   [5] Tit. i. 15.

named as in itself subject to evil. But as we shall see in the next chapter, this truth is everywhere implied in Scripture. According to the psychology of the Hebrews, the will was practically in the heart, which thus embraced the power not only of desire and feeling and affection, but also of action: and the heart of man is injured in its activity as well as in its inner life. The hint of antagonism struck out by the Apostle John when he says that the children of God are born "not of the will of the flesh nor of the will of man but of God," is confirmed by many statements which set the perversity and weakness and in truth the utter perversity of the human will beyond dispute.

CHAPTER III

THE INABILITY OF MAN THROUGH SIN—THE STATE OF THE UNREGENERATE

IF the question were raised as to which of the aspects of man's native corruption the first Reformers deemed most important for the maintenance of the truth, there would be no difficulty in giving the answer. They laid most stress on the depravity of the will.

How fully Luther expressed this conviction is seen in his treatise on *the Servitude on the Will*. His language was often so strong as to expose him to the charge of at least appearing to overstep the literal truth ; as when, for example, he says : " In his actings towards God, in things pertaining to salvation, or damnation, man has not free will, but is the captive, the subject, the servant, either of the will of God or of the will of Satan." Yet in the whole substance of his teaching, he was fully supported by Calvin, who says in his *Institutes*, as he also said more fully in his special *Treatise of the Will* : "We are all sinners by nature, therefore we are held under the yoke of sin. But if the whole man is subject to the dominion of sin, surely the will which is its principal seat, must be bound by the closest chains." [1]

This last position, however, was just that which the Romanists were not willing to admit. The difficulty they felt in the matter appeared very clearly at the sixth session of the Council of Trent and is stamped on the utterances then given. In the first three canons on the subject of justification, the Council in a general way followed the teaching of Augustine in his opposition to Pelagianism. But there were also present in the Council a large number of Franciscans and these, as being followers of Scotus, stood up very energetically for some recognition of the ability of man to help himself in the matter of salvation. The aim of the Council under the guidance of the papal legates was to please all parties ; and therefore on the back of these somewhat vague statements directed against Pelagianism, there follow several others which practically leave room for Semi-Pelagian views. Man's free will moved and touched by God does co-operate towards obtaining the grace of justification.

The fifth canon is in this connection specially worthy of notice ;

[1] *Institutes*, vol. i. p. 246.

"If anyone shall say that since Adam's sin the free will of man has been lost and extinguished or that it is a thing in name only, yea, a name without reality, in short, a fiction introduced into the Church by Satan : let him," etc.

The same two-sidedness is found in the first chapter of the decree, entitled, "On the inability of Nature and of the Law to justify man" : "It is necessary that each one . . . confess that, whereas all men had lost their innocence in the prevarication of Adam . . . they were so far the servants of sin . . . that not the Gentiles only by the force of nature, but not even the Jews . . . were able to be liberated or arise therefrom ; although free will attenuated as it was in its powers and bent down was by no means extinguished in them."

By such statements as these the Council evidently neutralised the more scriptural elements in the previous canons. Had the principles there enunciated been fairly carried out, no foundation would have been left for human ability or merit. But this would have been to undermine the whole system of teaching and practice that had grown up during the preceding millennium. For such a sacrifice the Council was not prepared ; and these really contradictory statements are left alongside each other to shelter Augustinianism on the one hand and Semi-Pelagianism on the other. Having regard to the whole attitude they took up in opposition to the Reformers, we can hardly err in thinking that the main tendency of the canons is to deny the servitude of the will in the sense held by the Reformers and to teach that fallen man has still some power to do that which may in some way and to some extent contribute causally to his own salvation.

In endeavouring to understand the position which the Protestant Churches came to take up against such declarations as this, it is needful to remember that the Reformers treated the whole question from the standpoint of theological doctrine. Any problem connected with the will inevitably branches out into many points that properly fall within the province of philosophy. With the metaphysical bent that characterised them, the Schoolmen of the Middle Ages had already raised almost every point in connection with the freedom of the will that has perplexed the human mind. But the Reformers spoke and wrote with an aim that did not require them to deal with these aspects of the subject. They were concerned with the extent to which the human will had been affected by sin and the measure of ability that still remained for effecting anything towards salvation. As we have seen, they found themselves constrained to believe and teach that the will of man was in a state of servitude as regards the performance of any spiritual duty ; and at first they never hesitated to use any form of speech, however extreme or paradoxical it might seem, that was fitted to leave a deep impression of that truth on the minds of men.

It is very evident, however, that when the various questions to which this discussion gave rise came to be disentangled, and the issues at stake were more clearly discerned, the Reformers were prepared to admit everything that philosophy could legitimately demand as requisite for the freedom of the will and human responsibility. Luther, for example, never averred that the Fall had made any radical change on the framework of man's moral nature. As he was created with the faculty of will, so he retained it in his fallen state. Nor when called upon to face the simple question as to whether the will of man was free to do what the reason selected as its choice, did he ever contend that either in itself or in the way of constraint put upon it from without, was there any obstacle that marred its entire freedom. Melanchthon was careful to set this beyond doubt. Calvin held precisely the same view. Although from the prejudices against evangelical truths which it had come to suggest, he preferred not to use the expression "free will," yet he never implied that sin had entailed on the will of man either in its own structure or in external compulsion anything that detracted from its full liberty of action. The same position is held by all the Churches that have followed his general system of doctrine. The Westminster Confession, for example, says: "God hath endued the will of man with that natural liberty that it is neither forced nor by any absolute necessity of nature determined to good or evil." This is a simple matter of consciousness. Man is endowed with the faculty of reason. He has the power of choosing that which on the whole meets the conjunct elements of feeling, desire, disposition and habit at the time; and he is conscious of being perfectly free to embody that choice in action. As the desire is dependent on the whole state of mind and the rational choice is governed by the desire, so the action is determined by the choice. There is no consequence of sin that in anyway obviates the interaction of this chain of desire, choice or volition and action. As the Scripture puts it, men have always done "what they listed."[1]

Holding these views on the essential nature of the human will, the Reformers could not avoid stating what they believed to be the truth concerning the faculty of volition in man's unfallen state. On this point of course, no direct statements of Scripture are available; nor are we able from our own experience to adduce any certain light upon it. We have only the guidance of general principles. Yet this is sufficiently distinct for determining all that it is needful for us to know. As made in the image of God and endowed with reason and conscience, man was able at once to distinguish betwixt the true and the false, the right and the wrong. He had a moral instinct that deterred him from evil and impelled him towards good. These faculties were given him in order that he might be able to fix his desires on that which was right in the sight of God, and guide his whole state of mind and feeling in the direction most likely to reach it. Since his moral nature as a whole was created so as to be disposed to good, if man had governed his desires and dispositions aright, he

[1] Matt. xvii. 12.

would not have fallen. But as endowed with a free will in the sense already explained, he had the liberty of letting his desires fasten upon evil, if it were presented to him, and of giving effect to any choice of it he might make. This is the substance of what all the Protestant Churches that have felt called on to deal with this stage of man's career have taught. The Westminster Confession says : " Man in his state of innocency had freedom and power to will and to do that which is good and well-pleasing to God ; but yet mutably, so that he might fall from it."

These views on man's will in the state of original integrity only prepared the Reformers for upholding more strenuously their characteristic position on its condition since the Fall. This they all held to be one of utter servitude to sin or entire inability to any spiritual good. Man, even as fallen, is still essentially a free agent, and therefore responsible for all his actions. He is still free and able to do what on the whole his desires prompt and decide him to do. But the corruption that sin has brought on his moral nature has tainted every faculty ; and in the case of the will, the evil done has been so deep that, to use the language of the Westminster Confession, man is now " utterly indisposed, disabled, and made opposite to all good and wholly inclined to all evil."[1] With this statement all the Lutheran and Reformed Confessions are in entire harmony.

How fully this position is supported by the utterances of the Bible may be very briefly shown. The prophets of the Old Covenant only anticipated the statements of the divine Master and the apostles echo His teaching. Jeremiah said : " Can the Ethiopian change his skin or the leopard his spots? Then may ye also do good that are accustomed to do evil."[2] The Lord Jesus taught that men could not become the children of God or enter into the kingdom save by a new radical change wrought in their heart only by the power of God Himself.[3] The apostles repeat the same truth : " Which were born not of blood, nor of the will of the flesh nor of the will of man, but of God " ; " For when ye were servants of sin, ye were free in regard of righteousness."[4]

In the face of such decisive statements as these, it is manifestly in vain to urge the Pelagian objection that certain duties are enjoined on sinners in Scripture, and this very fact implies the ability on their part to comply with them. It is true that natural men are commanded to keep the moral law, and that they are also summoned to repent and believe the gospel. But the existence of these counsels cannot overturn the series of strong testimonies already adduced. A sufficient explanation is found in the fact that the moral law is binding on man in whatever condition he may live, and that the knowledge of it may under grace be the starting-point of conviction and conversion : while the righteousness of the gospel may in like

[1] Ch. vi. 4.   [2] Ch. xiii. 23.
[3] John iii. 3, v. 40, vi. 44, 65.
[4] John i. 13 ; Rom. vi. 20, viii. 21, ix. 16 ; Eph. ii. 1, 8.

manner be the means of teaching men their helplessness and leading them to apply to God for mercy and grace to help in time of need.

Equally futile is it to say that if man be unable to do what God enjoins, he cannot justly be regarded as responsible for his actions or guilty in His sight. For it has never been affirmed in behalf of the Protestant view that man has not the natural ability to do what God commands. Rather has it been fully admitted and contended for that there is nothing in the structure of the will or in the shape of outward constraint that counteracts man's entire freedom of volition. All that has been asserted concerning man in his present fallen state and fairly proved is, that he has not the moral ability to comply with the divine commands; that he is morally not merely unwilling but actually unable to render obedience to His will. The fact that he has the natural, though not the moral ability is enough to make him responsible before God.

If, however, as a further objection to man's being held responsible for his actions, the fact be adduced that, besides being unable to do God's will, man is unable even to *will* to do what God commands, a more fundamental truth must be asserted. This is to the effect that as a member of a race which is not only an organic unity, but one also in its legal constitution and standing, man has inherited this inability through the sin of his head and representative. "The covenant being made with Adam not only for himself, but also for his posterity, all mankind descending from him by ordinary generation sinned in him and fell with him in his first transgression."[1] As Principal W. Cunningham has well pointed out, this means "that man is responsible for not willing and doing good, notwithstanding his actual inability to will and to do good, because he is answerable for that inability itself, having, as legally responsible for Adam's sin, inherited the inability as part of the forfeiture due to that first transgression."[2]

Holding these views on the inability of man through sin, the Reformers could not avoid coming into conflict with the Church of Rome on another point closely allied to it, namely, the character to be attached to the actions of men while yet unrenewed by the Spirit. This was indeed only the obverse side of the same question, though stated in different terms. Are the depravity of man's moral nature and the servitude of the will so complete, that every action is tainted with sin? Or is his nature left by the Fall in a condition that still makes it possible for him to do anything that is good and thereby deserve at the hands of God the grace that may enable him to make progress in the spiritual life? It was this latter view that prevailed in the Church of Rome. Broached and discussed at first by the Schoolmen, it had in the course of centuries worked its way into the heart of the priesthood and the people and moulded their whole conception of the manner in which the soul was to be saved. At the eve

---

[1] Westminster Sh. Cat. q. 16.
[2] *Historical Theology*, vol. i. p. 610.

of the Reformation, it was practically the source as well as the starting-point of all the ignorance and superstition that overshadowed the spiritual life of the Church.

This being so, Luther and his associates could not but direct their strongest attack against this aspect of the Romish position. The great Reformer saw that, unless the prevalent ideas about the nature and worth of human effort were overturned, there was no chance that the gospel of the grace of God would take root in the hearts of men. At any cost, men had to be stripped of their sufficiency in respect alike of free will, ability and merit. This accordingly was what he did. Leaving for the time the more minute determination of such questions as the relation of Adam to his posterity and the constituent elements of man's sinful condition, he bent his whole strength on breaking up the false foundations on which men were building their hopes for time and eternity. As the will of man was by nature in a state of servitude, so he could do no work that was not in itself evil. It was impossible for the sinner to commend himself to the grace of God by his own efforts. The more he endeavoured to build up a righteousness of his own, apart from faith in Christ, the more deeply did he sin against God. The other Reformers did not imitate Luther's vehemence and certainly did not always approve of every form of expression he used. But they unquestionably approved of and adopted the whole substance of his teaching.

When this side of the question came to be considered in the Council of Trent, the two parties that had already been so opposed on the correlative topic again came into conflict. Upholding the teaching of Augustine, the Dominicans maintained that the natural man had no power to do anything but sin. The Franciscans, on the other hand, held that the will of man was still able to do that which was good in the sight of God and that from their congruity or harmony with the will of God, these good actions might merit the bestowal of initial grace by Him on the soul (*meritum de congruo*). Seeing that unless such a position as this were taken up their whole method of dealing with men concerning salvation would be subverted, the Council leaned to the Franciscan side and wresting from its original connection a strong statement of Luther's framed a canon—the seventh under the decree on justification—in these terms : " If anyone shall say that all works which are done before justification, in whatsoever manner they may have been done, are truly sins or merit the hatred of God, or that the more earnestly anyone strives to dispose himself for grace, the more grievously he sins : let him," etc.

The arguments on which the Romanists of Trent based their position were chiefly those that had already been advanced by the Pelagians and Semi-Pelagians. They referred to the strong religious impulse of heathen nations and laid great stress on the apparently virtuous conduct of the Ninevites in repenting at the preaching of Jonah, of Naaman the Syrian and Cornelius the centurion, as implying that man was not wholly unable to do that which was in harmony with the divine will. In replying to such statements, the Reformers did not deny that heathen nations were under the striving of the Spirit and might in response to His influence move towards God. Yet wherever the soul was not actually born anew—and in this they did not limit the operation of the Spirit—there was no reason to believe that the power of sin had been effectually broken or that these actions were done from a right motive and to a right end. In the case of Cornelius, Luther held that, like the centurion Jesus met, he had accepted the grace of God in truth, and though not yet in full communion with Christ, had been really a child of God, before he called for Peter.

Apart altogether from such arguments, however, the Reformers could adduce evidence from the Scriptures that their opponents had nothing to meet. Strong proofs, equally applicable here, have just been indicated: yet even these are not all. Did not the Lord, speaking to Nicodemus of the natural man, say that "that which is born of the flesh is flesh"?[1] Did He not proclaim the great law that "the corrupt tree bringeth forth evil fruit" and that it was not possible "a corrupt tree can bring forth good fruit"?[2] His great apostle, knowing how deeply the Master's teaching was rooted in the Old Testament, taught the same truths in no less decisive forms: "In me, that is, in my flesh, there dwelleth no good thing";[3] "The carnal mind is not subject to the law of God, neither indeed can be."[4] If men are to be saved at all, it must be "according to God's mercy" and "the renewing of the Holy Ghost."[5]

It is this position, accordingly, that is taken up in all the leading Reformed Confessions. The Articles of the Church of England teach that "Works done before the grace of Christ and the Inspiration of His Spirit are not pleasant to God . . . neither do they make men meet to receive grace or deserve grace of congruity: yea, rather, for that they are not done as God hath willed and commanded them to be done, we doubt not but they have the nature of sin."[6] The Westminster Confession is still more explicit: "Man by his fall into a state of sin hath wholly lost all ability of will to any spiritual good accompanying salvation; so as a natural man, being altogether averse from that good and dead in sin, is not able, by his own strength, to convert himself or to prepare himself thereunto."[7] "Works done by unregenerate men, although for the matter of them, they may be things which God commands and of good use both to themselves and others; yet because they proceed not from a heart purified by faith, nor are done in a right manner, according to the word, nor to a right end, the glory of God, they are therefore sinful and cannot please God or make a man meet to receive grace from God."[8]

[1] John iii. 6.
[2] Matt. vii. 17, 18.
[3] Rom. vii. 18.
[4] Rom. viii. 6.
[5] Tit. iii. 5.
[6] Art. XIII.
[7] Ch. ix. 3.
[8] Ch. xvi. 7.

It is only doing justice to the teaching of the Reformers to add one or two remarks fitted to guard against the imputation to them of extreme views inconsistent with those they professed to hold.

1. It is a mistake, for example, to allege that even the first Reformers held that man has lost all traces of the divine image. Möhler snatching at some inconsiderate expressions of Luther has attributed this opinion to him: but not justly. Luther never denied that man still retained the rational moral nature in which chiefly man's likeness to God lies. He only affirmed that he was not now in a position to rise nearer to God owing to the bondage in which his nature was now held. Calvin expressly states that man retains traces of the divine image, but did not admit this in any sense that interfered with his views on the servitude of the will.

2. The Reformers thus held that man was after the Fall altogether capable of being redeemed, without any reconstruction of his moral and mental nature. All that he wanted was a new life; and this was the sovereign gift as it was the work of God alone.

3. They never ignored the fact that man might be filled with an intense longing for redemption. He was led captive by sin, but this servitude was not such that it made him incapable of cherishing the desire for deliverance. This yearning, however, was due to the striving of the Spirit and only by His power could it issue in liberty.

CHAPTER IV

SIN IN RELATION TO DIVINE PROVIDENCE

A VERY common feature of the manner of conducting controversy in the early Church was the habit of imputing to an opponent all the inferences that seemed capable of being deduced from his leading maxims. In the hands of the schoolmen, this artifice was reduced to a regular method. A writer was held responsible not only for his general principle but for all the consequences that seemed logically to flow from it. If a proposition were true, then the inferences it yielded would be true also. If the inferences deduced from it in logical form could be shown to be manifestly false, then the principle itself could not be true.

The element of philosophic fact in this method is obvious enough. It is one thing, however, to apply it to abstract propositions and another to use it in connection with revealed doctrines. In the one case, we can be sure of all the ideas with which we deal: in the other there will often be very much that we can but imperfectly understand. To prove the truth or falsity of a doctrine of Scripture by the consequences which it seems to our minds to involve, is an attempt full of the gravest risks.

Such, nevertheless, has been the spirit in which the Romanist theologians have dealt with the position laid down by the Reformers on the relation of sin to the divine providence. This was a topic that the teachers of the new movement could not avoid considering. The necessity of forming definite conclusions about it was forced upon them by the views which in common with all the theologians of the age they held on the reality of the divine agency in human life. The pressure in their case was increased by the views they held on the servitude of the will and the absolute dependence of man for salvation on the sovereign grace of God, coupled as they were with the cognate doctrines of divine foreordination and predestination. The deeper questions thus suggested have always been urged by the Romanists with great persistence. Pursuing the old method of argument by inference, they have asked: If the will is so enslaved that man by nature can do nothing to achieve deliverance, does not the evil condition of the unsaved sinner with all the sinful actions that flow from it, lay a heavy burden on the doctrine of the divine providence? Is it not necessary to draw as wide a gulf as possible betwixt the divine agency in the good actions of men and this agency in relation to sin?

With respect to the first of these questions, Möhler thinks that it presents a problem which Protestantism cannot solve aright. On the Romish view which regards the will of man as not wholly enslaved but only weakened and which therefore leaves man with some power to begin the process that will issue in salvation, there is not, he thinks, the slightest foothold left for anyone who should feel tempted to ascribe to Providence the permanent results of evil. But where man is regarded as alike utterly helpless and hopeless in bondage to sin and nothing in the shape of freedom for initiating or meriting the work of saving grace is left, the condition of human nature thus entailed seems to him to involve a view of human life and the world essentially akin to Manichæism. This indeed is the very charge that he again and again prefers against the teaching of Luther on original sin. Seizing upon certain extreme utterances of the Reformer that have never been embodied in any of the Protestant Confessions, and materializing his conception of sin beyond all due warrant, Möhler ventures to make statements like these: "If it is inconceivable how the image of God can be thoroughly rooted out of the human spirit, it is still more inconceivable how a new essence could be infused into it. And then the idea of making something substantial out of evil! After unspeakable efforts on the part of the Church, such representations had well-nigh disappeared along with those of the Gnostics and Manichæans and now once again they sprang up full of vigour and assumption. . . . But to what purpose is this act of violence that destroys the religious aptitude of man and therewith every trace of the divine image in him? Who in view of such facts would dare to attempt a vindication of Providence? Who would credit himself with the skill needful for justifying in any measure whatever the work of God in the history of the world?"[1]

The proper answer to be given to such charges has been already indicated. As we have seen, neither Luther nor the other Reformers held any such opinion as that the Fall had made a radical or essential change on the framework of the soul of man as originally created in the image of God. If man is in such a state of servitude to sin that in his natural state he can do nothing really good in the sight of God, this in no way relieves him of the abiding results of evil. For he himself is responsible for the enslavement of his will. He has inherited this as a part of the penalty attached to the sin of the human family. As Augustine so tersely said, "Man by his evil use of free will lost both himself and it."[2]

It was, however, the second form of the question just noted that the Reformers themselves had chiefly to deal with. In accordance with their principle of acknowledging the divine sovereign activity in the whole life of man, they did not hesitate to say that even the sins they com-

[1] *Symbolik*, ss. 73, 80.   [2] *Enchiridion*, cap. 30.

mitted fell within the scope of God's providence and that the Church was bound to ascertain all that the Scriptures taught on this point and give it a fitting place in her testimony. But it was no easy matter to adopt fitting forms of expression for the conclusions to which they were led. The Romanists on their part took care to avoid any decisive utterances on this subject, but watched every opportunity of turning the difficulties of their adversaries to the best account. Ever since the days of Augustine, the Latin Church had manifested a strong abhorrence of everything that seemed to savour of Manichæism or could be made to wear the aspect of giving it countenance. The Romanists knew that no heavier blow could be dealt at the teaching of the Reformers, than to be able to show in the face of the Church that their utterances involved something akin to the ancient heresy; and they seized eagerly the slightest grounds for launching the charge.

This is seen especially in the way in which they dealt with the teaching of Luther. After the Diet at Worms, the authorities at Rome had submitted a large number of his statements on the doctrines of grace and providence to the theological faculty of the Sorbonne at Paris. A committee of three well-known doctors gave in a report to the effect that they were chargeable with Manichæism. Luther was then in the Wartburg and not fully cognisant of what had taken place; but Melanchthon at once issued a vindication of Luther's position in which he claimed that it was fully sustained by Scripture. "You say: He is a Manichæan: he is a Montanist: let fire and faggots repress his foolishness. Who is a Montanist? Luther, who would have us believe in Holy Scripture alone or you, who would have men believe in the opinions of their fellow-creatures rather than in the word of God?"[1]

Melanchthon himself, it must be admitted, did not always write on this theme with perfect wisdom. In the first edition of his commentary on the Epistle to the Romans, while treating of the divine foreordination of all things, he had gone so far as to say that the treachery of Judas was as much the result of the divine operation as the calling of Paul. The Council of Trent did not formally discuss the question of foreordination, nor were they bound to exclude the doctrine of predestination. Yet such an opportunity of creating prejudice against the tenets of the Reformers on this subject was not to be let slip. It was this very utterance accordingly that they fixed upon for animadversion in one of their canons on Justification: "If any one shall say that it is not in man's power to make his ways evil, but that the works that are evil God worketh as well as those that are good, not permissively only, but properly and of Himself, to such an extent that the treachery of Judas is no less His work than the calling of Paul: let him," etc.[2]

This mistake of Melanchthon, which he did not fail to correct, did not prevent Calvin's continuing to maintain what he believed

[1] D'Aubigné, *History of Reformation*, vol. iii. p. 33.   [2] Canon VI.

SIN IN RELATION TO DIVINE PROVIDENCE 35

to be the whole truth of Scripture on the relation of sin to divine providence. From the canon just quoted, it is plain that the Romanist theologians were prepared to admit nothing more than that God permitted sin in the life of the world or did not actively interpose to prevent its being done. Such a statement, however, did not seem to Calvin to represent fairly what the Bible said on the matter. He remembered, for example, what Augustine had written on God's relation to the evil deeds of men. The great Latin theologian had always contended that the evil of men's deeds was not to be ascribed to God, yet he did not hesitate to say: "God does not command the wicked by ordering, in which case obedience would be laudable, but by His secret and just judgment He binds their will already bad by their own depravity, to this misdeed or that"; "God worketh in the hearts of men to incline their wills as He pleaseth, whether to good of His mercy or to evil, according to their deservings, and that by His judgment, sometimes open, sometimes hidden, but always just."[1] This was the position held by Calvin. He could not adopt the extreme language of Melanchthon, but he would not ignore the more direct guidance of sin in human life, which Augustine had acknowledged. Thus in his *Antidote to the Council of Trent*, he says: "As I abhor paradox, I readily repudiate the saying that the treachery of Judas is as properly the work of God as the calling of Paul. But they will never convince any man that God only acts permissively in the wicked, except it be one, who is ignorant of the whole doctrine of Scripture."[2]

What manifold evidence the Bible presents on this theme, is seen on almost every page. In two chapters of his *Institutes*, Calvin has reviewed it in detail.[3] Sinful men are spoken of as pursuing their own wicked ends, but God is represented as pursuing His own righteous ends by means of their inveterate propensity to sin. He overrules the sin of men to their own punishment: as when He hardened Pharaoh's heart not to let Israel go,[4] and the hearts of the Canaanites to oppose Israel's entrance into the promised land,[5] and the hearts of Eli's sons not to hearken to their father, "because the Lord would slay them."[6] He overrules the sins of men also for the chastisement or purification and advancement of His people. Joseph's brethren sought to do him evil; but, as he himself afterwards said, in selling him into Egypt, it was not they but God that sent him thither.[7] David, king of Israel, led on by pride took a census of Israel. Satan is said to have "provoked him to do this." But the higher explanation also given in Scripture is, that the anger of the Lord was kindled against Israel and He moved David against them to say: "Go and number Israel and Judah."[8] God overrules

[1] Cf. *Institutes, ut infra*.   [2] *Tracts* (Calvin Trans. Soc.), vol. iii. p. 149.
[3] Book I. ch. xviii.; bk. II. ch. iv.   [4] Ex. iv. 21.
[5] Josh. xi. 20.   [6] 1 Sam. ii. 25.   [7] Gen. xlv. 8.
[8] 2 Sam. xxiv. 1.

the sin of man also to carry out His purpose of redemption. The crucifixion of Jesus was the darkest crime that ever stained this sinful world, and as such it lay at the door of the Jews and Judas and the Roman governor. But the Scriptures teach that in the view alike of Jesus and His apostles, the deed was carried out in direct accordance with the will of God: "And truly the Son of man goeth as it was determined, but woe unto that man by whom He is betrayed";[1] "Thou couldest have no power at all against me, except it were given thee from above: therefore he that delivered me unto thee hath the greater sin";[2] "Him being delivered by the determinate counsel and foreknowledge of God, ye have taken and by wicked hands have crucified and slain."[3]

In the face of such testimonies, it is impossible to affirm that the Lord of heaven and earth has no more connection with the sins of men, than that which is implied in permitting them. Yet it is just as evident that He is in no sense the author of sin or chargeable with it. "God cannot be tempted with evil neither tempteth He any man. But every man is tempted, when he is drawn away of his own lust and enticed."[4] Here we are concerned only with the divine providence. If in creation as it came originally from the hand of God, there had been anything evil, it might have been justly laid to His charge. But in providence, where God has regard to the capacities and rights and responsibilities of His creatures, evil may emerge for which He is not responsible, but which He may overrule for His glory. As Augustine says, we must consider "to what end the will of each agent in the sin has respect. For the thing which God rightly wills, He accomplished by the evil deeds of bad men."

On this position the later apologists for the Council of Trent have never been able to make any effective assault. Bellarmin, for example, has at great length endeavoured to prove that all that can be rightly affirmed is that God simply permits evil to take place. Any other view seems to him inconsistent with the holiness of God and the freedom he claims for the human will. But against his reasonings, the Reformed theologians have always fallen back on the large body of Scripture proofs already outlined and have contended that these set it beyond doubt that the sins of men are not done without God's knowledge or consent or active interposition and superintendence, but that in a real sense and to a real extent (which however they could not define fully) His agency was at work in connection with them. No one can endeavour to combine the whole teaching of Scripture without having this conclusion forced upon him. Indeed, as Turretin pointed out, Bellarmin himself was unconsciously led to present this truth in terms almost strong enough to satisfy any Protestant theologian; for he wrote: "God not only permits the wicked to do many evil deeds and not only leaves the pious so that they are compelled to bear what is inflicted on them

[1] Luke xxii. 22.   [2] John xix. 11.   [3] Acts ii. 23.   [4] Jas. i. 13.

by the wicked, but even wields dominion over their evil wills and rules and governs, turns and bends them by operating invisibly in them, so that they are evil by their own proper fault, yet by divine providence, they are guided not positively but permissively, to one evil rather than another."[1]

When a Romanist could write thus, there is little room for surprise that the Reformed Confessions should make statements still more explicit. One of the best of these is found in the Westminster Confession: "The Almighty power, unsearchable wisdom and infinite goodness of God, so far manifest themselves in His providence, that it extendeth itself even to the first fall, and all other sins of angels and men, and that not by a bare permission, but such as hath joined with it a most wise and powerful bounding and otherwise ordering and governing of them, in a manifold dispensation, to his own holy ends; yet so as the sinfulness thereof proceedeth only from the creature and not from God; who, being most holy and righteous, neither is nor can be the author or approver of sin."[2] Beyond such a deliverance as this, it is needless to go. When the attempt is made, it only leads to that question of the origin of evil in the universe, which under every form of religion must here below remain a problem we cannot fully solve.

[1] *Opera,* Loc. VI. q. viii. § 7.   [2] Ch. v. 4.

CHAPTER V

THE METHOD OF CHRISTIANITY—REPENTANCE AND FAITH

AFTER drawing up their views on the Fall and its consequences, the theologians of Trent turned to the special blessings of the gospel. It was on these points that the greatest differences betwixt them and the Reformers emerged, and they felt it necessary to set forth the positions they were prepared to maintain with the utmost distinctness. At this stage we might have fallen in with the same order. But it will conduce much to a clear apprehension of the essential contrariety of the two systems, if we take up here the preliminary topic of the method of Christianity in dealing with fallen men and show how in their very first views of the nature and operation of the Christian redemption, Romanism and Protestantism took up a different attitude and proceeded on divergent lines.

The first and most distinguishing feature of mediæval Christianity was the prominence which it assigned to the teaching and declarations of the Church. This heritage it received from a very early period. By the leading theologians of the primitive Church, the whole Bible was regarded as a repository of intellectual doctrines. Origen, for example, regarded Christ not so much as a personal Saviour, manifesting His redeeming power in His death, resurrection and ascension into heaven, as a great teacher or lawgiver, or to use his own words, "the introducer of the saving dogmas of Christianity." It was these doctrines, including certain truths to be believed as well as a law to be obeyed, that constituted the real value of the Scriptures. To educe them in fitting order from this source was the supreme work of the Church; and intellectual assent to the resultant form or rule of faith, along with the endeavour to mould life and character in accordance with it, was the one duty binding on all who would become members within her pale. The same view came to prevail in the Western Church. Even Augustine was unable to cast off this bondage. The later mediæval theologians accepted it without demur. With Thomas Aquinas, the Scriptures are still the supreme source of doctrine:[1] but the special type of teaching recognised by the Church as a whole was the vehicle of instruction

[1] Cf. Prof. W. R. Smith, *What History teaches us to seek in the Bible* (*Inaugural Lecture*), p. 17.

with which every member of the Church had to do. All that was required was thought upon it with assent: this was faith. He that was prepared to yield a full mental assent to this rule was counted a believer: he that declined to receive it in its integrity was regarded as a heretic.

But it was not enough for the Church to put forth the form of doctrine which men were bound to accept. The principal element in this rule of faith was the power that had been conferred by God upon the Church. She herself was the object that was to bulk most largely in the eye of all her members and adherents: for by the grace of God, the Church had been made the supreme saving institute for fallen men under the heavens. This idea also was one of very early and gradual growth. After the apostolic age, the clergy began to exalt themselves and assume the functions of priests. This usurpation was naturally followed by the ascription of a very special value to the sacraments, when duly performed by them: even apart from the faith of the recipient, these ordinances were the channel of saving virtue. But if this were so, what view was to be taken of the Church, whose servants the priesthood were? Was she not, when regarded in connection with the whole hierarchy from the supreme Pontiff downwards, the one treasure-house in which all the grace and merits of the Lord Jesus had been deposited? Was not the Church, as the body of Christ, the visible counterpart of the Holy Roman Empire, and therefore entitled to wield over the spiritual life the same absolute authority that the Empire had over men in their social and civil relations? The whole efforts of such men as Gregory VII. were directed towards the realisation of this ideal; and, as time went on, every essential part of the project was attained. "Nulla salus extra ecclesiam"—no salvation outside the Church of Rome, was the postulate of mediæval Christianity. All who did not bow before it were apostates fit only for the dungeon and the stake.

It was a necessary result of this predominance of the Church that the aspirant to full communion with her had to put his whole case into the hands of the priesthood. The priest was the authorised "spiritual adviser" of the Christian community and no one could expect to be received into the Church or enjoy her privileges who did not submit the soul to his guidance. This authority was exercised in connection with a certain course of instruction, which, however, was often of the most meagre description when it was given at all; but very specially in the penitential preparation for receiving the sacraments. Whatever course of observances the priest set forth, the penitent had to obey it. Even though it involved austerities that could not fail to be painful, the sacerdotal prescription had to be carried out to its minutest details, or otherwise expressly compounded for.

The turning-point of entrance into the Church was the reception of baptism at the hands of the priest. In the case of the children of the faithful, this sacrament was administered as soon after birth as possible. In the case of the adult applicant, it was imparted, when the priest was satisfied that the requisite preparation had been fulfilled. Effecting as it did a complete union with the Church, baptism was regarded as the certain channel of redemption. By receiving it, the applicant was prepared for all other sacramental privileges the Church had to bestow.

Such were the leading features of the method of Christianity as practised by the Church of Rome up to the time of the Reformation. As the necessity for that great crisis showed, it had proved utterly ineffectual for the aim that the religion of the Lord Jesus had in view. To those who had been longing for a higher life, its multitudinous observances proved a burden too heavy to bear. Those who were worldly and indifferent, instead of opening their eyes and turning them from darkness to light, and from the power of Satan unto the living God, it only drew into a deeper bondage. As Luther put it, the mediæval form of the Christian religion as practised by the Papacy, had landed the whole Church in a state of "Babylonian captivity."

In view of a feeling so intense and widespread as this was, it might have been expected that the Council of Trent, when it assembled, would have endeavoured to vindicate in some decisive way the true spiritual liberty wherewith Christ has made His disciples free. But apart from the more evangelical strain of some of the earlier sections on the decree on Justification, this emancipation is not given. It is still the declarations of the Church that are to govern the beliefs of men : the words of Scripture "are to be understood in that sense which the perpetual consent of the Catholic Church hath held and expressed." It is still practically to the Church as the depository of grace that souls anxious to be saved must resort. It is still "by that penitence which must be performed before baptism," and therefore under the direction of the priesthood that men are to be prepared for the blessings of redemption. It is still "by the sacrament of baptism rightly administered in the form of the Church," that "the merit of Jesus Christ is applied both to adults and to infants." Where these principles are adhered to, true spiritual liberty is not to be enjoyed.

Nor has the Church of Rome modified her position in more recent times. It is true that in the hands of a theologian like Möhler, some sections of the decree on Justification are made to wear a very evangelical guise. He gives an account of the soul's first steps toward salvation that some Protestant theologians might not much stumble at. But it has to be remembered that Möhler was largely influenced by his wide acquaintance with Protestant theology, and that in such passages he is writing not so much out of his convictions as a Romanist as out of his own Christian experience. Other Romanist divines give the fullest prominence to the materialistic side of the Tridentine doctrine. The late Cardinal Manning, for example, did not hesitate to affirm that acceptance of the sacraments of the Church was all that was requisite to make men

Christians. "To become a Christian in the beginning of the gospel was a conscious act of the individual choice and will." Now "the whole body of Christendom by an act of God is made Christian without any conscious act of choice." "Baptism is God's appointed means for their first admission to the privileges of this mystical body." [1]

But now the question has to be faced: How does this representation of the Church of Rome square with the method of the Christian redemption as exhibited by Christ and His apostles?

What, for example, was the source of information set by the Lord and His followers before those who were anxious to know the nature and conditions of salvation? It was not the official declarations of the teachers of the Jewish people. He exhorted the people to "search the Scriptures." If His disciples were to be consecrated for His service, it could only be by the truth, and this truth was to be found only in the word of God: "Thy word is truth." From the written word, therefore, and not merely from the formulated teaching of men, were His disciples to derive that gospel of the grace of God, which was to be for the healing of the nations. "With all due reverence for the Fathers," said Luther, "I prefer the authority of Scripture." "The Church cannot create articles of faith; she can only recognise and confess them as a slave does the seal of his lord."

What again was the great theme of the gospel as proclaimed by the Lord and the apostles? It was the kingdom of heaven, that new reign of grace which had been promised by the prophets centuries before and had become a supreme object of desire among the nations. "Jesus went about all Galilee, teaching in their synagogues and preaching the gospel of the kingdom." [2]

In the later stages of His ministry, however, the Lord began to connect the kingdom more closely with Himself: "The kingdom of God cometh not with observation; neither shall they say, 'Lo! here,' or 'Lo! there': for lo! the kingdom of God is in the midst of you." [3] "My kingdom is not of this world." "Art thou a king then? Thou sayest (rightly) that I am a king." [4] This was tantamount to saying that it was He Himself who was the centre of the kingdom of heaven, and the supreme channel of all the grace God was to bestow by it. This at least was the view taken by the apostles. For when they began their work, they developed the doctrine taught by Christ into a special message concerning Himself. While proclaiming the kingdom of God, they also "preached Jesus and the Resurrection." [5] As the historian of the "Acts" puts it in describing Paul's work at Rome, "he received all that went in unto him, preaching the kingdom of God and teaching the things concerning the Lord Jesus." [6]

This view accordingly was a cardinal principle with the Reformers.

---
[1] *Unity of the Church*, p. 263. Cf. Litton, *The Church of Christ*, p. 231.
[2] Matt. iii. 1, iv. 23.   [3] Luke xvii. 20, 21.   [4] John xviii. 36, 37.
[5] Acts iv. 2.   [6] Ch. xxviii. 31; Col. i. 28; John i. 16, 18.

The evangelic order of truth, they held, was not, first the Church as a depository of grace and then Christ; but first the kingdom of heaven, Christ as the centre of it and then the Church through Christ. Luther wisely said: "To set forth the Church as the way to Christ, instead of setting forth Christ as the way to the Church was the fountain of unnumbered errors."

In entire harmony with their message concerning the heavenly source of salvation was the apostles' teaching on the way in which men were to enter on the enjoyment of it. Instead of insisting on submission even to their inspired guidance, they proclaimed at the outset the necessity of a new inward change on the part of men themselves, namely, repentance.[1]

What this repentance involves, we have no difficulty in determining. The first element in it is that which the literal significance of the word itself presents, namely, a change of mind or conviction. As men were by nature, they had wrong ideas of God, of themselves and of the duty they owed to Him. They were summoned to change and purify these views. They were to look on God as a righteous Judge as well as a source of blessing: they were to see themselves as sinful and guilty in His sight: they were to stand in awe of a coming day of judgment. Along with this change of mind, there was to be a change of heart or disposition. The connections in which "repentance" is used make this clear: the change of conviction through mind and conscience was to be so deep as to reach the heart, and break down the pride and self-righteousness cherished there into humility and love to God and man. The ultimate issue would be that there would be also a change of life: for the new heart, including as it does the will or source of action, would manifest itself in the whole conduct. The true penitent brings forth "fruit meet for repentance."

The discernment of this meaning of "repentance" was one of the turning-points of Luther's spiritual emancipation. Till he was thirty-six years of age, he was under the impression that "penitence," as the word was then rendered, was something to be done:[2] for "repent ye" was in the Vulgate translated "do penitence" or penance. It was regarded as a passing through the course of penitential discipline prescribed by the priesthood. But when he saw that the original Greek word of which "penitence" was an imperfect translation, really meant "change of mind," the joyful conviction took possession of his soul that it was not submission to the dictates of a priest that it enjoined, but a direct dealing with God as He called on men to humble themselves before Him, and be exalted in due time. With Luther and his friends, "repentance" was thenceforth a spiritual process which man was held by the gospel responsible for initiating and carrying out, but which could in reality be accomplished only by the power of the Holy Spirit.

The views of Calvin on the spirituality of repentance coincided

[1] Matt. iii. 1; Mark i. 15; Luke xiii. 3, 5.
[2] *Briefe* (De W.), i. s. 116. Cf. Beard, *Hibbert Lectures*, p. 118.

entirely with those of Luther. He held it right that men should be summoned to face this first great duty as one directly incumbent on them.[1] Only he was also most anxious to deliver men from the idea that they could develop this repentance themselves, or that it was confined only to the preparatory stages of the Christian life. Hence he laid great stress on the truth, that repentance was a lifelong process, and could be duly carried out only through that filial fear of God which took possession of the heart in saving faith and regeneration. In adopting this view, as we shall see in a later chapter, Calvin was justified by the language of Scripture. It is practically the same truth that is recognised, when, in the Westminster and other Catechisms, faith is made to stand first in the demands of the gospel, and repentance is placed next as "repentance unto life." Yet, with the method of the Lord and His apostles before him, the Christian preacher is called upon also to bring men face to face with the duty of repentance in the first appeals of the gospel. Without this indeed we can hardly be said to give the Holy Spirit the opportunity He needs for deepening the conviction of sin in the soul, and so hastening its entrance into the kingdom of heaven.

In the light of this view of repentance, the true way of actually appropriating salvation comes into full relief. It is not by mere submission to the ordinance of baptism, but by faith in Christ.[2]

It is true that baptism also was required of all that wished to enjoy the blessings of redemption, and to be received as members of the Christian community. It is needless to ignore the fact that this ordinance occupied a prominent position alike in the view of the apostles and the people they evangelised. This is seen in the condensed forms of expression used in connection with the offer of the special blessings of Christianity.[3] But when these expressions are examined, it becomes manifest that it is not mere acceptance of baptism that confers the blessing, but the believing in Christ Himself.[4]

As to what faith implies, it is not denied that there must be assent to the historic truth of the Scriptures and of the facts of the gospel. Without such a basis faith could not exist. But such belief is far from being an explanation of Christian faith. In its simplest form it is recognition of the higher world in which God rules, and of His beneficent activity there in behalf of the children of men. By thus laying in the soul a foundation for future blessing, and preparing it for intercourse with heaven, faith realises the description given of it in the Epistle to the Hebrews as "the substance of things hoped for, the evidence of things not seen."[5] But as now required by the gospel, it is primarily the acceptance of Christ as a personal Saviour given by the sovereign grace of God.[6] In this aspect, faith is not an

[1] *Institutes*, bk. III. ch. iii. p. 19.
[2] Matt. ix. 28; Luke vii. 50; John iii. 16, xiv. 1.
[3] Acts ii. 38, xxii. 16; Rom. vi. 3.   [4] Acts xxii. 16; Col. iii. 12.
[5] Ch. xi. 1.   [6] John i. 12.

act of the intellect merely, but the consent of the heart to the saving power of Christ. Since out of the heart are the issues of life, this trustful acceptance of the Saviour carries with it the surrender of the will and the whole conduct to His guidance. As a German Protestant theologian has put it, "faith is an unfolding of the heart, an opening up of the whole personal life to all the forces of the higher, eternal and blessed life that are now concentrated in Christ."[1]

How fully this view of the nature and operation of faith was acknowledged by the Reformers, we need not here show in detail. We shall find it expressed most sharply in connection with the doctrine of justification. It is either assumed or plainly taught in every one of their writings. From the divergence on this and the kindred points noted, a wide gulf began to open betwixt Romanism and Protestantism. How it became deeper and wider, the sequel will show.

[1] Vilmar, *Handbuch der Evangelischen Dogmatik*, s. 145.

CHAPTER VI

THE PRIMARY BLESSINGS OF THE GOSPEL—FORGIVENESS—
JUSTIFICATION

HAVING seen how Romanism and Protestantism diverge in their general conceptions of the nature and operation of Christianity, we are now prepared to compare the views they hold on the primary benefits it confers on men. It is at this point we enter on the field where the main conflict betwixt the two systems has been carried on. What is the most perilous element in man's condition as a sinner? What is thus his first and most clamant need? Through what channel, on what grounds and by what instrumentality on man's part, is this need met? These are the questions the Church has to raise and settle, if she would fulfil the task of saving souls. It is from the strong contrast in the answers they return that the wide chasm betwixt the Church of Rome and the Protestant Churches has been formed.

The period preceding the Reformation was not fitted to give birth to any thorough and accurate solution of the problem of the soul's salvation: the source of its failure lay in the fact that there was not then abroad in the minds of men any adequate sense of sin. This defect had been characteristic of almost every century since the time of Augustine. The growing secular feeling in the Church and the reception of so many members who were attracted only by social or political advantages, tended to lessen spiritual convictions of the heinousness of sin through many generations. No teacher arose of sufficient influence to stem the advancing tide of worldliness and ignorance. Save in the writings of Anselm and of such later followers as Thomas Aquinas, the apostolic teaching on sin and atonement received no adequate expression: and even these wielded influence over but a very limited area. The result was that except in the line of the chosen few who retained the light of primitive Christianity, any defects that human nature might be admitted to have or any transgressions into which men might fall, were sufficiently negotiated by the ordinances of the Church. The necessity of resorting to the facts or truths of the redeeming work of Christ as the guide of souls was becoming a thing of the past.

In the midst of this darkness, however, it pleased God to lead one great soul through a spiritual experience of sin so deep and abiding that there was awakened in him an intense craving to know the word of the truth of the gospel. Martin Luther had been chosen of God to be the bringer of light to the darkened peoples of Europe : but the conflict betwixt the two opposing elements had first to be fought out in his own soul. Through a terrible ordeal of suffering, temptation and doubt, the victory was at last won. Discerning the fruits that sin had borne in the life of men, he was at length also enabled to see and joyfully embrace the light and comfort God was prepared to dispense in the gospel of His Son. Where sin reigned unto death, grace now reigned through righteousness unto eternal life by Jesus Christ our Lord.

The first and most potent element in this discipline was his intense conviction of the guilt of sin. In this respect Luther advanced to a higher plane than Augustine. The Latin Father doubtless also discerned the penal consequences of transgression. Yet in his experience it was more with sin as entailing blindness, corruption and bondage that he had to deal. The great problem for Augustine was how to obtain a heart purified from the world and its lust. Luther, on the other hand, while feeling keenly the inveterate depravation sin had brought on every faculty of human nature, and especially the will, had his attention turned more to the judicial condemnation that God had pronounced on transgression. At this stage in the life of Europe, the idea of sovereign authority in connection with human law had taken a fuller possession of the minds of men. Luther had his eyes opened to see how completely this same idea governed the relations betwixt God and His creatures. Like Saul of Tarsus, trained under the theocracy of Israel, Luther saw sin first and chiefly as entailing on the transgressor guilt or the desert of punishment both in this world and that which is to come. The great question with him came to be how the conscience was to be liberated from the burden of this guilt, and the soul to be led into peace and friendship with God.

But along with this conviction of guilt, there was given to him a new view of the whole work of Christ as a Saviour from sin. This Luther owed, in the first instance, to Staupitz, the vicar-general of the Augustinian order in Germany. When, on making inquiry into the sadness that oppressed the young monk, Staupitz learned that he was burdened with a sense of his guilt, he directed him to look to what God had done to put away sin in the atoning sacrifice of His Son. "Why," said he, "do you torment yourself with all these speculations and these high thoughts? . . . Look at the wounds of Jesus Christ, to the blood that He has shed for you : it is there that the grace of God will appear unto you. Instead of torturing yourself on account of your sins, throw yourself into the Redeemer's arms. Trust in Him—in the righteousness of His life—in the atonement of His death. . . . If you desire to be converted, do not be curious about all these mortifications and all these tortures. Love

Him who first loved you." [1] As he listened to such words as these, Luther felt a new joy springing up in his soul. He began to see that the ground of peace lay not in what he himself was or could do, but in what God had done in the life and sacrifice of His Son.

There was still another truth, however, that had to be brought home with power, ere Luther could really tread the pathway of life. This was the way in which the sacrifice of Christ was to be appropriated and the immediate effect it was fitted to exercise on the soul. It was not till a second severe conflict with doubt had left him prostrate in body and mind that the great principle which was to sustain his heart was made known to him. Here Luther was greatly helped by an aged monk of the convent to whom he confided the cause of his trouble. After hearing his doubts, this pious friend repeated with great tenderness the words of the Creed : " I believe in the forgiveness of sins," and then added : "It is God's command that we should believe our own sins are forgiven. Hear what St. Bernard says: 'The testimony of the Holy Spirit in thy heart is this—Thy sins are forgiven thee.'" [2]

The joyful acceptance of this truth was the turning-point of Luther's whole career. From this time onwards, he never for any long period fell into the bondage under which he had formerly groaned. Yet he had to be more fully led into the recognition of the great principles that governed the spiritual life. This progress was made very specially in connection with a deeper insight into one great utterance of Scripture. When after his appointment to the chair of Biblical Theology at Wittenberg, he was devoting himself to the study of the Epistle to the Romans, Paul's quotation from Habakkuk in the first chapter arrested his attention : "The just shall live by faith." [3] There and then the connection betwixt faith and righteousness took possession of his mind. It is from righteousness that life flows ; but the righteousness and the life are both apprehended and sustained by faith. It was this same verse that restored his soul when he lay ill at Bologna on his way to Rome. It was still the same words that rung in his ears when he was toiling up Pilate's staircase to obtain an indulgence, and made him flee from the scene of superstition with horror. [4]

The result was that he was led to discern the first and most obvious application of this great maxim of Habakkuk by Paul to the problem of a sinner's acquittal at the bar of God. "By the deeds of the law shall no flesh be justified in His sight. . . . But now apart from the law a righteousness of God hath been manifested, being witnessed by the law and the prophets, even the righteousness of God through faith in Jesus Christ unto all that believe . . . being justified freely by His grace through the redemp-

[1] D'Aubigné, *History of Reformation*, vol. i. p. 176.
[2] D'Aubigné, *ut sup.* p. 181. [3] D'Aubigné, *ut sup.* p. 186.
[4] D'Aubigné, *ut sup.* p. 199.

tion that is in Christ Jesus."[1] "When, by the Spirit of God," said Luther, "I understood these words—when I learnt how the justification of the sinner proceeds from the free mercy of God through faith . . . then I felt born again like a new man; I entered through the open doors into the very paradise of God."[2]

After this vivid experience of the power of the doctrine, Luther could not help setting it in the forefront of his teaching. Very speedily there gathered around him a band of young men who imbibed the same truths. As the movement towards Reformation took shape in the various discussions that ensued, Luther's own convictions were more strictly defined. At Heidelberg, for example, in 1518, the thesis he maintained with such success was in these terms: "That man is not justified who performs many works, but he who without works has much faith in Christ." In commenting on the Imperial Edict in 1531, he said with still higher confidence: "I see that the devil is continually attacking this fundamental doctrine. . . . Well, then, I, Doctor Martin Luther, unworthy herald of the gospel of our Lord Jesus Christ, confess this article, that faith alone justifies before God; and I declare that it will stand and remain for ever."[3] As the Confessions of this period so clearly show, in this position, Luther only expressed the views of all the Reformers. The Augsburg Confession, for example, says: "The Churches also teach that men cannot be justified (obtain forgiveness of sins and righteousness) before God by their own powers, merits or works, but are justified freely (of grace) through faith, when they believe that they are received into favour and that their sins are forgiven for Christ's sake, who by His death hath satisfied for our sins. This faith doth God impute for righteousness before Him."[4]

We have been the more ready to dwell at the outset on the personal spiritual origin of the Protestant doctrine of justification, that it is in this way we are best able to appreciate the decree on this topic drawn up by the Council of Trent. Their statements are marked by a considerable amount of vagueness, arising from the attempt to give expression to many conflicting opinions. This want of precision is increased rather than removed by the thirty-three canons attached to the sixteen sections of the decree. Yet the great divergence of the Romanist doctrine from that of Protestantism is sufficiently plain.

The first feature of the Tridentine statement is the character of the change indicated by the word "justification." It is first set forth in general terms "as being a translation from that state wherein man is born a child of the first Adam to the state of grace and of *the adoption of the sons of God*, through the second Adam, Jesus Christ our Saviour: which translation indeed, since the promulgation of the gospel, cannot be effected, without the laver of regenera-

---

[1] Rom. iii. 21-24.   [2] D'Aubigné, *History of Reformation*, vol. i. p. 199.
[3] D'Aubigné, *ut sup.* p. 199.
[4] Art. IV. Cf. Schaff, *Creeds*, etc. vol. iii. p. 10.

tion or the desire of it, as it is written: 'Unless a man be born again of water and the Holy Ghost, he cannot enter into the kingdom of God.'"[1]

The way in which the blessing is to be received is next described. In the case of infants baptized by the Church of Rome, it is imparted in baptism itself, by which as an earlier decree teaches, "the guilt of original sin is remitted, and the whole of that which has the true and proper nature of sin is taken away." But in the case of adults who have not been baptized, justification is a gradual process the origin and course of which can be distinctly traced. "The beginning of this justification," the Synod declares, "is to be derived from the prevenient grace of God," so that men "may be disposed . . . to convert themselves to their own justification by freely assenting to and co-operating with that said grace."[2] This disposition or "preparation" is further aided first by "believing those things to be true which God has revealed and promised," then by "hope confiding that God will be propitious to them for Christ's sake," by "loving God as the fountain of all righteousness," and further "by that penitence which must be performed before baptism" and "by purposing to receive baptism and to begin a new life."[3]

After this preparation has been duly carried out, it is followed by justification itself, which is now described in more precise and specific terms as being "not remission of sins merely, but also the sanctification and renewal of the inner man through the voluntary reception of the grace and the gifts whereby man from being unrighteous becomes righteous, and from being an enemy becomes a friend, so that he may be an heir according to the hope of eternal life."[4]

As to the causes of this justification, the first we are concerned with here is the meritorious cause, which is stated to be "our Lord Jesus Christ . . . who merited justification for us by His most sacred passion on the wood of the Cross and made satisfaction for us unto God the Father." The instrumental cause is "the sacrament of baptism, which is the sacrament of faith, without which (faith) no man was ever justified." "Lastly, the alone formal cause," or as they seem to have understood it, "the vivifying principle," is "the righteousness of God: not that whereby He Himself is righteous, but that whereby He maketh us righteous, that, namely, with which we, being endowed by Him, are renewed in the spirit of our mind and are not reputed, but are truly called and are righteous, receiving righteousness within us, each one according to his own measure which the Holy Ghost distributes to every one as He wills and according to each one's proper disposition (preparation) and co-operation."[5]

That there may be no doubt about the operation of the meritorious cause of this blessing, an additional statement may be quoted, especially as it helps to set forth the real nature of justification in the Romanist sense: "Though no one can be righteous but he to

[1] Sess. VI. *On Justification*, ch. iv. [2] *Ut sup.* ch. v.
[3] *Ut sup.* ch. vi.   [4] *Ut sup.* ch. vii.   [5] *Ut sup.* ch. vii.

whom the merits of the Passion of our Lord Jesus Christ are communicated, yet this takes place in the justification of the wicked, when by the merit of that same most holy Passion, the love of God is shed abroad in the hearts of those that are justified and is inherent in them : whence man, through Jesus Christ in whom he is engrafted, receives in this very justification together with the remission of sins all these gifts infused at once, faith, hope and charity."

As to the function of faith in justification, a special chapter states "that we are said to be justified by faith on this account, that faith is the beginning of human salvation, the foundation and the root of all justification." [1] This statement is still further sharpened by one of the canons, which is to the effect that, "if any shall say that justifying faith is nothing but confidence in the divine mercy remitting sin on account of Christ, or that this faith alone is that by which we are justified, let him," etc.

In accordance with its nature as already described, justification is also expressly stated to be capable of increase : " Having been thus justified and made the friends and domestics of God . . . they, through the observance of the commandments of God and of the Church, faith co-operating with good works, increase in that righteousness which they have received by the grace of Christ and are further justified." [2]

Amongst the Romanist theologians who have most carefully studied and expounded the decree on Justification, Bellarmin occupies the chief place. In some respects, he has gone beyond the Council of Trent in adherence to mediæval doctrine ; as, when reviving a well-known distinction of Aquinas, he teaches that it is only the merit from desert that is denied by the Council to works preceding justification, but that they have still the merit of congruity. In this way he is able to claim a certain mysterious influence for the first Godward movements of the soul, although they should be hardly distinguishable from the common operations of the mind. It is he also that brings out most clearly the real spirit of the references the Council makes to the work of Christ as the meritorious cause of justification. There is no direct influence of Christ's atoning sacrifice on the forgiveness of sins. All that it merits is the communication to men of personal righteousness, which is therefore the only formal cause; or, as we must interpret it, the only ground of justification. For he says expressly : " If inherent righteousness is the formal cause of absolute justification, the imputation of the righteousness of Christ is then not required."

The more recent Romanist dogmaticians proceed on substantially the same lines. Möhler, Perrone, Dens, for example, differ only on minor points of phraseology. Cardinal Newman wrote his *Lectures on Justification*, while still a minister of the Anglican Church. But the influence of the Tridentine doctrine is everywhere apparent. For instance, instead of attempting to find out the one definite meaning

[1] Sess. VI. *On Justification*, ch. viii. [2] *Ut sup.* ch. x.

which the original word for justification bears, he indulges in such sophistical descriptions as these : " On the whole then it appears that justification . . . declares the soul righteous, and in that declaration on the one hand conveys pardon for its past sins, and on the other makes it actually righteous." [1] "If God's word and work be so closely united as action and result are in ourselves, surely as we use the word 'work' in both senses to mean both the doing and the thing done, so we may fairly speak of justification, as if renewal as well as mere acceptance." [2] S. J. Hunter exhibits strongly the tendency of recent Jesuitical theology. According to him, the Catholic Church defines faith to be "the readiness of mind to believe all that God has revealed, together with an explicit belief on certain points." Justification he describes as " a new birth by which one dead in sins receives the gift of life. . . . By this new birth, the sinner becomes truly just, participating in the justice of God." [3]

The only effect which the publication of this decree had upon the Reformers was to make them cleave to their distinctive doctrine more firmly, and stir them to define its various elements with greater precision. To this work Calvin made admirable contributions, especially in his *Antidote to the Council of Trent*. Later theologians, alike of the Lutheran and Reformed Churches, continued the task. The result is that there is no Christian doctrine which has been more completely exhibited in all its varied aspects than this of justification.

The distinguishing feature of the Protestant position is the prominence it assigns to the redeeming work of Christ. Accepting the guilt of sin as the first element in man's fallen condition that had to be put away, the Protestant theologians set over against it the perfect righteousness which Christ had wrought out in His obedience unto death. As they came to say in later Confessions, for example, the Formula of Concord, His whole atoning work consisted not only of His suffering for sin but His obedience to the will of God : it embraced an active as well as a passive righteousness.[4] This righteousness was completed in Christ's death on Calvary and was manifested in His resurrection. For " He was delivered for our offences and raised again for our justification." [5] As the Puritans put it, if in His life and death, the Lord finished His satisfaction to the righteousness of the Father, in His resurrection the receipt in full was put into His own hands. When, therefore, Christ ascended into heaven and sat down at the right hand of God, He entered on the public possession of a new sentence of life and acquittal, which, as belonging to the Son of God, was available for all who were to be united to Him. He is there as "an advocate with the Father, Jesus Christ the righteous," [6] or, to use the phrase of Jeremiah which the Reformers seeing it realised in Christ made the watchword of their gospel, " the Lord our righteousness." [7]

[1] *Lectures*, etc. p. 83.   [2] *Ut sup.* p. 99.   [3] *Outlines*, etc. iii. p. 130.
[4] Cf. Winer, *Confessions of Christendom*, p. 131.   [5] Rom. iv. 25.
[6] 1 John ii. 1.   [7] Jer. xxiii. 6, xxxiii. 16 : Heb. *Jehovah-Tsidkenu*.

On the way in which men participate in this righteousness, Protestant theologians are equally emphatic and united. They receive it by faith : which faith the Scriptures represent "as including or containing that state of mind which can be described only by such words as trust and confidence, and as involving or comprehending that act or those acts which are described as accepting, embracing, receiving and resting upon Christ and His work for salvation." [1] Moreover, faith alone justifies, that is, faith is the only instrument required for receiving justification. The Council of Trent, as we have seen, maintained that at least other six acts on man's part were equally necessary to justification, faith being only the first and most fundamental, namely, fear, hope, love, penitence, or purpose of receiving the sacrament and of beginning a life of obedience. Protestants admit that these are duties God requires of men, and are to be found in those He justifies. But we deny that they are ever in Scripture said to be instrumental in justifying the sinner as faith is : while faith is constantly set forth as the one thing needful in this connection apart from every other duty : "That He might Himself be just and the justifier of him that hath faith in Jesus." [2] "We reckon therefore that a man is justified by faith apart from the works of the law" ; "But to him that worketh not but believeth on Him that justifieth the ungodly, his faith is reckoned for righteousness." [3]

The supreme efficacy of faith is due to the fact that it unites men to Christ. Springing from a new life implanted in the heart by God Himself, it enables the soul to embrace the glorified Christ so fully as to be identified with Him. The Lord and the apostles charged men to believe in His name, that is, "into" fellowship with Him in all that He is and has for us. When this faith is yielded, the soul is thenceforth "in" Christ as the surety and administrator of the New Covenant.

Here accordingly comes distinctly into view the special immediate effect of this faith on man's condition as a sinner. As united to Christ in heaven, the believing soul is so completely identified with Him that it partakes of the very legal standing that Christ Himself has. In other words, the righteousness of Christ as a satisfaction to God is imputed to men and reckoned as theirs. No other mode of expression does justice to the Scripture statements on the point : "For as through the one man's disobedience, the many were made sinners, even so through the obedience of the one, shall the many be made righteous." [4] "Him who knew no sin, He made to be sin on our behalf, that we might become the righteousness of God in Him." [5] "That I may win Christ and be found in Him not having a righteousness of my own, even that which is of the law, but that which is through faith in Christ, the righteousness which is of God by faith." [6] Such language as this would never have been used, if Paul had not intended to convey the truth that through faith in

---

[1] Cunningham, *Hist. Theol.* vol. ii. p. 60.
[2] Rom. iii. 26, 28.
[3] Rom. iv. 5.
[4] Rom. v. 19.
[5] 2 Cor. v. 19.
[6] Phil. iii. 9.

Christ, the sinner is regarded and treated as having rendered the very obedience unto death which Christ finished on Calvary.

The real meaning and contents of justification are thus set beyond doubt. It is a forensic or judicial blessing, affecting and changing man's legal standing before God as a guilty sinner. The Council of Trent held it to refer to and include the regeneration and sanctification of the soul, and only as this was embraced could forgiveness be dispensed. Protestantism holds that in Scripture "justification" bears the single meaning of a forensic sentence or declaration of being righteous. This is the sense of the word itself in the numerous passages in which it is found: this is also the meaning demanded by the whole context in which it appears. As applied to men, it has the two sides of forgiveness and acceptance: "Through this man is preached unto you the forgiveness of sins, and by Him all that believe are justified from all things."[1] Through the passion and active obedience of Christ, the sinner is at once forgiven all his sins and received into the favour of God. As the Westminster Catechism puts it: "Justification is an act of God's free grace, wherein He pardoneth all our sins and accepteth us as righteous in His sight only for the righteousness of Christ imputed to us and received by faith alone." Like one who has been first condemned and then acquitted, liberated from prison and restored to his rights as a citizen, the believer is first pardoned and then welcomed to abide in the presence and favour of God. He is dowered with the very gracious sentence of life that rests on the glorified Son of God. No wonder is it that Luther said: "In truth, this very language of St. Paul was to me the true gate of Paradise."

With these facts before us, we have no difficulty in disposing of the objections that Romanists are wont to adduce against the Protestant doctrine.

The first is drawn from the teaching of the Apostle James on justification. He expressly asserts that man is justified not by faith only but by works, adducing Abraham and Rahab as cases in point. Luther in his day was so much perplexed by these statements that he was prepared to surrender the Epistle of James as uncanonical. But Protestants have long seen that there is no necessity for this course. We do not deny that James teaches a justification by works. But we affirm that there is not the slightest reason to believe that he is dealing with the same aspect of the subject as Paul. Paul discusses the question of a sinner's justification before God: James deals with that of a believer's justification before men and his own conscience. As one has said, they are not like combatants facing each other with swords crossed: they stand back to back and fight against different foes. Paul opposes the tendency of the human heart to self-righteousness: James, the temptation to antinomianism. Paul upholds the sovereignty and power of divine grace in dealing with sinners: James, the necessity of practical holiness on the part of

[1] Acts xiii. 38.

believers. Paul shows how the sinner is dealt with at the bar of God, in the court of heaven: James shows what is required of the believer who would win the sentence of acceptance from his own conscience and the hearts of men at the bar of the world.

Equally futile is it to say that the Protestant doctrine is contradicted by the fact that faith is a work. It is not denied that faith is a duty that we owe to God, as when it is said: "This is the work of God that ye believe on Him whom He hath sent"; "Without faith it is impossible to please Him." What we contend for is that it is not as a duty performed or a work done that faith is said to justify. It justifies only as the instrument or hand that apprehends Christ. Even in this respect, it is the gift of divine grace: " By grace are ye saved through faith and that not of yourselves: it is the gift of God."

Another objection is to the effect that justification by faith alone tends to relax man's sense of obligation to holiness and obedience, or that, when the favour of God is so easily obtained, men are tempted to be less careful about good works. In reply, it has to be said that there is nothing in the way Christ has interposed in behalf of men fitted to relax the claims of the law in the eye of the world. Rather is the law honoured: for sin met with its highest penalty when it was found imputed to the Son of God. Neither is there anything in the participation of Christ's righteousness on man's part that lowers the dignity of law; for this union with Christ is based on a principle of representation that runs through all human society. Besides this view really springs from a misconception as to what faith in the Protestant sense of the word really is and involves. It is the act of a soul that has been quickened by the Spirit of God. The believing soul is a living soul that has been awakened and enlightened to discern the guilt and heinousness of sin in the eyes of the divine Judge. When the sinner thus disciplined is enabled to feel that he is forgiven and accepted, the inevitable result is a new sense of gratitude to God, the direct tendency of which is to make him willing to recognise the will of God and yield his own will to it and no less to accept the divine commandments as the guide of his life.[1]

Hence also it is in vain to allege that on the Protestant system there is no real redemption from the power of sin. This objection is strongly urged by Möhler. It arises from the supposition that because Protestants hold justification to be only a forensic blessing, a deliverance from guilt, the announcement of a sentence of pardon and acceptance passing into the consciousness of the sinner, they are not concerned about emancipation from sin's bondage and power. It is not so. We maintain that in itself justification deals only with the problem of human guilt and not with the corruption of the heart: but we also contend that man can never be thus justified without at the same time having a new change begun in his spiritual condition. For, as we have seen, faith unites men vitally to Christ so as to identify them with Him. The moment a soul believes, therefore, not

[1] Rom. iii. 31.

only is the guilt of sin put away, but the carnal nature receives a mortal wound under which it is bound at last to die, while at the same time a new life, which is really the life of Christ, is implanted in the soul. Faith is the exercise of a newborn soul in whom the germ of a righteous nature has been implanted by the Spirit. Under the power of the Spirit of holiness, it is certain to issue in a righteous character and life. Probably this truth has not been sufficiently recognised in the theology of Protestantism. It forms a prominent element in the teaching of the Apostle John : "If ye know that He is righteous, ye know that every one that doeth righteousness is born of Him."[1] "Let no man deceive you : he that doeth righteousness is righteous even as He is righteous."[2]

On the same principle, the objection also urged by Möhler that the Protestant gospel requires no real appropriation of Christ is seen to be groundless. For, as faith is the first outcome of the life of Christ in the soul, so it can never abide there without being accompanied by all the other graces of the Christian character. In opposition to the Protestant truth that we are justified by faith alone, Bellarmin teaches that we are not justified by faith alone, but that faith may be alone. Such a faith, we reply, is not worthy of the name. The faith in Christ we contend for is a living faith, a vital principle of confidence, which, as involving the surrender of the will to Him, becomes a power in the whole character and conduct ; as Paul said : "The life I live in the flesh, I live in faith, even the faith of the Son of God who loved me and gave Himself for me."[3] Such a faith informed by the Holy Spirit receives the life of Christ into the heart and manifests His likeness in daily service. Giving all diligence, the believer adds to faith, virtue, knowledge, temperance, patience, godliness, brotherly kindness, love, till he is changed into the image of his Lord from glory unto glory.

While disposing of these objections to the Protestant doctrine, we can adduce certain counter-objections to the teaching of Rome to which no satisfactory answer can be given.

The Romanist doctrine does not give a full solution of the problem of man's guilt in the sight of God. Sin is regarded too exclusively as entailing corruption. Paul teaches that the whole world is "guilty" before God, and presents the doctrine of justification as the evangelic explanation of the method by which guilt is put away. The Church of Rome leaves this part of his teaching unaccounted for.

Hence, also, it derogates from the perfection of Christ's atoning work. This is indeed regarded as the meritorious cause of justification ; but only in the sense of obtaining the communication of what is necessary to prepare for justification,—that is, faith, fear, hope, love and penitence. The New Testament exhibits it as a real sacrifice offered to the righteousness of God, and thereby as the ground on which man is justified.

[1] 1 John ii. 29.   [2] 1 John iii. 7.   [3] Gal. i. 20.

Similarly, the Romanist doctrine fails to magnify the grace of God in the salvation of men. It does indeed say in so many words that we are justified *freely*; but this admission is neutralised by the statement that man himself merits the communication of this grace in the preparation for justification. According to the New Testament, "grace reigns" throughout as the only sovereign force to which salvation in all its parts is due.

Thus the whole teaching of the Church of Rome here tends to foster a spirit of self-righteousness. Men are taught that they can prepare themselves to receive righteousness and that by the growth of this righteousness inherent in themselves they are forgiven. This kind of righteousness is of the law and not of faith.

The worst result of this type of doctrine is that it leaves the soul in uncertainty. As the condition of the inner life fluctuates, so must the sense of forgiveness and reconciliation waver. Such uncertainty is not in harmony with the peace and gladness and assurance the New Testament teaches us to expect as the result of justification by faith.[1]

[1] Rom. v. 1, 2.

CHAPTER VII

REGENERATION—THE STATE OF THE REGENERATE—POST-BAPTISMAL SIN

THE preceding chapter has practically shown the view taken by the theologians of Rome of the whole method by which the effects of sin are undone in men as a fallen race. Identifying justification with regeneration and taking this term in the largest sense it bears, they regarded it as setting forth every essential feature of the change, "from that state in which man is born a child of the first Adam to the state of grace." To the Council of Trent, salvation was just this translation and nothing more : for it carried with it a new nature and on this basis, the forgiveness of sins.

The Reformers differed from the theologians of Trent not only on the meaning attached to "justification" but also on the ground on which the primary blessings of the gospel were bestowed and the order in which they were to be received. But never once did they ignore the absolute necessity for the implantation of a new life in the heart of the forgiven sinner or refuse to admit that this gift did effect a transition from the kingdom of fallen nature into the kingdom of grace. To their mind, this was just as essential an element of salvation as forgiveness or acquittal. By his exposition of the inner or subjective side of salvation as a new birth, Augustine had made the Christian Church his debtor for every age. The Reformers welcomed the heritage and gladly joined the Church of Rome in upholding what elements of truth on this point she still retained.

It is well for this Church that there is room in her doctrine for such evangelic features. It is their presence that gives her system any vitality it possesses. Without such gracious elements, she would never be able to retain any hold on the awakened conscience of her people. Yet even in exhibiting the special aspect of salvation which they chose to represent as the whole of it, the fathers of the Council did not escape serious error. Indeed, they took no pains to avoid it. Having erroneous conclusions to maintain, they started from erroneous premises and could not logically exclude the presence of vitiating elements in any intermediate doctrine they introduced. In this way they diverged at several points from the teaching of Augustine and adopted positions that are distinctly tainted with

Pelagianism. With the doctrine of regeneration in the strictly Protestant sense before us, we may now set forth these errors in detail.

The first point at which they went astray was the way in which the great change was originated. The position they took up is indicated in these terms : " If anyone saith that the free will of man moved and excited by God, by its assenting to God exciting and calling it, co-operates to no effect whereby it may dispose and prepare itself for obtaining the grace of justification ; and that it cannot refuse its consent, if it would, but as something inanimate does nothing at all, but merely holds itself passive : let him," etc.[1] Here, it is manifest, no attempt is made to exclude altogether the presence and operation of divine grace. An earlier canon denies "that man may be justified before God without the grace of God." In accordance with this utterance, the canon just quoted implies that God Himself must "move," "excite," and "call." The Council of Trent cannot thus be charged with teaching Pelagianism in its grossest form. Yet it is just as obvious that the taint of that system colours the whole statement. Man in his fallen condition has still a freedom of will to do that which is good: his will is not wholly passive at any stage of the process of regeneration : it is still able to play its own part in the change and operate towards the attainment of it. All that it needs is to be "moved and excited by God." If, as is stated in one of the chapters of the decree, men are only "excited and assisted by divine grace," they are also "freely moved towards God" in faith, hope and penitence.[2] In other words, regeneration is not effected by the grace of God alone, but by the will of man co-operating with divine grace from beginning to end of the process. In no sense is the grace of God in regeneration irresistible. Man might well refuse to be converted : it is only by his assent that the change is carried out.

On all the cardinal points of this statement the Reformers joined issue with the Church of Rome. The grace of God was indispensable. So far they and the Romanists were at one. But its whole operation was required to an extent and to an effect the theologians of Trent never acknowledged. The Reformers did not indeed hold, as their opponents averred, that the nature of man in relation to regeneration was inanimate as a stock or stone. Any incautious expressions which might be construed to imply as much, they repudiated. Fallen man has still mind and heart and conscience ; and under the preaching of the word, he may, by the striving of the Spirit, at once feel his need of redemption, and long for it. He may be convinced of sin and misery, and may also understand the work and claims of Christ so far as to appreciate the benefit of being united to Him. But his will is subject to the dominion of sin all the while. The point at which the grace of God

---

[1] *On Justification*, Canon IV. Cf. Mirbt, p. 139.
[2] *Ut sup.* ch. vi.

has to begin its real saving work is the renewal of the will. This is the work of God alone. The Spirit has not merely to "move," or "excite," or "assist," but to "create." The will of man must receive a new energy and a new bent; and it is only when the new life thus implanted by the Spirit in the will pervades every other faculty that Christ is embraced as a Saviour and the soul is born from above.

At the outset of the great change, therefore, or in regeneration in its narrowest sense of "quickening," the nature of man is entirely passive: the Spirit of grace has to take the initiative in quickening the will. But the Reformers held just as strongly that once this is done, the will of man does play an active part in embracing Christ, and responding fully to the divine call. So in the later process of sanctification, the renewed will puts forth its energy in turning from sin and following righteousness. Yet even throughout this stage, the grace of God must reign. Sanctification is as truly a work of God's free grace as justification is an act of it.[1] Whatever man does, is done by God with him and in him. Only, his renewed energies are called into action, and must be consciously and with a full sense of responsibility concentrated on the great results that the grace of God has in view to achieve.

Hence also it is evident that in a real sense the grace of God in regeneration may be said to be irresistible. The Holy Spirit does not compel men to accept Christ against their will: on the contrary, in His ordinary operations in the hearts of men, He may be resisted and thwarted. But no power of man can resist Him in carrying out the purpose of God, to impart grace in such efficacy to a soul that it shall be quickened and turned to Him. The grace of God is irresistible in the sense that He can infuse such life and energy into the soul as shall certainly cause it of its own accord to embrace Christ and follow Him. In other words, it is sovereign and efficacious in every one that is called into the fellowship of His Son Jesus Christ.[2]

How fully the Reformers were supported by the teaching of Scripture is manifest to everyone who recalls the terms in which the saving change implied in regeneration is there described. The action ascribed to God by the sacred writers is not adequately defined by saying that it merely "moves" or "excites" or assists" the free will of man. The Bible speaks of the change as "a creation," "a quickening," "a resurrection," "a renovation," "a new birth."[3] No language could more distinctly teach that the grace of God is the antecedent of every good movement in the soul, and that it alone is the sovereign agent in effecting the regeneration of fallen men.

The second element of error in the teaching of the Council of Trent on this subject is found in their views regarding the special

---

[1] Sh. Cat. q. 35.   [2] 1 Cor. i. 9.
[3] Ps. li. 10; 2 Cor. iv. 17; Gal. vi. 15; Eph. ii. 1; Rom. vi. 11; Tit. iii. 5; John i. 13, iii. 1.

instrument by which regeneration is imparted.[1] The Romish doctrine on the point has already been partly explained. Baptism alone is regarded as all-sufficient to bestow this saving change. Faith also may be said to be necessary, not, however, in the Protestant sense or to the same effect. It is requisite only as regards information about the truth and assent to it: not as a means of actually receiving the blessing.

In adopting such tenets, the Reformers held, the Council of Trent grievously erred. For, as we have already seen, if there is one truth announced in Scripture more clearly than another, it is just that the new birth is effected by faith in Jesus Christ exhibited in the gospel. The word presents the glorified Saviour to the soul: the soul quickened by the Spirit is enabled to receive Him: in this believing reception, the new life emerges in a new birth, whereby the soul passes from the realm of fallen nature into the kingdom of heaven. The statement just quoted from the Gospel of John sets this beyond doubt. Other Scriptures confirm it: "Of His own will begat He us with the word of truth, that we should be a kind of first-fruits of His creatures";[2] "Being born not of corruptible seed, but of incorruptible, even the word of God that liveth and abideth for ever";[3] "Ye are all the children of God by faith in Jesus Christ"; "Whatsoever is born of God overcometh the world, and this is the victory that overcometh the world, even your faith."[4]

Another point at which the theologians of the Church of Rome went far astray was the effect that regeneration or the baptism by which it was bestowed, had on the presence and operation of sin in the soul. The essential features of their statement are expressed in these words: "If anyone denies that by the grace of the Lord Jesus which is conferred in baptism, the guilt of original sin is remitted, or even asserts that the whole of that which has the true and proper nature of sin is not taken away, but says that it is only rased and not imputed, let him," etc.[5] "For in those that are born again, there is nothing that God hates because . . . they are made innocent, immaculate, pure, harmless and beloved of God . . . so that there is nothing whatsoever to retard their entrance into heaven. But this holy Synod confesses and perceives that in the baptized there remains concupiscence or an incentive to sin. . . . This concupiscence which the apostle sometimes calls sin, the holy Synod declares that the catholic Church has never understood to be called sin, as being truly and properly born again, but because it is of sin and inclines to sin."

In this canon, the Romanist view of the efficacy of the sacraments is carried out to its last consequences. The Church of Rome feels herself put to the test as to whether she can impart at once a perfect salvation from sin: she professes to be able to do so. As it was by participation of the fruit of the forbidden tree that sin came into the

[1] Cf. ch. v.   [2] Jas. i. 18.   [3] 1 Pet. i. 23; Gal. iii. 26.
[4] 1 John v. 4.   [5] Sess. v. *On Original Sin*, 5.

soul with its guilt and power, so by the use of the sacrament of baptism, duly administered by the hands of the priesthood, this guilt can be wholly taken away and everything that has the nature of sin purged out of the soul. It is indeed possible for men to sin after baptism. This is due to the fact that even after receiving baptism, concupiscence or evil desire—to which, however, in accordance with their views of the fall, a predominantly sensuous import is attached— still lingers in the soul. This desire acts as an incentive to sin, and has therefore to be resisted. Yet in its essential nature, it is not sin: it becomes sin only when yielded to in act. The Apostle Paul, it is true, does in the Epistle to the Romans seem to call it sin, but he does so only in a metaphorical sense and because it becomes the occasion of actual transgression. In this way the Council of Trent upheld the efficacy of baptism, and also laid a foundation for their doctrine of merit or the possibility of establishing a claim on God by works perfectly good.

Here again, the Reformers felt, there was a grave divergence from the Scripture doctrine which they had begun to teach. Had the theologians of Trent been content to emphasise the complete freedom from the guilt of sin which the baptized believer obtains, they would have raised no objection. For this would only have been to magnify, as it deserved, the atoning work of Christ. When the relation betwixt faith and baptism is rightly apprehended, the statement would only have been the expression of a great evangelic truth. But when the Council proceeded to maintain that by baptism a freedom from the power of indwelling sin was obtained to an extent equally complete, the Reformers were convinced that the Church of Rome was claiming for baptism more than the apostles had ever ascribed even to a full-orbed faith and were thus giving countenance to an unscriptural and dangerous exaggeration.

For what was it, they asked, that really took place when the soul was born again through faith in Christ? That it was vitally united to Christ, they maintained as earnestly as the Romanists. So truly and deeply is the believer united to the Lord in heaven, that every stage of His redeeming work may be said to be reproduced in the soul. As with Christ, he was crucified, so with Him He rose and ascended into heaven and sits at God's right hand in the heavenly places. But such ideal or representative descriptions of the believer's standing in union with the glorified Saviour, are not to be taken as necessarily implying that by faith he has got rid of all connection with sin. They have to be interpreted in the light of other statements equally explicit to the effect that the believer has still to maintain a conflict with indwelling sin;[1] that though no longer in the flesh or carnal nature as the sphere of his real inner life, the flesh is still in him and has to be incessantly mortified and subdued in the strength of the indwelling Spirit. The truth is that when a man through faith in Christ has the guilt of sin cleansed, the carnal

[1] Rom. vi. 12, vii. 17, viii. 9, 12, 13.

nature within him is affected only to the extent of having a mortal wound inflicted on it. This certainly secures that its dominion over the soul shall be broken, but it still leaves its presence and operation there. Its power is overthrown, but its activity is not extirpated. The believer is only assured that through the blood of Christ applied by the Spirit as the direct Agent at work, its power in the soul shall gradually wither, while the energies of the new nature shall as certainly be unfolded. That, however, is a great and blessed victory: "sin shall not have dominion over you, for ye are not under law, but under grace";[1] "Because I live, ye shall live also."[2]

In this way too the Reformers escaped the temptation to minimise the sinful nature of the evil desire which, their opponents admitted, still made itself felt in the souls of believers. Concupiscence is not only the result of sin and an incentive to it, but is also in itself essentially sinful. The Apostle Paul undoubtedly identifies it with sin: "Nay, I had not known sin but by the law: for I had not known evil desire (concupiscence) except the law had said, Thou shalt not lust"; "In me, that is, in my flesh dwelleth no good thing"; "O wretched man that I am, who shall deliver me from this body of death,"[3] that is, from the wounded carnal nature that still cleaved to him even as a believer. It is true that according to the Apostle James, it is only when evil desire conceives that "it brings forth sin."[4] But it brings forth after its kind: the offspring is, like its parent, stamped with the minding of the flesh that is enmity against God. When the Apostle John writes: "If we say that we have no sin, we deceive ourselves and the truth is not in us,"[5] he, to use the words of an eminent expositor, "marks the presence of something which is not isolated, but a continuous source of influence." The principle "to have sin" is distinguished from the act "to sin," but both are alike sinful.

On this principle also we are enabled to discern the invalidity of the distinction which the Church of Rome draws betwixt "mortal" and "venial" sins. According to one of the most popular Romanist manuals of instruction, "mortal sin is a thorough violation or breaking of a commandment of God with full knowledge and deliberation. Venial sin is either a slight infringement of the law, or, it may be, in some cases a great violation of the law, but rendered slight in the person who commits it, through his want of sufficient knowledge, deliberation, or freedom. Venial sin, although an offence against God, does not cause the forfeiture of God's friendship or the loss of justifying grace as mortal sin does. In short, it does not inflict like mortal sin, death on the soul. It causes a stain and a guilt in the soul of which one can easily obtain pardon; and therefore it is in that sense called venial, from the Latin, *venia*, pardon. We ought to avoid venial sin because it is always an offence against God; but we ought to be much more careful to avoid with horror mortal sin

---

[1] Rom. vi. 14. [2] John xiv. 19. [3] Rom. vii. 7, 18, 24.
[4] Jas. i. 15. [5] 1 John i. 8. Cf. Westcott, *in loc.*

REGENERATION—THE STATE OF THE REGENERATE   63

which offends God grievously, causes death to the soul and deserves everlasting punishment."[1] Of such sins, the chief are said to be "pride, covetousness, lust, anger, gluttony, envy and sloth." The priesthood claim the sole prerogative of deciding what special sins are to be considered mortal and what venial.

This is a distinction which has not the slightest countenance in Scripture. The passages that are usually adduced in support of it deal either with different degrees of punishment in the eternal world[2] or with the different kinds of Pharisaism into which superstitious religionists may fall.[3] When the Apostle John speaks of a sin that may be "unto death" as contrasted with a sin that is "not unto death," he refers to a sin that cannot be forgiven at all, because unlike other transgressions, it involves in one form or other the sin against the Holy Spirit.[4] Protestantism has never taught that all sins are equally heinous. The Reformed Churches proclaim that "some sins in themselves and by reason of several aggravations are more heinous in the sight of God than others" and therefore expose to a greater degree of loss and suffering in eternity. Yet are they equally united in teaching that in the strict sense of the words every sin is mortal. For every sin, however trivial it may seem in the eye of man, has its root in a heart that is sinful and proceeds from a subsoil of thought and feeling that is also sinful. This is enough to stamp it with the sentence which the perfectly holy God has passed on "every want of conformity unto or transgression of the law of God," in desire, thought, word or deed. Besides, it is not true that one who is really a child of God will knowingly and habitually commit sin against God or that if he happens to be ensnared in such sin, he thereby loses the new life which was implanted in him by the Holy Ghost and led him through faith into vital union with Christ.[5] For the life of Christ in the soul is progressive and imperishable : " I give unto them eternal life and they shall never perish ";[6] "Whatsoever is born of God sinneth not."[7] The new birth is a permanent introduction into a new sphere of life, where all the resources of divine grace are made available for the everlasting salvation of the soul.

The only other point of difference that falls to be noticed here is concerned with the maintenance and increase of that fellowship with God into which the regenerate soul is introduced. The Romish view is set forth partly in the decree on Justification and more fully in the chapter on Penance.[8] The root of it is found in the position that when a baptized believer sins, forgiveness can be dispensed to him only through an ecclesiastical channel. From the moment of baptism, the whole life of a believer is regarded as belonging exclusively to the Church and under the supervision of the priesthood as

---
[1] Di Bruno, *Catholic Belief* (14th ed.), p. 59.   [2] Matt. v. 22.
[3] Matt. xxiii. 24 ; Luke vi. 42.   [4] 1 John v. 16.
[5] John vi. 36, 37, 39, 40.   [6] John x. 27, 29.   [7] 1 John iii. 9.
[8] *On Justification*, ch. xiv. ; *On the Sacrament of Penance*, Sess. XIV.

the accredited guardians of her purity. When therefore he falls into sin, he must go to the priest under whose jurisdiction he lives and comply with the ordained conditions ere he can receive pardon.

These conditions according to the Council are contrition, confession and satisfaction: which "are as it were the matter of the sacrament."[1] Contrition is defined as "a sorrow of mind, a detestation of sin committed with the purpose of not sinning for the future." Confession is the secret personal "enumeration" to the priest at certain stated times of all the mortal sins of which the penitent is conscious, "even though the sins may be most hidden." Satisfaction is the performance of the acts of humiliation or self-denial enjoined by the priest as the punishment of the sins enumerated "according to the quality of the offences and the ability of the penitent." Only when the satisfaction imposed by the priest is duly rendered can absolution be pronounced by him. For in dealing with the sins of believers under his care, the priest sits as a judge on a tribunal and his sentence must be executed, ere he can bestow the blessing.

In support of this method of forgiveness, almost the only Biblical statements adduced are those passages in which the apostles are authorised by the Lord to bind or loose and to remit or retain sins.[2] "Our Lord Jesus Christ, when about to ascend into heaven, left priests, His own vicars, as presidents and judges, unto whom all the mortal offences into which the faithful may fall should be carried, in order that, in accordance with the power of the keys, they may pronounce the sentence of forgiveness or retention of sins."[3]

What a system of tyranny, deceit, and imposture sprang from this evil root in the course of the Middle Ages, has already been partly seen and will yet be exhibited more fully. Meanwhile it is only necessary to show how, according to the Reformers, this chain of opinion and practice is alien alike from the whole spirit of the gospel and the express teaching of Scripture.

There is not the slightest indication in the writings of the apostles that the sins of believers are to be forgiven on any other ground than that on which they rested when they first went to the Saviour or that this forgiveness is to be obtained otherwise than directly from God.[4]

It is true that from the time when a believer professes his faith in Christ and is baptized, he no longer lives an isolated life, but is to regard himself and be treated as a member of the Christian community. But this fact does not bring him into subjection to those who may have been set apart for the work of the ministry, otherwise than "in the Lord." They are not priests in any sense that he is not. Believers are one and all of them on the same footing before God and "through Christ have access by one Spirit unto the Father."[5]

---

[1] *On Penance*, ch. iv.   [2] Matt. xviii. 18; John xx. 22, 23.
[3] *On Penance*, ch. v.
[4] Ps. xxv. 11; Isa. xliii. 25; Eph. i. 7; 1 Pet. i. 2; 1 John i. 7, 13, ii. 1.
[5] Eph. ii. 18.

There is but one atoning Priest in the Church of Christ, and He, after pouring out His soul as an all-sufficient offering for sin, sat down at the right hand of God, having obtained eternal redemption for us.[1]

In the light of these statements, it is manifest that, when the Lord gave to the disciples authority to remit and retain sins, He had in view offences that were doubtless sins against God, but came under their cognisance, because they were also offences that publicly militated against the reputation and spiritual life and progress of the Christian society. That such transgressions do occur, is a matter of constant experience. Members of the Church are continually falling into sins that publicly convict them of failure to fulfil their obligations as members of the Church ; and the Church as an organised society must, by her office-bearers, deal with such offenders in a way that shall be for their salvation, the edification of fellow-Christians and the glory of God. But such a method of ecclesiastical discipline is far apart from a secret tribunal of which a single so-called priest is the only judge. When the Lord empowered the disciples to exercise this authority, He dealt with them as representatives, either of the Church as a whole, or the presbyterate appointed and ordained by the Church. In either case, it was a corporate and disciplinary authority, not one that was individual and judicial.

In the light of these truths, we are able to form a right estimate of the conditions which the Church of Rome has attached to the forgiveness of sins. Contrition is everywhere regarded in Scripture as indispensable to forgiveness. But it must be manifested in the sight of God, and spring not only from a true sense of sin, but also from an apprehension of the mercy of God in Christ, and thus include along with grief for sin and hatred of it an actual conversion from sin " with full purpose of and endeavour after new obedience."[2] Sin has also to be confessed, but save in the case of offences that fall under the cognisance of the Church, to God alone. The passages [3] which Romanists adduce in support of sacramental confession, refer either to what is due to God only, or to that mutual acknowledgment of failure which is necessary to the reconciliation of friends that have been estranged.[4]

On the same principles, the alleged necessity for any satisfaction as a condition of forgiveness is seen to vanish like mist before the rising sun. Even if the sufferings which the presence of sin in the world entails in such manifold forms on the life of God's children had been of a penal or judicial character, that would have been no sufficient ground for the institution of a similar system of inflictions on the part of the ministry of the Church. For what may be right and just for God with His absolute authority and infinite wisdom and love to send or permit, may be utterly unrighteous in frail fallible men to

---

[1] 1 Cor. xi. 3 ; Heb. v. 14, x. 19 ; 1 Pet. ii. 4 ; Rev. i. 6.
[2] Sh. Cat. q. 87.   [3] Prov. xxviii. 13 ; Mark i. 5 ; Acts xix. 18.
[4] Num. v. 6, 7 ; Jas. v. 16,

determine or inflict on however low a scale. But as a matter of fact, the sufferings endured by God's children in the world are in no sense penal. The judicial element in the suffering attached to sin has for them been fully borne and entirely done away in the cross of Christ. The Christ was "to make an end of transgression."[1] The Lord said on the tree, "It is finished." "There remaineth no more sacrifice for sin," because none is needed. Since those who are forgiven and saved by the blood of the Cross are introduced into the friendship of God and made and recognised as His children, any sufferings they may undergo are to be regarded as His fatherly chastisements, sent not only for the correction of sins committed, but also to preserve from future sin, to test and develop faith, to influence others and prepare for future and more strenuous service. "Whom the Lord loveth He chasteneth and scourgeth every son whom He receiveth."[2] God as the Father of our spirits chasteneth us "for our profit that we may be partakers of His holiness." "Ye have been put to grief in manifold trials, that the proof of your faith, being more precious than gold that perisheth, though it is proved by fire, might be found unto praise and glory and honour."[3] "As many as I love, I rebuke and chasten."[4]

It is as reproducing and reflecting the spirit of such fatherly corrections that the Church is authorised to exercise the power of suspending or cutting off from the enjoyment of the privileges of communion those that may bring overt reproach on the cause she represents. But such publicly recognised exercise of ecclesiastical discipline is distant as the poles from the secret arbitrary devices of an irresponsible priesthood. These can only tend to degrade alike the officials that impose them and the people who are so forgetful of the dignity of God's regenerate children as to submit to them.

[1] Dan. ix. 24; John xix. 30; Heb. x. 36.
[2] Heb. xii. 6, 10.
[3] 1 Pet. i. 6, 7.
[4] Rev. iii. 19.

CHAPTER VIII

THE HIGHER BLESSINGS OF THE GOSPEL

THE identifying of justification with regeneration by the theologians of Trent, and the immediate errors into which they fell, are not the only results of their failure to discern the real nature of that blessing. Not merely did they fail to appreciate the way in which the redemption of Christ bears on the primary effect of sin : they were also led to overlook the deeper results of sin and the value of the relative blessings which the victorious Christ confers on all that are united to Him. The fruits of sin are seen in their magnitude only when the various aspects of fallen man's nature and life are regarded distinctly. In the light of his relation to God as creature and subject, sin has entailed guilt. On his moral nature, it has brought corruption. As God's vicegerent in the world, man has been visited with loss of dominion and inheritance. As originally called to live in close fellowship with God, he has suffered the withdrawal of His Spirit and lost the assurance of being under His favour, embraced in His purpose and ordained to reach a higher destiny. The redemption of Christ meets all of these results with special corresponding blessings. But notwithstanding their avowed purpose "to expound the true and sound doctrine" of salvation as taught by Christ and His apostles, the Tridentine dogmaticians did not distinguish the different elements in salvation aright and, even when they mentioned them, did not give them the prominence and value assigned to them in the Scriptures.

The Reformers on the other hand paid special attention to the apostolic teaching on these topics ; and even though their method of exhibiting the various aspects of redemption has since been developed and improved upon, we find in the Confessions of the Reformed Churches a fair recognition of all the higher blessings of the gospel. It will be fitting to present here some indication of the contrast presented by the way in which the two Churches deal with these points.

1. With respect to sanctification, it would be very unfair to ignore the fact, that the Church of Rome has always laid the utmost stress on the reality and necessity of the blessing. This has been made manifest in the preceding chapter. The Council of Trent erred in identifying justification with regeneration ; but the decree on that

subject is quite consistent in holding that regeneration includes and leads to deliverance from the love and power of sin, and to a new life. The justified or regenerate are said "to be renewed day by day, that is, by mortifying the members of their own flesh and by presenting them as instruments of righteousness unto sanctification, they, through the observance of the commandments of God and of the Church, faith co-operating with good works, increase in that righteousness which they have received through the grace of Christ and are still further justified."[1] The defects in this description are patent on the surface. The source of sanctification in the grace of God is not indicated as it ought to be; and in consequence the attainment of the blessing is here as elsewhere represented too much as a matter of human effort and compliance with the observances of the Church. With the Reformers, on the other hand, sanctification is exhibited as specially the fruit of divine grace, the work of the Holy Spirit renewing the whole man, and the root whence all good works inevitably spring. This view may be seen even in Luther's Small Catechism (1529) in which sanctification is a prominent topic. It is stated with notable precision in the Scotch Confession (1560): "As we utterly spoil ourselves of all honour and glory of our own creation and redemption, so do we also of our regeneration and sanctification. For of ourselves we are not sufficient to think one good thought, but He who has begun the work in us, is only He that continues us in the same, to the praise and glory of His undeserved grace."[2]

2. As sanctification undoes the results of sin in man's moral nature, so adoption with its correlative blessing of heirship, is intended to restore him to the higher destiny and inheritance which man by his sin forfeited. This fruit of union with Christ is barely mentioned in the Tridentine decree. It is evidently regarded as a mere result or aspect of justification in the sense of regeneration, and not as a new and higher relationship to God the Father, obtained through faith in Christ His Son. The same defect is seen in the teaching of several of the Reformed Confessions, with this difference that like justification, adoption is exhibited as the fruit of God's free grace. A marked exception is found in the *Consensus Tigurinus*, written by Calvin (1549), in which it is said: "Accordingly it must be held that Christ, being the eternal Son of God, of the same essence and glory with the Father, put on our flesh, in order that by right of adoption, He might communicate to us what by nature was solely His own, to wit that we should be sons of God. This takes place when we, ingrafted through faith into the body of Christ and thus by the power of the Holy Spirit, are first justified by the gratuitous imputation of righteousness, and there regenerated into a new life, that, new created in the image of the heavenly Father, we may put off the old man."[3] Here adoption is put in its rightful Pauline position as in the order

---

[1] *On Justification*, ch. x.
[2] Art. XII. *Of Faith in the Holy Ghost.* Schaff, vol. iii. p. 451.
[3] Art. III. Cf. Appendix to *Outlines of Theology*, by A. A. Hodge, p. 651.

of faith posterior to sanctification and identifying the believer with Christ in the sonship that belongs to Him as the incarnate Saviour. Among modern theologians, the late Principal Candlish has the distinction of reviving and more fully expanding the view held by the great teacher of the Reformation.[1]

3. As man by sin lost the indwelling of the Holy Spirit and the privilege of intimate fellowship with God in all his life, so in union with the glorified Son through faith, he receives once more the presence and power of the Spirit and therewith a fuller preparation for spiritual service. It is this blessing that the Reformers meant by the Christian priesthood and modern Protestant evangelism knows as consecration. It is needless to prove that this blessing is not recognised as it ought to be in Tridentine teaching. It would have been foreign to the whole spirit of the system to admit it in anything but the name. But as Luther showed, if a believer is admitted to free, full and uninterrupted access to God in union with His Son, and living in the holiest of all is there baptized in the Holy Spirit, he is prepared to exercise under Christ according to his measure, the office of a priest, king and prophet in the world. It is the unction from the Holy One that makes him a Christian and it is the same grace that makes him a priest unto his God and Father.[2] It is the recognition of this truth that is so prominent a characteristic of modern evangelical activity. Consecration is not the work of man but of God. It is the work of God's free grace whereby through the Spirit He takes a growing possession of our mind and heart and conscience and will as His children, and so makes our souls a fit dwelling-place for Himself for His own glory and our present fruitfulness and everlasting reward.

4. At this point, however, the question arises : If such be the blessings which God bestows on those that believe in His Son, in what manner or to what immediate effects are they received in the heart? Does God impart them in such a way as to make those who enjoy them practically assured that they are saved for ever? Or, in other words, is it practicable, expedient and obligatory that men should be assured of their everlasting salvation? This was a question that could not but be suggested to the Reformers as well by the study of the Scriptures as by their own intense Christian experience. When they examined the utterances of the apostles, for example, they could not help seeing that it was possible for believers to be assured of their salvation. They all spoke with a tone of unwavering certitude on this point. Repeating and confirming the expressions of patriarch, psalmist and prophet, Paul, for example, said : "The Spirit beareth witness with our spirit that we are children of God" ;[3] "The life I live in the flesh, I live in faith, the faith of the Son of God who loved me and gave Himself for me" ;[4] and, when His career was coming to an end : "I know Him whom I have believed and I am persuaded that He is able to guard that which I have committed unto Him

---
[1] *The Fatherhood of God (First course of Cunningham Lectures)*.
[2] Rev. i. 6.   [3] Rom. viii. 16.   [4] Gal. ii. 20.

against that day"; [1] "The Lord will deliver me from every evil work and will save me unto His heavenly kingdom." [2] The apostles took it for granted that other Christian disciples might enjoy the same certitude that they had. The writer to the Hebrews urges his readers to show the same diligence to the full assurance of hope to the end. Addressing his brethren of the dispersion Peter said that believing in Christ, they rejoiced with joy unspeakable and full of glory. Speaking for his fellow-believers as for himself, John said they knew they had passed from death unto life and were in Christ, because they had the legitimate fruits of this change in their character and conduct.

The grace which God thus gave to the primitive disciples, He no less fully imparted to His witnesses at the Reformation. Luther and his friends found their experience in harmony with that of the apostles and contended that from the courage and hopefulness and gladness it imparted, this assurance should be enjoyed by every disciple of the Lord. It was indeed the very emphasis they laid on this truth that brought them into collision with the Romanists. The Church of Rome had always gloried in the certainty on every vital matter which she professed to be able to afford her adherents. It was by her alone that they could be assured of the authenticity of the Scriptures or of the meaning of their statements. It was she alone in like manner that could give men any real certitude of ultimate salvation. When therefore the Reformers proclaimed that they themselves enjoyed this assurance, their opponents did not indeed deny that such assurance was possible; but they contended that it could not be enjoyed with a divine certainty of faith, apart from the testimony of the Church or a special revelation from heaven. The question betwixt the two parties as put by Bellarmin was in this form: "Whether anyone without a special revelation ought to be or can be certain with the certitude of a divine faith in which a false element can by no means be found, that his sins are forgiven." [3]

The Reformers were led and as they thought on sufficient grounds to accept this challenge. They did affirm that they were assured of forgiveness with a divine certainty, and that this was the normal attainment of all true believers. So confident indeed were they of having the sanction of Scripture for this position that they went the length of saying that this assurance was an essential element of justifying faith. True faith embraced the persuasion not simply that Christ was able to save a soul on condition of trust in Him, but that He did actually save the soul of the believer Himself. This view was constantly repeated by them in their teaching, and though not embodied in the most important Confessions, was undoubtedly held by the majority of the Reformers. To put the ground of their assurance beyond doubt, not a few of them presented the action of the Spirit on the soul of the believer as being practically as explicit as the testimony of Scripture or the Church.

[1] 2 Tim. i. 12. [2] Ch. iv. 18.
[3] Cf. Cunningham, *Reformers and Theology of Reformation*, p. 144.

It is now generally admitted by Reformed theologians that in taking up this position the Reformers and their successors made a mistake. They were not really called upon to charge themselves with the duty of showing that believers ought to be and could be assured of salvation with the certainty of divine faith. It was enough for them to prove that, through the ordinary operations of the Spirit working faith in the heart and enabling it to transform the character and life, the believer might and ought to arrive at a moral certainty regarding his salvation. Assurance of necessity introduces the element of reflection on personal experience; and, with the manifest liability of man to error, it is not possible to reach a certainty that can fitly be compared with the certainty of truths taught in the Scriptures. Similarly, it is going beyond what Scripture fairly warrants, to hold that saving faith essentially includes a conviction that the believer's own sins are forgiven. As Principal Cunningham pointed out, "God requires us to believe nothing that is not true before we believe it and which may not be propounded to us to be believed accompanied at the same time with satisfactory evidence of its truth; and, if so, the belief that our sins are forgiven and that we have been brought into a state of grace, must be posterior in order of nature, if not of time, to the act of faith by which the change is effected and cannot therefore prove a necessary constituent element of the act itself, cannot be its essence or belong to its essence."[1]

In accordance with this view, the Westminster Confession, for example, expressly states that "this infallible assurance doth not so belong to the essence of faith, but that a true believer may wait long and conflict with many difficulties before he be partaker of it."[2] It also admits that "true believers may have the assurance of their salvation divers ways shaken, diminished and intermitted." But none the less does it hold forth the privilege and the duty of being thus assured. "Such as truly believe in the Lord Jesus, and love Him in sincerity, endeavouring to walk in all good conscience before Him may in this life be certainly assured that they are in the state of grace, and may rejoice in the hope of the glory of God."[3] The faith that first attaches the soul to Christ carries with it an element of certainty from the very fact that it is based on the infallible truth of the divine promise of salvation. In those that embrace the Son of God, and receive in His fulness the Spirit of adoption, the cry of "Abba, Father," which consciously rises from the soul, is an additional element of experience that makes for certainty: for though blended with the soul's own voice, it is essentially a joint testimony of the Spirit corroborating that which we already enjoy by simple faith. When on the basis of this experience a believer is also enabled to bring forth in actual life the fruit required by the gospel, he has all that is needed to impart to him a real assurance that he is being saved by the Lord.

Our Romanist opponents spare no pains to break down the force

[1] Cunningham, *ut sup.* p. 119.   [2] Ch. xviii. 3.   [3] *Ut sup.* i.

of these last two lines of evidence. "Certainly," says Möhler, "according to the sentence of the apostle, the Spirit witnesses with our spirit that we are the children of God. But this witness is of so tender a nature and needs a handling so delicate, that in the feeling of his unworthiness and frailty, the believer approaches the matter only with timidity and scarcely ventures to receive it into consciousness. It is a holy joy which would fain hide itself from its own view, and remain even a secret to itself."[1] So with respect to the fruit of the new life, he says: "As they (Catholics) do not regard fallen nature to be so devoid of all moral and religious rudiments and signs of life, they lack a criterion entirely beyond the possibility of illusion, whereby they can distingish the workings of that element in man which is akin to God and not destroyed by the Fall, from those of divine grace."[2] On both of these points Möhler lags behind the spirit and teaching of the New Testament. According to Paul, the very aim that God has in giving the Spirit of adoption is just to banish the bondage that leads to fear. The co-witness of the Spirit is no mere evanescent feeling, but a strong joyful persuasion that demands expression in prayer and praise, and is sure to come out in testimony to others. The fruits of the Spirit on the other hand stand sharply discriminated in the word of God from the meagre and superficial imitations of the natural man. Springing from a deeper root, and drawing strength from a divine source, they are governed by a higher motive, directed to a nobler end, developed in richer abundance, and preserved in the face of sterner adverse influence. With the evidence of such graces in heart and life before his eye, a believer is guilty of no presumption in being assured that he is and shall be saved. Such assurance cannot be characterised as being in the language of the Council of Trent "vain confidence and one alien from all godliness";[3] for alike in the teaching of Scripture and Christian experience it is invariably found associated with humility, gratitude, watchfulness and ever-growing ardour and activity in the service of God.

5. Amongst the Reformers there was no doubt as to the primary foundation on which the grace of assurance was based. It rests on the divine purpose of love to choose a people out of the world for everlasting life. Paul was persuaded of the Thessalonians' election of God.[4] Peter addressed his fellow-believers as "elect according to the foreknowlege of God the Father."[5] The Christians of the Reformation felt in their own hearts that they had been dowered with the same blessings and possessed by the same assurance; and they could not do justice to the sovereign grace of God without believing that they too had been embraced in the same purpose of mercy. On this broad platform all the Reformed Churches were prepared to take their stand.

Such convictions concerning the eternal foundations of the

[1] *Symbolik*, ss. 195, 196.   [2] *Ut sup.* s. 193.   [3] *On Justification*, ch. ix.
[4] 1 Thess. i. 4.   [5] 1 Pet. i. 2.

spiritual life did not meet with the approval of the theologians of Trent. There was nothing in their system of doctrine that obliged them to ignore or deny the truth of predestination, yet they never viewed it with favour. They would have had men rely on the stability of the Church and the efficacy of her ordinances as administered by the priesthood, rather than on the counsel of God's will. Hence, in the decree on justification, they affirm that "no one as long as he is in this mortal life, ought so far to presume as regards the mystery of divine predestination, as to determine for certain that he is assuredly in the number of the predestinate . . . for, except by special revelation, it cannot be known whom God hath chosen unto Himself."[1] Against this position rises the whole strain of the apostolic teaching. Believers are led step by step into the recognition of their election, because it is only thus that they can explain how from death and helplessness they have been quickened and enabled to enter into fellowship with God. Their salvation is entirely to the praise of the glory of His grace, and it is no " rash presumptuousness " but only full submission to the truth to acknowledge that it is God that worketh all in all.

6. On the same principle the Reformers proclaimed the gospel of final perseverance. If God had chosen men to salvation through sanctification of the Spirit and belief of the truth, it was impossible for Him not to fulfil His purpose. So Christ and His apostles taught. The Lord gave unto His sheep eternal life, and they were never to perish. No power was to pluck them out of the Father's hand. Having begun a good work in His people, God would perform it unto the end.[2] These utterances are so plain and forcible that the Council of Trent could neither neglect nor pervert them. Yet even while quoting them, they try to strip them of all efficacy by warning the believer against promising himself "anything as certain with an absolute certainty." Such a restriction is contrary to their manifest scope. It is true that men are called to endure, to be self-distrustful, self-denying, and ever watchful. Yet this should not prevent their being entirely confident, that in the midst of this diligent and strenuous effort they shall certainly persevere in the path of righteousness to the end. Perseverance on man's part means preservation by God. Peter teaches that believers are kept in the power of God through faith unto salvation.[3] Jude, who charges men to keep themselves in the love of God, nevertheless exults in God as able to keep them from falling, and present them at last "faultless in the presence of His glory with exceeding joy."[4]

Thus in the higher as well as in the primary blessings of the gospel, Protestantism approves itself as the only system that is faithful to the truths of Scripture and the facts of a vital Christian experience.

[1] *On Justification*, ch. xii.
[2] John x. 38 ; Phil. i. 6 ; 2 Thess. ii. 13 ; 1 Pet. i. 2.
[3] 1 Pet. i. 5. [4] Jude ver. 24.

CHAPTER IX

GOOD WORKS

FROM what we have seen of the tendencies of Romanist doctrine, we might fairly conclude that it would not avoid laying stress on the necessity of Christian obedience. If, while contenting themselves with a meagre form of faith, the theologians of the Romish Church required works from those that are looking forward to justification, much more were they likely to urge "good works" on those that had been justified. This expectation is not disappointed. Her most eminent teachers in every age have given the utmost prominence to this obligation. Starting from such precepts concerning "good works" as that of the Lord in His Sermon on the Mount, or of Paul to Titus, they have charged their followers to remember that Christianity is a religion not of the mind or feeling only but of the will and the life.

With all this teaching, so far as it is based on the word of God, the Protestant Church stands in full harmony. The Reformers never attempted to lessen the value of any contribution to Christian ethics made by the Latin Church, nor did they in their teaching do aught to weaken men's sense of responsibility for leading a holy life. Modern Romish apologists would fain have us believe otherwise. Möhler *e.g.* adduces such passages as the following from Luther and contends that the Reformer "maintains an inward and essential opposition betwixt religion and morality": "The conscience must have nothing to do with law, works and earthly righteousness. So the ass remains in the valley but the conscience ascends with Isaac up the mountain and knows nothing either of the law or of works, but seeks and looks only for the forgiveness of sins and the pure righteousness which is proffered and imparted to us in Christ. On the other hand in civil government we must most rigidly exact and observe obedience to the law. . . . Thus both things, to wit, the law and the gospel are to be severed as far as possible, the one from the other, and each is to remain in the separate place to which it appertains. The law is to remain out of heaven, that is to say, out of the heart and conscience."[1]

But it is manifest that in this and all similar passages, Luther is dealing in his usual intense manner, not with the question of Christian

[1] *Symbolik*, ss. 233, 234,

obedience to the law of God in itself, but only with the method by which a soul is to be reconciled to God and enter on the enjoyment of true peace of conscience. His representation as a whole may be somewhat onesided and some of his expressions incautious, but the essential truth of his statements when viewed in this light cannot be denied. It is no part of his intention to disparage the necessity or value of Christian good works.[1] As he himself says in his *Table-Talk*: " If at the commencement I spoke and wrote with such asperity against good works, it was because Christ had been hidden and obscured in the Church and buried under a load of superstitions. My desire was to liberate from this tyranny pious and God-fearing souls. But never, never have I rejected works." "The obedience towards God is the obedience of faith and good works : that is, he who believes in God and does what God has commanded, is obedient to Him."[2]

The whole aim of the Reformation, indeed, was to establish a closer and more stable union betwixt a living faith and a genuine Christian morality. However little he may have discerned it, it was the true spirit of Luther that animated Möhler when he wrote these words: "The law is God's declared will : and with alienation from God, there came also alienation from His law. Through the appearance of the Son of God in our midst and His reception into our hearts, the disunion betwixt God and man terminated: in Christ both become one and are reconciled. Shall then the law which had been extraneous not penetrate also into the interior of man, and there become living and consequently be fulfilled? Yea, by reconciliation with God, we are reconciled and become one with His law also. By the living reception of God into our hearts by means of faith, we likewise, and inevitably, receive His law also. For the law is God's eternal will and one with Him : so that where God is, there also is His law for evermore."[3]

In spite of this apparent harmony, however, in the general strain of their practical teaching, it is undeniable that there is a grave divergence betwixt Romanism and Protestantism alike in the elements of their doctrine of Christian obedience and the practical issues to which they gave rise.

1. In the first place, there is a difference as to the sense in which any works of believers can be called "good." This epithet occurs very frequently in Scripture and must bear a very definite and substantial meaning. Yet in view of other statements on the life of God's children, it is impossible to avoid the question as to the extent to which this "goodness" applies to such works. Are we intended to regard them as good in the sense of being entirely and absolutely free from sin in the sight of God? Or is this epithet applied in such a sense as still leaves room for the existence in them of elements that are sinful?

[1] Cf. Bungener, *History of the Council of Trent*, p. 141.
[2] *Table-Talk* (Bohn), p. 293.   [3] *Symbolik*, s. 237 ; Rom. viii. 3, 4.

The Church of Rome upholds the former view: according to her tenets, it is possible for believers to do works that are wholly good. This is a natural consequence of her doctrine of justification. If in this change men have been wholly freed from sin, then it is possible for them to do works free from any admixture of evil. This is plainly implied in the chapter of the Tridentine decree "On keeping the commandments and on the necessity and possibility thereof." "No one ought to make use of that rash saying, one prohibited by the Fathers under an anathema,—that the observance of the commandments of God is impossible for one that is justified. For God commands not impossibilities; but by commanding, both admonishes to do what thou art able and to pray for what thou art not able to do, and aids thee that thou mayest be able. . . . For although during this mortal life, men, how holy and just soever, at times fall into at least light and venial sins, not therefore do they cease to be just. . . . Those are opposed to the orthodox doctrine of religion, who assert that the just man sins, venially at least in every good work; or, which is yet more insupportable, that he merits eternal punishments; as also those who state that the just sin in all their works."[1] To the same effect also wrote the leading Romanist divines, as, for example, Möhler who says: "As in the man truly born again from the Spirit, the Catholic Church recognises a real liberation from sin, a direction of the spirit and the will truly sanctified and acceptable to God, it necessarily follows that she asserts the possibility and reality of truly good works. . . . We are bound to believe that the justified are enabled through works performed in God to satisfy the divine law according to the condition of this present life."[2]

In support of this position, Romanists adduce various statements of Scripture. Besides the very numerous passages[3] in which the works of believers are spoken of as "good," they refer, for example, to saints who are said to be practically free from sin, as Noah who "was a righteous man and perfect in his generations";[4] Job, who "was perfect and upright, and one that feared God and eschewed evil";[5] and Zechariah and Elizabeth who "were both righteous before God, walking in all the commandments and ordinances of the Lord blameless."[6] They adduce also statements in which saints of God claim to be free from sin, as that of the psalmist, who appeals to God to see "if there be any wicked way in him,"[7] and of Paul who said that he knew nothing against himself.[8]

Indeed, so satisfied are the Romanist divines with the validity of these proofs, that they have not hesitated to take even a further step in recognition of the goodness of works done by justified persons. They hold that man, after being made righteous, can do more

[1] *On Justification*, ch. xi.   [2] *Symbolik*, ss. 197, 198.
[3] Matt. v. 16; 2 Cor. ix. 2; Eph. ii. 10; 1 Pet. ii. 12.
[4] Gen. vi. 9.   [5] Job i. 1.   [6] Luke i. 6.
[7] Ps. cxxxix. 24.   [8] 1 Cor. iv. 4.

than perfectly fulfil the law. In addition to the ordinary commands given in Scripture which are binding on all Christians, they profess to discover there certain higher injunctions which are not absolutely obligatory but are proposed for observance only to those who wish to reach a higher grade of perfection. The chief of these "counsels of perfection," as they are called, are the vows of voluntary poverty, chastity and obedience, which are seen in their fullest form of operation in the monastic and conventual institutions of the Roman Church. In performing such works, believers are held to do more than God can righteously require of them. They are paying out to Him, as it were, more than can be strictly regarded as His due, and hence are doing deeds that, from the Latin phrase for paying more than enough out of a public treasury, are called "works of supererogation." The main arguments in behalf of this distinction are drawn from those passages of Scripture in which such works are supposed to be enjoined : as, for example, the direction given by the Lord to the rich young ruler,[1] the advice of Paul to the Corinthians concerning marriage,[2] and the precept to the Hebrews to obey those that had the rule over them.[3]

Amongst the Reformed Churches, on the other hand, there is entire unanimity in the view that good works in the sense of works absolutely free from sin are not possible to man in this present life. The Articles of the Anglican Church agree with the Westminster Confession in saying that, "as they are wrought by us, they are defiled and mixed with so much weakness and imperfection that they cannot endure the severity of God's judgment."[4] In speaking thus, Protestant theologians have no desire to disparage the character of good works or minimise their value in the sight of God or man. Since they are called "good" in the word of God, they must, like those that do them, be good in their general character and leading elements. They are indeed worthy of being so called, because they are the fruits of a new nature implanted in the soul by God Himself, and are brought forth in the power of the Spirit. Yet such epithets as "fair" or "good" whether applied to men or their works are of themselves quite insufficient to maintain the sweeping assertions of the Church of Rome. In order to arrive at the divine truth on this matter, we have to combine the whole evidence found in the Scriptures, and this includes statements that when duly weighed prevent our regarding the epithet "good" as implying freedom from sin.

For, in the first place, is there not the broad fact that nowhere in Scripture is it claimed for any man called "good" or "perfect" or "upright" that he did not do that which is evil, nor for any one deed of any such man that it was entirely free from evil? On the contrary, some of the best men that ever lived, such as Noah,[5] Job,[6] and David[7] are expressly shown to have sinned against God ; while

[1] Mark x. 21.   [2] 1 Cor. vii. 26.   [3] Heb. xiii. 17.
[4] Art. XII. Conf. of Faith, ch. xvi. 5.   [5] Gen. ix. 21.
[6] Job xl. 4.   [7] 2 Sam. xiii. 13.

the way in which they are spoken to and dealt with by the Lord proves that they needed continually His infinite forbearance and pardoning love.

The absence of such testimony is fully confirmed by the utterances of saintly experience. Job declares that he is prepared to abhor himself and repent in dust and ashes. David's idea of blessedness turns on the assurance of being forgiven all his iniquities. Solomon declared that there is no man that sinneth not;[1] one of the psalmists adds that "there is none that doeth good, no not one";[2] and the Preacher summed up both when he said that "there is not a just man upon earth that doeth good and sinneth not."[3] Paul testified that he did not approve of what he actually did and that he was ever encompassed with a sense of failure and imperfection: "What I hate, that do I"; "To will is present with me, but how to perform that which is good I find not."[4]

The explanation of these facts has been already given. It is found in the truth fully established in a previous chapter that even when a man believes in Christ and is born of the Spirit, he is not thereby wholly freed from the dominion of sin. The corrupt nature has been "crucified" and so mortally wounded, but it is by no means extirpated. Out of it arises concupiscence or evil desire, which is itself sin, and cannot but taint every thought, word and deed of which the soul is capable. Tried by the standard of a law that demands nothing short of absolute perfection in desire, motive and conduct, the saintliest man that ever lived must acknowledge that he continually comes short of the glory of God. If sin is not merely any "transgression of the law of God," but also any "lack of conformity unto it,"[5] every saint does sin against God in every good work he performs. The statement of the Apostle John that "whosoever is born of God doeth no sin, because His seed abideth in him: and he cannot sin, because he is begotten of God,"[6] does not affect the general position; for it means only that a regenerate soul has within it an inveterate antagonism to sin and will never willingly or habitually indulge in it. That there is no countenance given to the possibility of a sinless life is abundantly shown in the earlier statements in which John denounces those who claim to "have no sin" or to "have not sinned,"[7] as guilty of transgressing the ninth commandment. As James says, "In many things we all stumble."[8]

The mode in which the Church of Rome tries to repel these proofs is indicated in the quotation from the decrees of Trent already given. The Council drew a distinction betwixt sins that are mortal and sins that are venial. It is to the latter kind that the sins of believers are said for the most part to belong.

This, as we have seen, is a distinction that all evangelical Protestants practically reject.[9] No sin is of such a nature that it can of

---

[1] 1 Kings iv. 46. [2] Ps. xiv. 3. [3] Eccles. vii. 20.
[4] Rom. vii. 15, 18. [5] Sh. Cat. q. 14. [6] 1 John iii. 9.
[7] 1 John i. 8, 10. [8] Ch. iii. 2. [9] P. 63.

itself be called venial. The law under which man was placed at creation, and under which as a Christian he must still live, demands entire perfection in heart and conduct. The whole law is pervaded by the spirit of love : if therefore it be broken in one precept, it is broken in all. " For whosoever shall keep the whole law and yet offend in one point, he is become guilty of all."[1] Strictly speaking then, every sin is in its own nature and proper effects mortal ; that is, it does, when left to operate fully, entail spiritual death on the soul. Here, however, it has to be remembered that in the case of believers sin is not suffered to bring forth its proper fruits. As it is repudiated by the regenerate soul, so it is forgiven by the blood of Christ. "There is no condemnation to them that are in Christ Jesus."[2] "The blood of Jesus His Son cleanseth us from all sin."[3] It was only with this provision consciously and fully in view that John said that we love God and keep His commandments and that His commandments are not grievous. It is only by the constant use of it that any works of God's children can be rendered acceptable to Him at all.

If this be the view we are bound to take of the best of man's good works, we need not stay to prove that works of supererogation are purely fictitious. Möhler insists that the minds of the Reformers were too coarse-grained to appreciate duly the fine distinction which the Church of Rome draws. It should be enough to say in reply that after duly searching the Scriptures neither the Reformers nor their successors found any warrant for it there. There are no mere counsels of perfection in the New Testament. The Lord Jesus laid on the rich ruler an obligation that was needful to show him his failure and remove a positive defect in his preparation for ordinary discipleship. So far as Paul recommended the renunciation of marriage at all, it was only as a practical expedient in view of the existing widespread persecution of the Church, and the greater trouble which the necessities of family life would entail. Neither in the Epistle to the Hebrews nor anywhere else are men called on to surrender the exercise of reason and conscience and judgment at the will of a superior official.

2. This accordingly leads to the second point of divergence, namely, *the value which good works possess in the sight of God*. It is beyond question the doctrine of the Church of Rome that the works of justified men are meritorious before God. After alluding to the vital union betwixt Christ and believers, the Council of Trent says : " We must believe that nothing further is wanting to the justified to prevent their being accounted to have by those very works which have been done in God fully satisfied the divine law according to the state of this life and to have truly merited eternal life, to be obtained also in its due time, if so be, however, that they shall depart in grace."[4] It is true that in a succeeding statement, men are warned against trusting in themselves on the ground of their

[1] Jas. ii. 10. [2] Rom. viii. 1.
[3] 1 John i. 7. [4] *On Justification*, ch. xvi.

works, for such works flow from the grace of God, "whose bounty towards all men is so great that He will have the things which are His own gifts to be their merits." Yet, lest it should be supposed for a moment that works are in any sense to be lessened in influence or value, the Fathers of Trent added a canon on this very point : " If any one saith that the good works of one that is justified are in such manner the gifts of God that they are not also the good merits of him that is justified; or that the said justified by the good works which he performs through the grace of God and the merit of Jesus Christ, whose living member he is, does not truly merit increase of grace, eternal life and the attainment of that eternal life—if so be, however, that he depart in grace—and also an increase of glory : let him," etc.[1]

It does not fall within our scope to indicate here at length how such views have affected the practical life of the Romish Church as a whole. But it cannot be overlooked that they have led to the multiplication of duties to which the Church is prepared to affix the name of "good works"; and that too often stress is laid on the performance of such works to the detriment of more important scriptural obligations. The wearing of symbolic ornaments, the observance of certain forms of devotion, the use of special prayers, charities to images in churches, attendance at festivals, pilgrimages to shrines and so-called holy places and fasting, are amongst those that are best known.

It is also from the prevalence of such views that so many members of the Romish Church are induced to attempt performing works that have already been described as works of supererogation. For if ordinary good works are meritorious, these must be held to lay up before God in heaven a yet larger stock of merit.

The leading proofs adduced in support of this doctrine are those passages in Scripture in which special blessings are attached to the cultivation of certain graces, as the beatitudes of the Sermon on the Mount; and, in particular, the very numerous statements in which believers are said to receive reward at the hand of God.[2]

To all this teaching the Reformers and their successors offered the most strenuous opposition. Falling back on the truth already vindicated that every saved man still retains a source of corruption in his heart and that every work performed by him must be tainted by sin, they contended that even in order to be acceptable to God at all, the best of man's works had to be presented through the atoning sacrifice of Christ. To Him and Him alone therefore could any merit belong. There is not the slightest hint in Scripture that Christ permits any works of men that have to be cleansed by His blood to be reckoned for righteousness to them. It is faith alone that receives righteousness and that only from Himself.

[1] Canon XXXII.
[2] Matt. v. 11, 12; Heb. xi. 27; Rev. xxii. 12; 1 Pet. i. 17; Rom. ii. 7; 2 Tim. iv. 9.

Besides there can be no merit in simple obedience to what is commanded. The discharge of duty incumbent on a servant from the very position he occupies cannot be reckoned to his account as entitling him to special reward. He simply does his duty or what is due from him to his master. This truth was enunciated with unmistakable clearness by the Lord Jesus Himself. A disciple is in the household of God as a servant is in the family of his master. When a servant devotes his whole life to his master's service, does he owe special thanks to him on that account? "I trow not," says the Lord; and then He adds: "Even so ye also, when ye shall have done all the things that are commanded you, say: We are unprofitable servants; we have done that which it was our duty to do."[1]

Moreover it is plain that the word "reward" cannot bear the strict special meaning which Romanists attach to it. It does not always imply "merit": for the one is not necessarily the correlative of the other. Its real meaning is gracious acknowledgment. The Apostle Paul, for example, says: "Now to him that worketh the reward is reckoned not of grace but of debt": but the whole strain of his argument goes to show that such "working" is not possible to man; and that the same reward, which is therefore purely of grace, is given to him that believeth. "Therefore it is of faith, that it might be of grace, that the promise might be sure to all the seed."[2] It is true indeed that such recompense is fitted to act as a stimulus to Christian diligence, and that, with that fact in view, eternal life is promised "to those that seek after glory, honour and incorruption."[3] But we have other passages where the source of eternal life in the grace of God is so strongly emphasised that the possibility of meriting it by works is overthrown. "The wages of sin is death": the sinner works for strict hire; but it is not so with believers: "The gift of God is eternal life through Jesus Christ our Lord."[4]

To these considerations there also falls to be added the truth that, even if the good works of men were really meritorious, the reward attached to them would have to bear some proportion to the service rendered. This is a condition of merit strictly so called. But it passes all bounds of equity to hold that any works such as man can do are in themselves deserving of "eternal life." This is the greatest reward that God can give,—a blessing so rich that the heart of man cannot receive it,—a recompense that is immeasurable and inexhaustible. No enlightened conscience can even for a moment imagine that the actual worth to God of a lifetime of service really stained by sin, and at the best very imperfect, demands from Him the inheritance of heaven. It is the grace of God alone that can bestow it, and this grace is as sovereign and full as it is undeserved.[5]

It is only in accordance with this general position that the Reformed Churches should decline to give the name of good works to any duties that are not expressly indicated in Scripture. For both

[1] Luke xvii. 7-10. [2] Rom. vi. 4, 16. [3] Rom. ii. 6.
[4] Rom. vi. 23. [5] Cf. Tennyson's Dedication of *In Memoriam*, st. 9.

Christ and His apostles warn their followers to beware of "vain traditions,"[1] "the leaven of the Pharisees,"[2] "the rudiments of the world,"[3] as conferring no real honour on the Christian life, but tending only to the gratification of the corrupt heart. The Reformers also repudiated with equal earnestness the idea of enjoining works of supererogation as tantamount to binding on men's shoulders burdens too grievous to be borne, and tending to self-delusion, fraud and fanaticism.

3. This being so, there is no need at this stage for dwelling at length on the third great divergence betwixt Romanism and Protestantism on this topic, namely, *the possibility of men's being benefited by the merits of good works performed by others*. Both Churches of course agree that men may confer blessing on others by their good works. Prayer has power with God and prevails to obtain mercy even for the unworthy, where it assumes the form of direct intercession in the name of Christ. Christian beneficence stirs up the world to praise God and follow a good example. But not even the Church of Rome teaches that such blessings are bestowed on the ground of the meritoriousness of these acts.[4]

Yet Romanists have come to hold that there is a method by which the merits of the just can be made available for others less worthy. This notion began to take root in apparently simple and innocent ways. It is seen, for example, in connection with the merit early ascribed to martyrdom. When a prominent member of the Church was condemned to death, some of those who had been subjected to a long discipline for gross sin would ask a recommendation from them to the ecclesiastical authorities, that they should be restored to the privileges of membership in the Church.[5] The idea was that the superior merit of the martyr might cover the sin of the excommunicated. This opinion took deeper root in the susceptible mind of the early Christian centuries. The priesthood saw that it could be turned to advantage for the progress and authority of the Church. At last the doctrine was elaborated that the inexhaustible grace of the Saviour, together with the superabundant merits of the Virgin mother and all the martyrs, confessors and saints formed a treasury of grace placed at the disposal of the chief bishop of the Roman Church which he could dispense to men at his own will in the shape of remissions of punishments due to sin either in this world or in that which is to come. The only proviso was that such remissions should be given only on terms befitting the condition of the penitent, the value of the gift, and the needs of the Church.

To what a lamentable extent the Roman pontiffs availed themselves of this supposed treasury is seen stamped on the very beginning of the Reformation. It was this shameless traffic in such "indulgences" carried on by Tetzel, the agent of the archbishop of

[1] Matt. xv. 6, 9.
[2] Matt. xvi. 6.
[3] Col. ii. 8.
[4] Cf. Hunter, iii. p. 157.
[5] Cf. Maclear, *Introduction to the Articles of the Church of England*, p. 185.

Mainz, that first opened the eyes of Luther to the iniquities of the whole Romish system.

The Reformer was right. Not a single trace of a foundation for such opinions and practices can be found in the word of God. The grace that reigns through righteousness unto eternal life is wholly in the hands of the Most High, and cannot be dispensed by or through any other than "Jesus Christ our Lord." By this channel men may obtain it directly from God " without money and without price."

CHAPTER X

THE STATE AFTER DEATH

THE grave contrast betwixt the doctrine of the Church of Rome and that of the Protestant Churches on the state after death has been already alluded to. It arises from the divergent views held on the forgiveness of post-baptismal sins. According to evangelical Protestantism, when a man believes in Christ as a Saviour, the whole penalty of his sins is remitted. The sins of his whole life, past, present and future, are for ever blotted out. This forgiveness is to be realised growingly every day, but the blessing itself is secured once for all, through faith in Christ. Hence nothing that he may be called on to endure in the shape of trial or suffering can be regarded as having a penal element in it. That is for ever done away in the sacrifice of Christ, the Lamb of God's right hand. Whatever suffering he may encounter is only the discipline of the Father of mercies that he may be partaker of the divine holiness. Death itself is robbed of its originally penal character. It becomes the gateway of heaven. For, as the Westminster Catechism says, "The souls of believers at death being made perfect in holiness do immediately pass into glory."[1] For those that are in Christ, there is no state intermediate betwixt earth and heaven. Dying in the Lord, they enter at once into what is in all its essential elements a condition of perfect bliss in which they await the manifest glory of the resurrection. Those that have not received here on earth the gift of eternal life enter at once into a state in which they are for ever bereft of the presence and blessing of God. Even the resurrection of the dead can only bring them a deeper degradation and a more intense remorse. "Besides these two places for souls separated from their bodies," adds the Westminster Confession, "the Scripture acknowledgeth none."[2]

According to the Romanist theology, on the other hand, a man is by no means done with the penalty of sin, when he believes and is baptized. The liability to eternal punishment is indeed for ever annulled through the death of Christ applied in the sacrament of penance. But the sins he may commit after baptism expose him to a temporal punishment which the Church, acting in the spirit and after

[1] Q. 37. [2] Ch. xxxii. 1.

the manner of a judge, is bound to impose. If a believer should die without having fully satisfied the demands of the Church as to the temporal punishment judicially annexed to his mortal sins, or as to that due to his venial sins, then, according to the Church of Rome, he cannot enter at once into heaven. Such souls are detained in an intermediate state and place to which the name of "Purgatory" has been given, because there they are made to endure all the suffering needed to cleanse them from the last traces of the sin in which they die.

This is the doctrine distinctly stated in the decree of the Council of Trent on Justification and more fully in that on Purgatory itself. " If anyone saith that after the grace of justification has been received, to every penitent sinner the guilt is remitted and the debt of eternal punishment is blotted out in such wise, that there remains not any debt of temporal punishment to be discharged either in this world or in the next in Purgatory, before the entrance to the kingdom of heaven can be opened to him : let him," etc.[1] " Whereas the Catholic Church, instructed by the Holy Ghost has, from the sacred writings and the ancient tradition of the Fathers, taught in sacred Councils and very recently in this œcumenical Synod, that there is a Purgatory and that the souls there detained are helped by the suffrages of the faithful but principally by the acceptable sacrifice of the altar ; the holy Synod enjoins on bishops that they diligently endeavour that the sound doctrine concerning Purgatory, transmitted by the holy Fathers and sacred Councils, be believed, maintained and everywhere proclaimed by the faithful of Christ."[2] Here no attempt is made to define the precise locality of Purgatory or the nature of the punishment inflicted in it. This generality of statement is probably due to the influence of certain more moderate members of the Council, who declined to commit themselves to views that had no support either in reason or revelation. The distinctively Romanist doctrine is expressed with less reserve in the Catechism of Trent where on the question as to how many are the places in which souls kept out of bliss are detained after death, it is said : " There is also the fire of Purgatory in which the souls of the just are purified by punishment for a stated time to the end that they may be admitted into their eternal country into which nothing defiled entereth."[3]

The devotional manuals of the Church have been written under the guidance of the Catechism rather than the decrees of Trent. With a minuteness and an extravagance for which the Church of Rome cannot escape responsibility, the tortures of Purgatory are to this day constantly set before the people. In the hands of the priesthood, this doctrine has become the most potent instrument for maintaining dominion over the minds of men and for drawing large sums of money into their treasury. For if, as we have seen, the duration of punishment in Purgatory can be shortened by the suffrages of the faithful, " to wit, the sacrifices of masses, prayers, alms

[1] Canon xxx, [2] Sess, xxv, [3] Pt. i. ch. vi. q. 3.

and other works of piety, which have been wont to be performed by the faithful for the other faithful departed"; [1] and further, "endowments of testators" are received for this purpose ; and yet again, the power of remitting or shortening such punishment is left in the hands of the supreme Pontiff ; it is plain that there is practically no limit to the terrific power which the Church wields over the minds of her members alike for securing submission to her authority and obtaining revenues for the maintenance of her observances. It is not indeed necessary to believe that the extortionate procedure of such men as Tetzel is anywhere reproduced in the present day. The light of the Protestant Reformation has probably rendered that impossible. But it cannot be gainsaid that the sale of indulgences was only the legitimate fruit of principles that are as firmly held now as they were in the days of Martin Luther.

How did this doctrine of Purgatory come to take root in the Church? It was evidently a very gradual growth. For the first origin of the idea, we have to go to the religious teaching of the ancient Persians. Fire was the supreme element by which the successive changes in the life of souls were effected. From the Persians the idea passed into the doctrine of the Stoics and later into the philosophy of Plato. He taught that no one could enter into abiding happiness who did not expiate his sins after death. If they were too great to be thus atoned for, the suffering would have no end. Some of the Jewish Rabbis probably imbibed their similar views at this source.[2]

Amongst the earliest Fathers of the Christian Church, the doctrine of a purifying fire is not distinctly broached. The first to give it vogue was Origen.[3] He, however, fixed the time of purgation after the resurrection and held the doctrine in relation not to believers only but to all mankind, who would thereby be restored to fellowship with God. Later writers worked on this basis and developed Origen's doctrine in various forms. In the time of Augustine it was not at all generally accepted as a Biblical position, that there was a possibility of purification from sin before entering heaven on the part of those whom death overtook in a state of imperfect sanctification. But already this view had begun to exercise so much influence on the minds of men and for the time not without instilling into them a measure of awe, that Augustine went so far as to say that there might be an element of truth in the view, and that in any case he at least was not prepared to argue against it.

Such surmises were but a very meagre foundation on which to rest a definite doctrine. Yet when Gregory the Great saw that it could be made to blend with the growing practice of praying for the dead and so exalt the influence of the Church and the priesthood over the minds of the people, he did not hesitate to adopt the view that there was a distinct place and state into which the souls of men that were

---

[1] Sess. xxv.   [2] Cf. C. Hodge, *Syst. Theol.* iii. p. 767.
[3] Cf. E. H. Browne, *Exposition of the Thirty-nine Articles*, pp. 499–502.

not in this life perfectly freed from sin were received and in which they were kept till they had made satisfaction for their guilt.

From this time onwards, through all the Middle Ages, the necessity and reality of detention in a Purgatory took the firmest hold of the mind of Europe. When the Council of Florence, separating from that of Basle, tried to unite the Churches of the East and West, it did not hesitate to promulgate the doctrine that there was a Purgatory. The Council of Trent, we have seen, took the doctrine as a matter of course and while making a show of repudiating abuses, only riveted the whole system of which Purgatory forms a part more firmly on the life and service of the Church.

For a doctrine which so manifestly owes its existence to the ideas of pagan philosophy blending with the superstition and prejudice of immature Christian thought, the Fathers of Trent could not adduce any Scriptural evidence. The utmost they could attempt to do was to quote certain statements which were capable of being perverted into an apparent recognition of the doctrine.

On the first of these, taken as it is from the Apocrypha,[1] it is needless to dwell. It has only to be remarked that the Latin Vulgate from which the Douay Version is made, has foisted on the original Greek an interpretation the words will not bear. It was simply a sacrifice for sin that Judas offered and not a sacrifice for the dead.

The passage quoted from the Sermon on the Mount has evidently no bearing on the question: "Agree with thine adversary quickly, whilst thou art with him in the way; lest haply the adversary deliver thee to the judge and the judge deliver thee to the officer and thou be cast into prison. Verily I say unto thee, thou shalt by no means come out thence, till thou have paid the last farthing."[2] The only conceivable reason why Romanists should quote this utterance in favour of Purgatory is that its last clause happens to be coincident with the kind of expression they most frequently use in speaking of the place of purification. Our Lord here is really giving a parabolic illustration of the necessity of immediate reconciliation with God. Man by nature is in His hands as a resister of just claims is in the hands of a more powerful adversary. For his own safety man ought at once to come to terms of peace with God. To one who dies out of fellowship with Him there is no hope of restoration. Thus, if the passage has any reference to the future at all, it is to the place not of Purgatory but of irremediable woe.

Equally perverted is the use made of another statement of Christ: "Whosoever shall speak a word against the Son of Man, it shall be forgiven him; but whosoever shall speak against the Holy Spirit, it shall not be forgiven him, neither in this world nor in that which is to come."[3] Here there is no reference to the possibility of forgiveness in a future life: least of all in a place of purification. As those that heard the words would at once understand, it is simply a

[1] 2 Macc. xii. 46. [2] Matt. v. 29. [3] Matt. xii. 32.

proverbial expression of the certain fact that there will be no forgiveness whatever for those who consciously and wilfully persist in rejecting the presence and power of the Holy Spirit. It is impossible for such to be forgiven, simply because they deny the only Agent by whom the grace of God can be imparted.

Nor is there any reference to Purgatory in the statement of Paul: "If any man's work shall be burned, he shall suffer loss; but he himself shall be saved: yet so as through fire."[1] Here again there is a very close approximation to the forms of speech Romanists use in reference to Purgatory. But the reality itself is wanting. The apostle has in view a trial that is to take place, not after death, but at the final judgment. It is the teachers of the Christian Church that he refers to and it is the results of their service that are to be searched by the eye of the Lord, as the substance of everything that can be burned is searched by fire. If a teacher's work can endure the test of the divine judgment, he shall be rewarded accordingly in heaven. If his work has elements in it that have been unsound, to that extent his service is consumed and his reward in heaven is less abundant. He himself is saved: but in view of the large portions of his service that have failed to endure the divine scrutiny, it is as one who has lost much of his substance by fire.

When in writing to the Philippians Paul says: "In the name of Jesus, every knee shall bow, of things in heaven and things on earth and things under the earth,"[2] he cannot be regarded as having any place of purification in view. It is simply a comprehensive way of saying that Jesus shall receive the homage, not only of angels in heaven, but of men living on the earth and even of those who have passed into the unseen world.

No theologian who has had to grapple with the vast difficulties that surround Peter's statement on Christ's preaching to the spirits in prison would ever presume to claim it as evidence in favour of Purgatory.[3] Whether it is to be interpreted of an actual passage by the Lord Jesus into the region of the unseen world where the spirits of the disobedient are gathered together, or of an ancient proclamation of judgment by His Spirit to the rebellious antediluvians, it is not the place of purification, but that of final exclusion from God that the apostle has in view. For these "spirits" are the representatives of the highest form of antagonism to the gracious will of God that has ever been manifested on earth; and, according to the teaching of the Church of Rome, cannot be in Purgatory at all. As the willing perpetrators of mortal sin up to the time of death, they must be in final perdition.

The statement of the Apostle John concerning the Holy City that "there shall in no wise enter into it anything unclean,"[4] does not carry with it the slightest suggestion of a Purgatory. It is simply a warning to all men that heaven is a region only for those that are

---

[1] 1 Cor. iii. 15.
[2] Phil. ii. 10.
[3] 1 Pet. iii. 18-20.
[4] Rev. xxi. 27.

holy and that those who here on earth do not wash their robes and make them white in the blood of the Lamb, shall find no entrance into it.

It is not enough for us, however, simply to show that there is no foundation for the Romanist Purgatory in the passages usually adduced in its behalf. The doctrine itself is directly overthrown by many statements in the Bible that bear not only on the grace of God towards men and the character of the Christian life here on earth, but also on the change effected by death and the entrance into His presence which He has prepared for them that love Him.

What place is left for Purgatory, for example, in the face of such statements as these on the freedom, fulness and everlasting validity of the forgiveness which God extends to those that receive His grace? "As far as the east is from the west, so far hath He removed our transgressions from us."[1] "Though your sins be as scarlet, they shall be as snow."[2] "I will forgive their iniquity and their sin will I remember no more."[3] "Who is a God like unto Thee that pardoneth iniquity? He will tread our iniquities under foot and Thou wilt cast all their sins into the depths of the sea."[4] "Speak ye comfortably to Jerusalem and cry unto her that her iniquity is pardoned; that she hath received of the Lord's hand double for all her sins."[5] Here is forgiveness without reserve, and without limit, as it is "without price." In the face of such statements, the Romanist superstitions about a place of purifying by suffering after death fall to the ground.

The foundation on which this grace rests is the perfection of Christ's atoning work. There is no necessity that men should suffer for sin after death, because Christ in His death bore all the curse attached to the sin of the world. Every penal element in the suffering due to the sins of His people was poured into the cup of Calvary. Having been quaffed to the dregs by Christ, it is now emptied of wrath and transformed into a cup of blessing and victory for all that obey Him. "Christ hath redeemed us from the curse of the law, being made a curse for us."[6] "The blood of Jesus His Son cleanseth us from all sin."[7] "There is no condemnation to them that are in Christ Jesus."[8]

This prospect of deliverance from penal suffering here and hereafter is fully confirmed by all that the Bible teaches us of the real nature of the Christian life, as it is imparted and guided by God. The fire that is to purify the souls of His people is really ministered to them here on earth. The new birth itself is but the kindling of that light of life which is to burn in the heart for ever. The new nature thus given is constantly being purified by a fresh baptism in the Spirit and in fire.[9] The word of God when received into the heart acts similarly as a purifying agent. "Is not My word as a

---

[1] Ps. ciii. 12. [2] Isa. i. 18. [3] Jer. xxxi. 34.
[4] Micah vii. 18, 19. [5] Isa. xl. 2. [6] Gal. iii. 13.
[7] 1 John i. 7. [8] Rom. viii. 1. [9] Matt. iii. 11; Luke xii. 49.

fire and as a hammer that breaketh the rock in pieces?"[1] To these forces is added the fire of holy parental discipline: "I will turn My hand upon thee and thoroughly purge away thy dross and will take away all thy tin."[2] "He is like a refiner's fire and like fuller's soap: and He shall sit as a refiner and purifier of silver: and they shall offer unto the Lord an offering in righteousness."[3] What may not be expected from this divine process in the way of separating sin from the affections of the soul?

The supreme deliverance from sin, however, is effected in death. As might be expected, Romanists refuse to believe this and argue strenuously against it. "In case we leave this earthly world," says Möhler, "still stained by some traces of corruption, how shall we be purified from them? Shall it be by that mechanical deliverance from the body of which the Protestant symbols speak so much? But it is by no means evident how sin is to be purged away from the sinful spirit, simply by the fact that the body is laid aside. It is only to one who does not hold fast the idea of moral freedom in sin or who has fallen into Manichæan or Gnostic errors that anything like this doctrine can be acceptable."[4] This objection, it might be said in reply, could never be put forward by anyone who fully realises the meaning of the Biblical statements on God's forgiving love and Christ's atoning sacrifice and the nature and discipline of the Christian life. But it is also based on a misconception of the real nature of the change effected in the redeemed by death. For all such, death is not merely a mechanical or chemical dissolution of the union betwixt body and soul. It is really a birth of the regenerate spirit into a higher sphere of life; the new birth indeed carried out into its highest development. Remembering the essential separation from sin and the dominion over it that were imparted in regeneration, can we wonder that in the last great crisis of human existence, in which the gracious discipline of heaven is consummated, the Spirit of the Lord should finish His sanctifying work and send the soul out of this world absolutely free from sin? The principle that Peter announces as governing the progress of history to its goal is no less true of the completion of man's deliverance from sin: "But forget not this one thing, beloved, that one day is with the Lord as a thousand years and a thousand years as one day."[5] In the hour of death the Lord can finish His sanctifying work in the soul, not by any such "sudden or magical change" or "mechanical course of operation" as Protestants are held to believe in, but by the same omnipotent energy of the Holy Spirit by whom it was at once raised into life from death in trespasses and sins.

In urging this objection, the Church of Rome is grievously inconsistent with her own extravagant views of the new birth. If, as she teaches, her own act of baptism by a consecrated priest really frees

---

[1] Jer. xxiii. 29.　　　[2] Isa. i. 25.　　　[3] Mal. iii. 3.
[4] *Symbolik*, s. 218.　　[5] 2 Pet. iii. 8.

the soul from sin and enables it to fulfil the law of God, why should it be thought incredible that in the dissolution of natural life, when the last links of connection with a sinful world are being severed, the soul itself already ransomed and sanctified at the core, should be finally delivered from corruption? As Delitzsch says, "the spiritual life begotten and nourished in us by word and sacrament is in itself actually and sufficiently powerful, when it has rid itself of the world lying in the wicked one or is suddenly withdrawn from it, to break forth in the view of the manifest reality of that which has been believed here below, with such intensity that it drives out the sin which is still dwelling in human nature, even to the last trace of its consequences."[1] Received in this faith, death may be the occasion of a baptism in the Spirit and in fire that shall present the soul faultless before the throne of God.

If anything were wanting to establish this hope and overthrow the Romanist fiction, it is found in the scriptural delineations of the entrance into heaven which God grants to those that have trusted in His Son. Neither the Lord nor His apostles give us the slightest reason to believe that the souls of believers are kept in any outer court. On the contrary, there are many statements that seem intended to teach that, as the Westminster Confession says, "they are received into the highest heavens, where they behold the face of God in light and glory, waiting for the full redemption of their bodies."[2] It was thither that the Lord Jesus went when He died: it was thither that He took the soul of the robber who hung by His side: "To-day shalt thou be with Me in Paradise."[3] It was to this blessed issue Paul looked forward: "To die is gain"; "To depart and be with Christ which is very far better."[4] The redeemed now in heaven ascribe their perfect cleansing to the once crucified Saviour: "They washed their robes and made them white in the blood of the Lamb."[5] The condition of those that have entered heaven is described as one of peace and blessing: "Blessed are the dead which die in the Lord from henceforth: Yea, saith the Spirit, that they may rest from their labours."[6] Such statements do not imply that the spirits of just men made perfect may not be the subjects of growth and advancement. This is rather an element in their blessedness. Freed from all encumbrances, the immortal spirit is filled with a more intense life and must be making inward progress towards the fuller glory that awaits it at the coming of the Lord. In accepting this truth, modern evangelical Protestantism fully vindicates itself from Möhler's charge of doing violence to human nature: for "it recognises alike the power of sovereign grace" and "the eternal law of the human spirit."

[1] Delitzsch, *System of Biblical Psychology*, p. 488. [2] Ch. xxxii. 1.
[3] Luke xxiii. 43. [4] Phil. i. 21.
[5] Rev. vii. 14. [6] Rev. xiv. 13.

PART II

THE CHARTER OF PROTESTANTISM

DIFFERENCES CONCERNING THE SOURCE OF TRUTH—THE FORMAL PRINCIPLE

CHAP.		PAGE
I.	The Contents and Use of the Scriptures	95
II.	The Responsibility of the Individual Christian towards the Scriptures	102
III.	The Source of Certainty respecting the Authority of the Scriptures	111
IV.	The Perspicuity of Scripture	119
V.	The Perfection of Scripture	127
VI.	The Perfection of Scripture—Tradition (*continuation*)	138
VII.	The Doctrinal Study of Scripture—The Theory of Development	145

CHAPTER I

THE CONTENTS AND USE OF THE SCRIPTURES

IN our exposition of the first principles of the Protestant gospel, we have tacitly assumed that the Scriptures are the only authoritative guide of the spiritual life. It is out of the Bible as the source of truth that the gospel springs, but it is with this spoken word of God in the first instance that the inquiring soul has to deal. Luther himself may be said to have got his first right impressions of the truth from the personal address to him of his friend Staupitz. It was only after he heard and believed the gospel of forgiveness at his lips, that he could read the Bible intelligently. It was later in his career that he found it to be a means of grace to his soul, and later still that he learned to wield it as a divine weapon against his adversaries. In studying the evangelical application of the truth, therefore, we were entitled to take for granted the divine foundation on which it rested. Now that these first principles have been set forth, we are at liberty to survey more carefully the basis on which the gospel of Protestantism rests. Thus also shall we be prepared for the discussion of other topics in which the Scriptures must hold their ground against the claims of human authority.

The most precious legacy that the apostolic age transmitted to succeeding centuries was a complete Bible. Bringing in one hand the Scriptures of the Old Testament, collected and preserved by successive generations of pious Jews, the primitive Church presented in the other the writings of the evangelists and apostles with the plain indication that they were of equal value for the education and development of the Christian life. The post-apostolic Church welcomed all these Scriptures and treated them as occupying the same supreme place as parts of the revelation of God.

This conviction speedily showed itself in the most practical way. In the Septuagint and the Greek New Testament, the greater part of the Eastern Church found the Scriptures in a language they could at once understand. It was soon manifest, however, that if the Western Church was to enjoy the same knowledge of the word of God, the whole Bible would have to be rendered into Latin. Many Latin versions accordingly soon appeared. In course of time one was adjudged superior to all others, on account of the extensive scholarship of its author and the eminent position he occupied in the Church. This was the version of Jerome, the bishop of Jerusalem, now commonly known as the "Vulgate." The Old Testament was translated directly from the original Hebrew, the New Testament partly from an older version named the "Itala," but corrected throughout by the original Greek. It was this version of the whole Scriptures in Latin that became the Bible of the mediæval Church, as it is indeed the authorised version of the Church of Rome over the world to this day.

Nor should it be forgotten that even in the Middle Ages the Bible was treated with the respect due to its origin and character as a divine revelation. The theologians of that period frequently referred to it as the supreme authority in matters of Christian faith. Rupert, Abbot of Deutz, for example, in the twelfth century, laid the utmost stress on the duty of studying the word of God. "To him the Bible appeared the great text-book for all ages and peoples and the field where the precious pearl of salvation lay concealed which every person whose vision faith had enlightened might there discover."[1] Thomas Aquinas also wrote in the beginning of his great theological treatise: "Our faith rests on the revelation made to the apostles and prophets who wrote the canonical books, not on such revelations as may have been given to other teachers."[2] It is true that in the Church as a whole the Bible was often practically thrust into the background; but at first there was no other formal authority set alongside it or on the same level. When Luther was first brought face to face with his opponents, he could take it for granted that the Bible was acknowledged as the supreme source of doctrine, and at the outset they were not unwilling to try to meet him on that ground.

Yet it is plain that this tacit acknowledgment of the supremacy of the Scriptures did not then wield the influence it should have had. For well-nigh a whole millennium before the Reformation, the Bible was regarded and used in a fashion that really nullified its authority in the Church.

For one thing, no effective or widespread effort was made to study and expound the Scriptures in the original languages. One scholar here and another there might urge candidates for the priesthood to study Hebrew and Greek. But the clergy as a whole were never called on to make this work an essential element of their duty. The result was that, except in the case of a few learned dignitaries, the original Scriptures were utterly neglected. Copies of the Vulgate were being continually made with manifold variations and not a few gross errors, alike in translation and interpretation. Yet these were never corrected, but rather openly admitted and even sometimes seized upon as the foothold of new superstitious additions to doctrine or practice.

[1] Kurtz, *Ch. Hist.* i. § 134. 3.   [2] *Summa*, i. 1.

Besides this, a very defective view of the real nature and purpose of the Scriptures came to prevail almost universally. Several of the most eminent Fathers of the Church had embraced Christianity after their minds had been deeply imbued with the spirit and method of Oriental philosophy. Origen is a notable example of this class. He and others like him regarded the Scriptures as really beyond the mental reach of plain men and women. Jesus Christ in His highest function was a new spiritual lawgiver, and in their view the only way of treating the Scriptures with adequate reverence was to look upon them as a repository of intellectual truths and moral principles. These were most distinctly set forth in the New Testament; but, coming from the same source, the Old Testament must teach essentially the same things. If in the earlier Scriptures these truths were presented in a more obscure form, this fact only laid on the philosophic interpreter the duty of piercing beneath the surface of the letter and bringing the hidden treasure to light.

Accordingly, there sprang up alongside of this view of the Bible a system of interpretation exactly consonant with it. The simple meaning which the words of Scripture naturally suggested was in this view of but little value. " Litera gesta docet," it was said in a well-known Latin couplet of the time: the letter teaches only things that have taken place. If there were no other sense but the literal one, these teachers thought, then whole books of Scripture, such as the books of the law or the Chronicles of the kings of Israel, would be almost worthless, for they were only records of what was past and gone, dead histories with which no one had now to do. The real meaning of Scripture, its actual contribution to eternal truths and ethical principles, must be sought in a higher mystical sense which the words bore. This sense was in turn taken to be threefold: an *allegorical* meaning which showed the bearing of the statement on the truths of the faith; a *figurative*, which exhibited its lessons on duty; and an *anagogic*, which indicated its suggestions as to the future. In the hands of Thomas Aquinas, for example, the words, " Let there be light," besides their literal historical reference to the creative act of God, have a threefold mystical meaning. Allegorically, they mean, " Let Christ be love"; figuratively, " May we be mentally illumined by Christ"; anagogically, " May we be led by Christ to glory."

The first issue of such a method of interpreting the Scriptures could only be an undue reliance on tradition. In the case of writers who had ingenuity or learning enough to impose on the words of Scripture the ideas and fancies in which they took chief delight, the work of exposition might be carried out in any form or to any extent. But with those who had not the requisite gift of imagination, it was far otherwise. They could only fall back on the array of opinions held by their bolder predecessors and select that which seemed on the whole to have most support. Thus arose gradually that veneration for the Fathers of the Church to which in principle the Church of Rome still cleaves. What one or more of those old teachers thought and taught, however much it might be contradicted by others, proved basis enough for the introduction and final adoption of opinions and practices of the most extravagant kind.

The ultimate result was still more unfortunate. The Bible fell more and more into disuse throughout the Church. When a book is such that the interpretation of it is reserved only for those who have undergone a special training, or when its language is not thought to yield readily a simple and salutary meaning, it is no longer sought for and used by ordinary people. Even the higher clergy failed to study the Bible as it deserved. A multitude of the priests were grossly ignorant of it, while for the laity almost the only source whence they could readily gain any knowledge of its contents was the meagre portions of Scripture printed in the manuals used in the ordinary worship of the Church. Even when the Scriptures were translated into the vernacular language of different nations, the interest in them was never keen enough to secure adequate study or circulation of the sacred volume.

While this process of obscuration was going on, however, there were other influences at work that were destined to counteract it. When the treasures of classical learning became scattered in Europe and scholars began to take delight in the literature they contained, the thought gradually took hold of the minds of many that the Bible itself also might well be interpreted in the same way as other writings. If the language and thoughts of Homer, Virgil and Cicero were to be taken in their plain literal sense, was it not worth while to read the Scriptures for the meaning which the words themselves, when duly pondered, were at once found to bear? It was this conviction that really underlay the zeal with which such Hebrew scholars as Reuchlin, and such students of Greek as Erasmus were inviting the youth of Europe to return to the examination of the original Scriptures. If the Bible had but one single simple sense, whatever other special applications certain passages might admit of, then it was indispensable to study the language in which its documents were at first written and to take heed to the events narrated in them.

In this way, the various parts of Scripture came to bear a new significance. The chief theme of the Bible as a whole was seen to be the history of the redemption accomplished for fallen men. The Old Testament set forth the preparation for this work: the evangelists narrated the fulfilment of it: the apostles taught the way in which it bore on the mind and conscience and life of those who accepted it. These ideas, fostered by the new interest in the history of the world and illumined by the great evangelical convictions disseminated by the teaching of Wiclif, Hus and Jerome of Prague, were at the time of the Reformation rousing the minds of serious students to go back to the Scriptures as the source of a more glorious light than had ever yet fallen on the eyes of men.

Amid such influences it needed only a deeper conviction of sin on the one hand, and a richer experience of divine grace on the other, to initiate a widespread movement in favour of a return to the apostolic gospel as the only vehicle of salvation, and to the Scriptures as the only source at which this gospel could be found in its purity. We have seen already how his spiritual experience led Luther in this direction. Under his preaching and that of his coadjutors, many thousands of every rank of society in Germany were led by the same path to this goal: so that when the deputies at the Diet of Speier expressed their intention of cleaving to the word of God as the only source of life and peace as well their only guide in Christian doctrine, they but formulated a decision that was destined to be characteristic of Protestantism in all its after history.

With these facts before us, the Protestant view of the contents and purpose of the Scriptures may now be more precisely defined than it has often been in the controversy with Romanists. A very common way of stating the main difference betwixt the two Churches on this point has been to say with Chillingworth that "the Bible and the Bible only is the religion of Protestants." This is indeed true, and indicates a position we shall have to make good in a later chapter. But it leaves untouched what the preceding pages have shown to be a yet more fundamental difference, namely, *that which arises from what Protestants find in the Bible*. The Reformers saw in the Bible what the mediæval theologians had neglected to seek for, and thus found it to be to them practically a different book, disclosing new contents and wielding a higher power over all their thought and life. To the fruits of this discovery, the Protestant Churches still cleave as their richest heritage.[1]

1. We receive the Bible, in the first place, then, as the primary source of *the word of God*. This is what the quickened soul longs for. If we are really redeemed by the blood of the Son of God and brought into direct communion with God through Him, then it is possible for us to hear the voice of the heavenly Father. Nothing short of this will meet the craving of the renewed heart. But it is just this divine message that through the Spirit is ministered to man from the Scriptures. "The seed is the word of God."[2] "So belief cometh of hearing, and hearing by the word of Christ."[3] "God having of old time spoken unto the fathers in the prophets by divers portions and in divers manners, hath at the end of these days spoken unto us in His Son."[4] "Wherefore, even as the Holy Ghost saith, To-day, if ye shall hear His voice, harden not your hearts."[5] "For the word of God is living and active and sharper than any two-edged sword."[6] These words represent the attitude that Luther took up. Having been made free by the Son, he contended, we are entitled to live in the atmosphere of spiritual liberty, and this can be had only by hearing the voice of

---

[1] Cf. Prof. W. R. Smith, *What History teaches us to seek in the Bible*, (*Inaugural Lecture*, 1870).
[2] Luke viii. 11. [3] Rom. x. 17. [4] Heb. i. 1.
[5] Heb. iii. 7, 8. [6] Heb. iv. 12.

God speaking to us in the Scriptures. "The soul has no other thing either in heaven or on earth in which it can live pious and free and Christian, but the holy evangel, the word of God, preached by Christ.... So we must be sure that the soul can lack everything but the word of God, but without that word it is helped by nothing."[1] And further: "If thou askest, What then is the word that gives such rich grace, and how shall I use it? the answer is: It is nothing else but the preaching that is given of Christ, as the gospel contains it, which is so to be presented as it has been, that thou mayest hear thy God speaking to thee."[2] This was a view of the Bible which as a whole the mediæval Church had never consciously reached.

2. It is only taking a step farther in the same direction when we say that as Protestants *we use and study the Bible as a means of grace.* Under the conception of the Bible as a storehouse of eternal abstract truths and ethical principles, the Church of Rome removed it as far as possible from the rubric of appointed channels of divine grace. It was the sacraments alone that practically held this position. Even to Carlstadt, the friend and coadjutor of Luther, the Scriptures were largely an authority lying outside the Christian life, a codex of law by which it was to be governed, but which on that account was not to be inwardly appropriated and enjoyed. Luther on the other hand strenuously maintained that the Scriptures are entitled to be placed alongside the Lord's Supper as a channel by which through the Spirit God operates directly on the soul. The word of God held in the Scriptures and continually sounding forth as a living voice from them, was the indispensable food of the soul. This claim the Bible itself everywhere makes. "Man doth not live by bread only, but by everything ("word," Matt. iv. 4) that proceedeth out of the mouth of the Lord, doth man live."[3] "For it is not a vain thing for you, because it is your life."[4] "How sweet are Thy words unto my taste!"[5] "Receive with meekness the implanted word which is able to save your souls."[6] "As newborn babes long for the spiritual milk which is without guile, that you may grow thereby unto salvation."[7]

3. Last of all, the Protestant Church adheres to the Scriptures *as the source of Christian doctrine.* This claim, we have seen, was, to some extent admitted by the theologians of the mediæval Church. But it was nullified by the form in which the teaching of Scripture was put. So long as doctrine was formulated in the mould of abstract truths and principles, the Bible could only appear to be a heap of miscellaneous fragments. It could not be properly treated as the final court of appeal for utterances that might distinguish truth and error. When, however, the Scriptures were found to be a

---

[1] *Sermon von der Freiheit eines Christen-menschen,* § 5 (*Werke:* Pfizer, s. 232).
[2] *Sermon, ut sup.* s. 6.   [3] Deut. viii. 3.   [4] Deut. xxxii. 47.
[5] Ps. cxix. 103.   [6] Jas. i. 21.   [7] 1 Pet. ii. 1.

thoroughly progressive, united and luminous history of redemption, a record of historic facts by which through faith the soul could be brought into direct fellowship with God their author, and Christ their living subject, the doctrines drawn from them could be stated in a form directly fitted at once to nourish and establish the soul and protect it from error. It was this conception of the Bible that gave Luther his marvellous facility in exhibiting the baseless character of so many of the corrupt opinions and practices of the Papacy. As the great historian of Protestant theology has said, "The apostolic and prophetic writings only came to be regarded by him as the decisive rule and judge, after the saving matter, which the Church still had in common with the Scriptures, had approved itself to his heart by its own inherent power."[1] By this method the Protestant Church abides still. Embracing the Scriptures as the source of the gospel, using them as a perennial means of grace, we find in them also a storehouse of truths which we can marshal in forms fitted alike for the comfort and defence of our spiritual life and the demolition of error. "But Jesus answered and said unto them, Ye do err, not knowing the Scriptures, nor the power of God."[2] "Ye became obedient from the heart to that form of teaching whereunto ye were delivered."[3] "The sacred writings which are able to make thee wise unto salvation, through faith which is in Christ Jesus." "Every scripture inspired of God is also profitable for teaching."[4]

[1] Dorner, *History of Protestant Theology*, vol. i. p. 221 (Clark).
[2] Matt. xxii. 29.   [3] Rom. vi. 17.   [4] 1 Tim. iii. 15, 16.

CHAPTER II

THE RESPONSIBILITY OF THE INDIVIDUAL CHRISTIAN TOWARDS THE SCRIPTURES

IT is not difficult to see that, with the views of the Scriptures they held, the theologians of the mediæval Church could not encourage the people to carry on private personal investigation of their meaning. The Bible being a storehouse of truths and principles, it was only those that had passed through a special discipline and had otherwise the sanction of the Church that were at liberty to continue such studies. The ordinary members of the Church of Rome were not regarded as having any call to do this work or any fitness for engaging in it. It was rather a thing to be eschewed. Such, for example, was the view sternly held even by such an advocate of reformation as Jean Charlier de Gerson, chancellor of the University of Paris. While he was prepared to appeal to the Bible as the only source and rule of Christian knowledge, he nevertheless strongly protested against the laity's having access to the Scriptures in the vernacular. The interpretations of the Church were inspired ; and everyone that was not prepared to receive them was to be branded as a heretic and even legally punished.

With Luther and his followers a widely different view was sure to prevail. If in the Scriptures men had a revelation whereby they could hear a direct message from God to their souls, a natural inference was that they should have unfettered access to them. It was a duty they owed to God to hear what He might speak, and they had a right to the full use of the special means by which this duty could be best fulfilled. Luther himself clung to this position with the utmost tenacity. At a very early stage of his career, he wrote to Pope Leo X. to this effect : " I cannot bear with laws for the interpretation of the word of God, since the word of God which teaches liberty in all other things ought not to be bound."[1] In spite of manifest wavering on the part of some of his associates, Luther upheld this claim to the end. "To ascertain and judge concerning doctrine," he says, " appertains to all and to every Christian ; and it appertains in such a way that let him be anathema who shall injure this right by a single hair."[2]

[1] D'Aubigné, *History*, ii. p. 262.
[2] Köstlin, *Luthers Theologie*, vol. ii. s. 61 (1883).

Against such a position as this, it is easy to see, the Roman Church could not but set her face. In the earliest Councils of the Church, there was no express direction as to how men were to deal with the Scriptures. But at a very early period before the Reformation, her theologians had been accustomed to limit their interpretations of Scripture by the opinions of the Fathers. Even they had no right to exercise their own judgment on the sense of any passage of the word of God. How could such a privilege be extended to the laity? At the first appearance of Luther before the Diet of Worms, it was set beyond doubt that in the view of the Romish authorities no such liberty existed. When, after the Reformation had begun, they had to define their position in the Council of Trent, the privilege was expressly denied : "Furthermore, in order to restrain petulant spirits, the Synod decrees that no one relying on his own skill shall—in matters of faith and of morals, pertaining to the edification of Christian doctrine—wresting the sacred Scripture to his own senses, presume to interpret the said sacred Scripture contrary to that sense which holy mother Church—whose it is to judge of the true sense and interpretation of the holy Scriptures—hath held and doth hold, or even contrary to the unanimous consent of the Fathers."[1]

The decision as to which of these divergent views is right can be obtained in the last resort only by an appeal to the Scriptures themselves. Before producing their testimony, however, it may be well to make plain what this responsibility of the individual Christian in relation to the Bible for which Protestantism contends, really involves. It will help to disentangle the real question at issue, if we begin by setting aside some views of the obligation which are constantly attributed to Protestantism but do not belong to it in fact.

1. Let it be understood, for example, that no claim is here made for the individual Christian to think *what he pleases* concerning the teaching of Scripture. Romanists have often imputed this pretension to upholders of the Reformation. The claim may have sometimes been advanced by sceptical thinkers, especially when they have been combating some attempt to assert authority over the conscience. But it is not to be confounded with the position of Protestantism. The Reformation was not a movement for mere freedom of thought. No man is at liberty to think as he pleases, where facts are to be had that point clearly to the direction earnest thought should pursue. This is true of every subject of human investigation. We are free to think as we list only where there are no well-ascertained facts to guide us. The moment that definite data come into our possession, mental liberty is limited, and the conscience is bound to take cognisance of them in forming a decision. It is a characteristic of Protestantism that it sees in the statements of Scripture facts presented in language about the meaning of which there can be no doubt in any reasonable mind ; and to these truths it charges men

[1] Sess. IV. *On the Canonical Scriptures.*

to attach all the weight they deserve. It stands to the honour of Luther that he was one of the first to discern in the historical facts of the Old Testament as well as the New a real history of redemption and to mould his views of doctrine on the indubitable basis thus supplied. The same spirit characterises Protestantism still. It holds it to be as unreasonable as it is unscientific to give the reins to fancy, caprice or prejudice, when data are supplied, sufficient to lead into all the truth.

2. It is also plain that this responsibility of the individual Christian to the Scriptures does not imply that he is to take no account of what the Christian Church has been taught and has been enabled to testify for during her past career. It has often been charged against Protestantism that it counsels an utter breach with the past and that, in its desire for reformation, it would ignore and nullify the lessons and the discipline of all past Christian history. Cardinal Newman, whilst still an Anglican, went so far as to say: "This one thing at least is certain: whatever history teaches, whatever it omits, whatever it exaggerates or extenuates, whatever it says and unsays, at least the Christianity of history is not Protestantism."[1] It is thus, he also says, that Protestants "are forced, whether they will or not, to fall back upon the Bible as the sole source of revelation and upon their own personal private judgment as the sole expounder of its doctrine." That we do thus ultimately resort to the Scriptures cannot be gainsaid: but we deny that Protestantism has at any stage of its career ever made any such breach with historical Christianity truly so called. The Reformers never ignored the divine education and discipline of the Church in the endeavour to ascertain the mind of the Spirit in the Scriptures. There are many most important elements of Christian doctrine taught by the Church of Rome in common with the other Churches of Christendom. Luther and his associates clung to these after they left her pale as earnestly as ever they did while within it. They had no wish to part with any doctrine that could be shown to be contained in the Scriptures or to be deduced from them by just and necessary consequence. Only they taught that neither these doctrines nor the formulas in which they were stated by the wise and learned of other days either as individuals or in Councils of the Church, were to be regarded as of equal value with the Scriptures themselves or as possessing permanent authority over the minds of men in their interpretation of them. Vincentius of Lerinum had laid down the principle that "the line of interpretation should be guided according to the rule of the ecclesiastical and Catholic sense." Luther, on the contrary, held that as a Christian theologian he was entitled "to be free—to live in the kingdom of the truth and to confess as truth whatever he saw to be truth." "A layman who has the Scripture," he said, "is more to be trusted than Pope or Council without it." This is the spirit of Protestantism still. The past attainments of the Church in the

[1] *An Essay on the Development of Christian Doctrine*, p. 7 (pop. ed.).

elucidation of Christian doctrine are not barriers beyond which the mind of the individual student of the Bible is on no account to penetrate. They are to be valued as aids to personal study of the Scriptures and only to be accepted by each man as he finds them taught there.

3. Equally manifest is it that this responsibility does not imply that every individual Christian is called on to throw overboard all the ideas and principles he may have inherited in early Christian instruction and to build again his own doctrinal conceptions from the foundation. Protestantism has no interest in discarding the elements of truth imparted in Christian education, by whomsoever they may have been taught, so far as these are in accordance with the Scriptures. Nothing is to be gained by the attempt to make the mind a mere *tabula rasa*, and to insist that the first principles of Christianity shall be learned again under new auspices. There are certain great elements of truth and duty drawn from the Scriptures that are happily common to all Churches professing Christianity and where these have been suffered to exercise an unbiassed influence on character and life, they should remain undisturbed. What Protestantism desires to protect the soul against is the claim on the part of separate denominations of the Church to impose their characteristic articles of belief as final and authoritative for the conscience. Every branch of the Church is at liberty to take measures by which only those that hold the truth as she propounds it, shall become office-bearers in her communion. But it is one thing to exercise such administrative authority and another to assert a right of jurisdiction over the individual judgment. Protestantism claims for the individual adherents and members of every Church the duty and the right of bringing to the test of Scripture whatever may have been taught them as distinctive points of faith, so proving all things, while holding fast that which is good.

4. Last of all, this responsibility of the individual Christian does not imply that everyone is entitled to rely simply on his own gifts or abilities as an interpreter of the Scriptures. It has often been said that, according to Protestantism, every member of the Church, however ignorant or unlearned, is placed on the same level as another and permitted to wield the same influence in connection with the acceptance and dissemination of the truth. It is not so. We acknowledge that grades of knowledge and wisdom must prevail in every age of the Church. As children at school occupy lower and higher forms, so must men stand on planes of varying power of understanding and interpreting the word of God. This is due to difference in natural ability, in providential opportunities and spiritual gifts. The divine intention in this diversity is doubtless to bind the members of the Church together in mutual dependence and helpfulness. It thus becomes the duty of every disciple to avail himself of all the helps to growing knowledge that may come to his hand. There are definite rules for arriving at the real meaning of the written word; and in the course of the Church's work in the world,

many helps of various kinds have been framed for facilitating the understanding of the Scriptures. It would be a violation of the laws of providential progress and Christian fellowship for any individual disciple to ignore these. In the acquisition of ordinary knowledge, we gladly take account of all that has hitherto been acquired in each department, without thereby binding ourselves to the statements of special writers or teachers. Any other course would expose us to the charge of conceit and self-will. The same principle must govern our growth in spiritual knowledge. Luther not only studied the rules for interpreting the Scriptures aright but read diligently the expositions of earlier writers as an aid to arriving at their meaning. The only proviso that Protestantism makes here is that we are not to accept the dicta of any writers, however eminent, as final or authoritative, but constantly preserve an attitude of mental and moral independence towards men, while we cherish as deep a confidence in the teaching, authority and grace of God alone.

The responsibility of the individual Christian towards the Scriptures may therefore be defined as the obligation resting on every man of hearing the word of God as addressed to himself, and of exercising his own faculties on the Scriptures which contain the word, that he may ascertain their meaning and be led into the full assurance of understanding. It is thus also seen to involve what has been so long called "the right of private judgment," in the special sense of immunity from ecclesiastical or civil domination in matters of conscientious belief and therewith freedom to ascertain what the word of God itself teaches on every point of doctrine and practice. As one has well said, "It is the most sacred of rights, because it guarantees the most sacred of duties."[1] It is a right as well as a duty of which men cannot strip themselves. It is a responsibility from which no man or Church should attempt to relieve the conscience of mankind, because it is clearly implied alike in the general principles and express statements of the word of God.

1. It is implied, for example, in that longing for direct communion with God which lies in the depths of every soul. Man feels that he is dependent on the God that made him, and has both a capacity for receiving communications from Him and a craving for them. The great Swiss Reformer, Zwingli, indeed regarded this endowment as the most essential element of the image of God in man. "We discover then," he said, "that the image of God in us is to be identified with something much more special than the mere intellect, will and memory. The chief element in it is longing for God and His word. This is the most certain token that there exists between God and us something in the shape of kinship, likeness and form and that we were glorified at the first with this image according to the Scriptures."[2] When, therefore, man comes into direct contact with

[1] Dr. R. W. Dale, *Protestantism: its Ultimate Principle*, p. 37 (2nd ed.). Exeter Hall Lecture, 1874.
[2] *Von Klarheit u. Gewüsse des Worts Gottes*, Werke, i. ss. 57, 58.

the word of God in the Scriptures, he is only discharging a duty and receiving a privilege that are his by the indefeasible rights of creaturehood. It is on this ground that he is held responsible for learning something of God from the work of creation. Why should it not also make it incumbent on him to exercise reason and judgment on His written word?

2. All the more readily should this be admitted that the revelation of Himself which God has given in the Scriptures is actually designed and intended for all men. The longing for the knowledge of God which in spite of sin is still preserved in the heart of man, is met by a corresponding longing on the part of God to reveal Himself to His fallen creatures. The attitude of the Creator is everywhere represented as one of forbearance and long-suffering, of compassion and love towards the whole race. The Scriptures were indeed written by holy men of old connected with one nation, but the entire strain of their utterances shows that they were the custodiers of the divine communications for all mankind. The reason assigned for the special covenant with Israel is : " For all the earth is mine."[1] The apostles were charged to preach the gospel that springs directly from the Scriptures to every creature under heaven. The Scriptures were the ground of public appeal to every man for the verity of the good tidings they brought ; and never did they leave anyone under the impression that the written source of their message was not to be as accessible as the message itself.

3. This position is also abundantly confirmed by the fact that, when men do accept the grace of God, they are received into the closest fellowship with Himself. Under the old covenant men had to deal with Jehovah through the mediation of the priests, at least in external worship. They did not enter into the high calling offered them of being a kingdom of priests, and had therefore to be so far dependent on the closer intercourse with Him extended to others. Under the new covenant, as we have seen, every believer in Christ is equally a king and a priest unto God. " Through Him we all have our access in one Spirit unto the Father."[2] This privilege carries with it a corresponding right of access to His word. He that welcomes every child of His into the holiest of all will never close the door of communication with the Scriptures He has provided. Rather will He encourage them to enter every chamber of the temple of truth and, as heirs of God and joint-heirs with Christ, to appropriate all the riches of wisdom they find there.

4. These considerations are clenched by the additional fact that to all who study the Scriptures God has everywhere expressed His willingness to impart the special illumination of the Holy Spirit.[3] No higher testimony could be given to the reality of the obligation to study the Scriptures and to the desire of God that every disciple should enjoy the comfort they alone can give. This blessing is to be obtained in answer to prayer : " If ye then, being evil, know how to

[1] Ex. xix. 5.   [2] Eph. ii. 18.   [3] Ps. xxv. 9 ; Isa. lix. 21.

give good gifts unto your children, how much more shall the heavenly Father give the Holy Spirit to them that ask Him?"[1] This gift has been actually enjoyed by God's children from the beginning. It was not of Himself as an apostle but of his fellow-disciples as a whole that John wrote : "Ye have an anointing from the Holy One and ye know all things."[2]

What is thus taught by the general principles of Scripture is expressed in varied forms in the devotional and didactic utterances of many of its books. The constant perusal of God's word is commended in the most pointed way. "Man shall not live by bread alone, but by every word that proceedeth from the mouth of God."[3] "This law is no vain thing for you : because it is your life."[4] "His delight is in the law of the Lord ; and in His law doth he meditate day and night."[5] "Let the word of Christ dwell in you richly in all wisdom," wrote the Apostle Paul.[6] He congratulates Timothy that from a child he had known the Scriptures which were able to make him wise unto salvation.[7]

Moreover, the Scriptures are to be used as a standard for testing the claims of individuals or classes to be teachers and leaders of the people of God. Christian disciples are often in Scripture warned to be careful in the performance of this duty. No one insisted on it more sharply than the Lord Jesus. We are to beware of false prophets :[8] we are to guard against thieves and robbers.[9] The Apostle John says that we are not to believe every spirit, but to try the spirits whether they be of God.[10] Cardinal Newman quotes these words as presenting the only kind of judgment Christians are to exercise. "The great question which Scripture puts before us for the exercise of private judgment is,—Who is God's prophet and where? Who is to be considered the voice of the holy Catholic and Apostolic Church?"[11] This is an utter misrepresentation. The Scriptures themselves are to be the primary subject of consideration : men are to be judged of only under their guidance. To call upon disciples to test teachers instead of studying the word of God, would be to put a more difficult duty in the place of a simpler one, and at the same time to take away the only means by which it can be duly performed.[12]

In view of such an array of Biblical testimonies in favour of the duty of personal study of the truth and the right of private judgment, how vain is it for Romanists to adduce the only verse of Scripture that can be perverted into an apparent utterance against them. Writing to the brethren of the dispersion regarding the word of prophecy and urging them to take heed to it as unto a light shining in a dark

[1] Luke xi. 9, 13.   [2] 1 John iii. 20.   [3] Deut. viii. 3.
[4] Deut. xxxii. 47.   [5] Ps. i. 2.   [6] Col. iii. 16.
[7] 1 Tim. i. 21 ; cf. 1 Pet. ii. 2 ; Jas. i. 21 ; Rev. i. 3.
[8] Matt. vii. 15.   [9] John x. 4, 5.   [10] 1 John iv. 1.
[11] *Essays Critical and Historical*, vol. ii. p. 355.
[12] Isa. viii. 20 ; John v. 39 ; Acts xvii. 11 ; 1 Cor. ii. 15, iii. 22, x. 15 ; 1 Thess. v. 21 ; 2 Tim. ii. 7.

place, Peter reminded them that "no prophecy of Scripture is of private interpretation."[1] Such a conjunction of words is too precious to be let slip by the hard-pressed controversialist: the text is quoted as a clear denial of "the right of private judgment" in relation to Scripture. The view is quite untenable. For, in the first place, Peter is dealing here, not with the Scriptures as a whole, but simply with the Messianic prophecies of the Old Testament. He says also to his readers that they do well to take heed to these: which surely implies the perusal of them. Then he bids them remember this caution in dealing with these prophecies, namely, that they were not "of private interpretation." This restriction cannot possibly refer to his readers who were urged to read and so interpret, but only to the prophets themselves who uttered the prophecies. The apostle evidently means that no prophecy is to be limited in its interpretation simply by the views, convictions or feelings of the prophet who was enabled to utter it. Every prophecy has a wider range of application than its first spokesman may have attached to it. For, as imparted by the Spirit of Christ, it stands in relation not only to the circumstances of the time in which it was spoken, but also to God's redeeming work in the world, and has a bearing on the sufferings of Christ and the glory that should follow.

How deeply these views of the responsibility of the individual Christian to the Scriptures roused the antagonism of the Church of Rome must be left to be shown in the sequel. Meanwhile it will be in place to indicate the fruits they began to bear in the action and administration of the Protestant Churches in connection with the Scriptures.

i. In the first place, no doctrinal value was attached to any book that was not of distinct canonical authority. The Apocrypha which formed part of the Septuagint was received by the primitive Church as practically on the same level with the Hebrew Scriptures. Several of the Eastern Churches expressly rejected them as without authority. But the Latin Church continued to show them some favour. The Reformers, on the other hand, set them utterly aside; and, though they were still, unhappily, printed in the same volume with the other Scriptures, no Protestant Church ever regarded them as inspired or authoritative for doctrine and practice.

ii. New translations of the Scriptures were made into the vernacular language of all the countries in which the Reformation took root. As we have seen, certain versions of the Bible had been in circulation before that era. But in many respects they were very imperfect. In his noble German version made from the original Hebrew and Greek Scriptures, Luther set an example which was speedily followed by all the Reformed Churches.

iii. The people were encouraged and exhorted to read the Scriptures for themselves. To the great majority of the members of the Church, the Bible had been a sealed book. When they

[1] 2 Pet. i. 20.

received it in their own speech, it became to them a new revelation. Every book and every page became radiant with the light of heaven. Many could say with Jeremiah: "Thy words were found, and I did eat them; and Thy words were unto me a joy and the rejoicing of mine heart."[1]

iv. The clergy of the Churches were trained to preach the word of God from the whole Scriptures. Luther followed a method of vigorous, popular address, based on the word of God that recalled the preaching of the apostles. His example fired all the teachers of the Reformed colleges. The students who looked forward to the ministry were bound to exercise their minds on the exegetical study of the Scriptures; and, when ordained, they made the Bible the chief nutriment of their congregations.

[1] Jer. xv. 16.

CHAPTER III

THE SOURCE OF CERTAINTY RESPECTING THE AUTHORITY OF THE SCRIPTURES

IT is not unreasonable to suppose that, where the real use and intention of the Scriptures as well as the right of direct access to them have been thoroughly grasped, all Christian disciples might well be left to fulfil their duty unfettered by further doubts. What interest could any Church have in keeping men back from her supreme public possession? The Church of Rome has never seen the matter in this light. It has not suited her policy to leave men free for the personal study of the Scriptures: she has continually endeavoured to introduce into their minds the idea of the paramount authority of the Church in connection with their use. Seeing clearly that, if the privilege of access to them were once conceded, their whole system would speedily crumble to the ground, the Romanists began soon after the Reformation to insinuate doubts about the Scriptures themselves which, they thought, would have the effect of deterring men from direct investigation of their contents. The point at which the attack was made was the authority of the Bible. This, it was contended, had no existence independently of the Church. So far were men from being able to dispense with the authoritative utterances of the Church in connection with Scripture, that, apart from her decision, they could have no valid persuasion that the Scriptures were really the word of God. How could men dare to ignore the voice of the Church, when it was required for imparting to the Bible any authority it could wield as the divine word?

In order to understand the exact incidence of this objection, as well as to put ourselves in a position for dealing effectively with it, it will again be well to adopt the method of separation and set aside certain points on which there is no question at issue.

1. It is to be understood, for example, that we are not to discuss here the question as to what it is that gives the Scriptures their claim on the assent and obedience of men. They derive their authority entirely from the fact that they are the word of God. As the Creator, Lord and Redeemer, of men, God exercises supreme authority over the mind and conscience. Every utterance of His

necessarily carries with it the same power. The moment that any message or injunction can be certified as having proceeded from the mind of God, it is at once clothed with an authority that is not to be gainsaid.

On this point Romanist and Protestant can hardly be said to be now at variance. It was indeed not always so. Turretin, the Genevan theologian, reminds us that in the century before his own there were men who did not hesitate to say that the whole authority of Scripture was derived from the testimony of the Church.[1] In more recent times, however, Romanists have felt inclined to abandon their former position. Most of them attempt to draw a distinction betwixt the authority of Scripture in itself, and its authority in relation to us. In the former aspect of it, they are willing to admit, the authority is due to the fact of its being the word of God. But they still join issue with us as to what constitutes the basis of its authority *over us*, and how we are to be assured that this authority is real.[2]

2. Moreover, on neither side is there any dispute as to the desirability of being assured that the Scriptures wield divine authority. To the Romanist, it is true, this can hardly be said to be such a vital attainment because he has what professes to be an equally valuable and authoritative source of guidance. Still the Church of Rome is not prepared to deny that men may and should desire to be assured that the Scriptures are divine alike in their origin and authority. To the Protestant, on the other hand, this confidence is desirable, because it is practically indispensable. If we have no persuasion emanating from an absolutely trustworthy source that the Scriptures are or contain the word of God, and are thus entitled to our assent and reverence, we are left without any foundation on which to build our faith now or our hopes for eternity. This is not a matter of mere speculative doctrine : it concerns the reality, growth and comfort of our spiritual life.

3. Hence also there is no question betwixt us as to whether the source of our firm persuasion concerning the divine origin and authority of Scripture should be human or divine. It is agreed on both sides that merely human testimony on a point of such moment would not be an adequate basis for such a conviction. The wiser theologians of the Roman Church admit as fully as Protestants that there is much evidence to be gleaned from many quarters in behalf of the divine authority of the Scriptures ; and in dealing with unbelievers, they are willing to give it all due weight. Only they hold, as we do, that this evidence is not in itself fitted to produce that full certitude concerning Scripture which men ought to have as the foundation of their religious life. It is sufficient to strip unbelievers of all excuse for their reluctance to acknowledge Christianity ; but, being such as man in the exercise of his ordinary faculties can collect and consider, it does not necessarily and of itself

[1] Loc. II. q. vi.   [2] Cf. Cunningham, *Theological Lectures*, p. 321 (Nisbet).

carry full certitude as its direct consequence. Both sides admit that what man requires is a faith in the divine authority of Scripture that shall rest on divine testimony. The divergence betwixt Romanism and Protestantism here is solely concerned with the question as to what is the precise source or channel through which this divine assurance is ministered, and whether it is sufficient for the purpose.

At this point accordingly, we are able to state the position of the Romanists on this question in the most precise form. They contend that the sole and sufficient source of a divine assurance respecting the authority of Scripture is to be found in the testimony of the Church to the effect that the Scriptures are the word of God; or, as the Council of Trent expressly says, "that God is the author of them." To their mind, this is a divine testimony which therefore furnishes not a mere part of the evidence that the Scriptures are the word of God, but in itself a truly divine basis of the whole proof, and one that is sufficient as the ground of a full conviction. So, for example, Cardinal Wiseman taught. Following the line taken by earlier theologians he said: "The Church stands forth with that authority wherewith she is invested by Christ—and proclaims: 'Under that guarantee of divine assistance which the words of Christ, in whom you believe, have given me, I pronounce that this book contains the revealed word of God and is inspired by the Holy Spirit; and that it contains all that has a right to enter into the sacred collection.' And thus the Catholic at length arrives, on the authority of the Church at these two important doctrines of the canon and inspiration of Scripture. . . . Supported by all the evidence of his divine mission, He (Christ) has appointed this authority to teach; and then that authority not merely advises, but obliges us, by that power which Christ has invested in it, to receive this sacred book as His inspired word."[1]

The main argument advanced in support of this position, as it is also indeed the foundation of the whole system, is of course that the Church is the divinely appointed organ of the Holy Spirit on earth, and therefore endowed with the gift of infallibility. No one presented this form of the doctrine more strongly than J. A. Möhler. "Since the word spoken by Christ (taken in its widest meaning) entered with His Spirit into a circle of men, and was received, it has taken flesh and blood, it has assumed form; and this form is the Church, which consequently is to be regarded by Catholics as the essential form of the Christian religion itself. . . . For this reason, the Church, according to the Catholic mode of looking at her, can fail in that part of her task which consists in the pure maintenance of the word, as little as she can in any other: she is inerrable."[2] This is an intelligible ground, and we must admit that if it can be established, the Romish position is entirely defensible. If there is an infallible Church acting as the mouthpiece of the Spirit of God and that

[1] *Lectures on the Catholic Church*, vol. i. pp. 65, 66. [2] *Symbolik*, ss. 333, 335.

Church says that the Scriptures are to be received as the word of God, men cannot be denied the privilege of accepting her statement, and resting upon it as the basis of their deepest convictions.

But is there such a Church on earth, or has the Church of Rome, in particular, any claim to stand in this place? The whole question falls to be discussed at a later stage of the exposition. When we come to deal with the teaching of the Church, we hope to be able to show that no Church on earth, and, least of all, the Church of Rome, is entitled to lay claim to the attribute of infallibility. Neither the Scriptures nor the facts of Christian history furnish the slightest proof that the Romish Church, whether acting in general Councils, or speaking judicially by the lips of her chief bishop, has any such endowment. Here it must suffice to insist that the Church cannot be said to be the organ of the Spirit in any sense, or to any extent, that warrants us in receiving her utterances as clothed with absolute truth. God did indeed give through holy men of old many promises of the presence and guidance of His Spirit; and these are essentially applicable to the Church of Christ in all ages. But the apostles who received and repeated these promises, never indicate that the Church was to be so united to Christ and identified with Him, as to become thereby for all time the source of an infallible testimony. Under the divine Master they too were so filled with the Spirit, that they were enabled to write the Scriptures which were necessary to complete the revelation of the mind of God. But when this task had been finished, and the Church was left with the Scriptures in her hands, the Lord did not see meet to maintain any living inerrable source of instruction longer upon the earth. His word charges us in manifold ways to cherish the indwelling and operation of the Holy Spirit; but it nowhere indicates that in the Church as a whole, or in any part of it—such as the Church of Rome at the most is—any further infallible witness of the truth is to be found. There is simply the promise that, in gracious recognition of study and prayer and service, believers shall certainly be led into all the truth they need to know for the salvation of the souls of men, and the accomplishment of the work of Christ in the world.

This being so, it is no valid argument in behalf of the Romish position to say that the Church existed prior to the Scriptures, and may thereby be presumed to surround them with the dignity and the authority over us, that are, as is alleged, inherent only in her own constitution. This assertion is not in accordance with fact. It is by the word that the children of God have been born into the kingdom from the beginning. The word spoken by holy men of old, coming as it did from the lips of the Eternal, existed before any constituted society of the saints of God on earth. If it was only after such organisation was given that the word of God was preserved in written form, that change did not affect the substance of the truth, but merely made provision for its permanent use by the people of God.[1]

[1] Eph. ii. 20.

No less futile is the argument derived from the special functions assigned in Scripture to the Church in connection with the word of God. Romish controversialists lay great stress on the fact that in one of his pastoral letters Paul speaks of the Church as "the pillar and foundation of the truth."[1] The reference of these figures to the pillars and foundation of a building is not to be evaded. Protestantism has no interest in minimising the dignity of the Church, or in taking up any attitude that appears to lessen her responsibility. But in this statement there is really nothing that favours the claim to pronounce on the divine authority of Scripture advanced by the Church of Rome. Taken in their most obvious sense, Paul's words refer not so much to the Scriptures as to "the word of the truth of the gospel," "the truth as it is in Jesus," which is based on them. To the Church is assigned the task of proclaiming the truth, and preserving it from the erroneous admixture of Gentile philosophy. So closely is the discharge of this duty bound up with her origin, existence and progress that she may be truly said to be to the maintenance of evangelic doctrine what pillars and foundation are to a building. It is on the continued presence in the world of the Church of the living God as a community of called, faithful and chosen souls that the spread and preservation of gospel truth depends. An assertion like this, however, is far from implying that the Scriptures from which this gospel is derived owe the acknowledgment of their authority to the Church. The Church upholds the evangelic system simply because without it she herself, like a roofless building exposed to the tempest, would be left without protection against the errors of a world lying in the wicked one. It is just because the Church of Rome has failed so grievously to fulfil this duty, that her form of Christianity presents the many points of likeness to the philosophy and worship of ancient paganism that we find in it to this day.

But if the Romish view of our source of certainty concerning the authority of Scripture has no real basis, what is that of Protestantism? It too puts the testimony of the Spirit in the forefront, but it maintains that the divine testimony is given, not through a so-called infallible Church, but directly to the individual believer in and with the word in his heart. This is the position so strongly asserted by Calvin. "If," said he, "we wish to make adequate provision for consciences, if they are not to be agitated in perpetual doubt, it is necessary for us to take the authority of Scripture from a higher source than the reasons or proofs or conjectures of men. That is to say, we must have it on the inner testimony of the Holy Spirit. For granted that in its own majesty there is sufficient ground for its being revered, it nevertheless begins really to touch us, when it is sealed on our hearts by the Holy Spirit. Being thus illumined by His power, we believe neither on our own judgment nor on that of others that Scripture is of God : but above all human judgment, we decide with-

[1] 1 Tim. iii. 15.

out dubiety that it has been given to us from the very mouth of God. . . . I say nothing but that which every believer experiences in himself, unless indeed it be that the words are far beneath the dignity of the argument."[1] With this statement all the other Reformers were in full sympathy: so also are the Reformed Confessions, though they express their views with varying precision. Amongst the most decided are the Scotch Confession (1560) and the Westminster (1647). The latter says: "We may be moved and induced by the testimony of the Church to an high and reverend esteem of the Holy Scripture . . . yet, notwithstanding, our full persuasion and assurance of the infallible truth and divine authority thereof, is from the inward work of the Holy Spirit, bearing witness by and with the word in our hearts."[2]

How thoroughly consonant this view is with all that Scripture itself teaches concerning the relation of the soul to the Spirit and the truth, as well as of these to one another, a little consideration will show.

It is obvious, for example, that, according to Scripture, the Spirit of God can deal directly with the heart of man. It is only as He works first in the heart of individual believers that the Church can become an habitation of God through the Spirit.

But this inward work of the Spirit in connection with the believer's view of the Scriptures is not carried on independently of the word of God itself but by means of it. Protestantism lays no claim to any testimony of the Spirit apart from the personal use and study of the Scriptures. The Spirit Himself uses the word they contain in bearing His testimony to their divine origin and authority. To this purpose the Scriptures are divinely adapted.

i. For, in the first place, are not the Scriptures in the last resort, the work and product of the Holy Spirit? They were indeed written by holy men of old in the full and unfettered exercise of their own faculties. The writers of the books of Scripture were responsible for the scope and plan of their special contributions as well as for the language in which they were composed. But the work of each was so done in the strength of the Spirit of God that His divine breath exhales from them continually. Thus Paul could say that "every Scripture is inspired of God."[3] What instrument can be so well fitted for the Spirit of God to use in convincing men of the divine origin of the Scriptures as the word of truth contained in these writings themselves?

ii. All the more readily should this principle be conceded that the more fully the illumination of the Spirit is ministered to men, the more clearly do they discern in the Scriptures many unmistakable tokens of their divine origin. The incomparable simplicity, concise-

---

[1] *Institutes*, bk. 1. ch. vii. 5. The French version is here fuller. The original, from which the above passage is translated, may be seen in Reuss, *History of the Canon*, p. 303.
[2] Ch. i. v.   [3] 2 Tim. iii. 16 (marg. in R.V.).

ness and energy of their language; the marvellous unity of design maintained in books written by men that lived whole centuries apart; the harmony that prevails in the representation given of what man is to believe concerning God and what duty God requires of man; the consistent statements everywhere made on man's condition and needs as a fallen creature; and especially the views presented of the wisdom, power and grace of God, in solving the problem of his redemption: these become "arguments" whereby the divine origin and authority of the Scriptures are set beyond dispute. Yet, as the Westminster Confession states, the highest testimony that the Spirit gives, is ministered not so much even by these features of the Scriptures as by the felt power of the truth operating in the heart.

iii. For it is by the word of God based on the Scriptures and springing from it, that the Spirit quickens the soul. He deals directly with the soul, but we hear no voice of the Spirit that is independent of the word. We are born of the Spirit, but, at the same time, not of corruptible seed, but incorruptible, even the word of God that liveth and abideth for ever.[1] If by the word the Spirit can impart life, can He not also by it impart a true and abiding conviction concerning the Scriptures themselves? If the Spirit can bear witness with our spirit that we are the children of God, what can prevent His bearing witness with the word that it is the word of the living God?

iv. This truth is still further confirmed by the fact that it is by the personal use of the Scriptures that the Spirit leads the soul into the higher ranges of Christian experience and knowledge. The Spirit and the word are the divine elements that are to work out the consummation of the kingdom of God in the hearts of men : " My Spirit that is upon you and my word that I have put in thy mouth shall not depart out of thy mouth nor out of the mouth of thy seed, nor of thy seed's seed, from henceforth even for ever." [2] This promise of Isaiah is echoed in the words of Paul : " God chose you from the beginning unto salvation in sanctification of the Spirit and belief of the truth." [3] It is only as we use the Scriptures that we can grow in wisdom, love and joy or be fitted for every good work. Why may we not also through the Spirit arrive at a firm conviction that the Scriptures by which He achieves this progress are themselves divine in origin and authority?

Nor can it be said that the Scriptures thus attested are here exalted to a position they are not fully entitled to occupy in the thoughts and life of mankind. When men have begun to taste their power, the Scriptures are felt to fit into their whole moral and spiritual nature as the elements of our physical life fit the senses. Light does not need to be proved to the eye, nor sound to the ear, nor food to the taste : the senses detect these at once. In like manner do the spiritual senses of quickened souls learn to feel the power of the Scriptures as the word of God : "The entrance of Thy word giveth

[1] 1 Pet. i. 23.   [2] Isa. lix. 21.   [3] 2 Thess. ii. 13.

light"; "So then faith cometh by hearing and hearing by the word of God";[1] "How sweet are Thy words to my taste";[2] "Thy words were found by me, and I did eat them; and Thy words were unto me the joy and rejoicing of my heart."[3] Who would not choose as their ultimate authority a book that through the Spirit plainly sustains its own claim to be divine, rather than an infallible Church fabricated out of ever fallible men?

[1] Rom. x. 17.   [2] Ps. cxix. 103, 130.   [3] Jer. xv. 16.

CHAPTER IV

THE PERSPICUITY OF SCRIPTURE

A FURTHER expedient resorted to by the Church of Rome for deterring men from direct reliance on the Scriptures, as a means of acquiring a knowledge of divine truth open to all, is to assail the form and substance of the books themselves.

Looking at the Scriptures as a collection of higher truths and principles rather than a historic revelation of the divine purpose of love to the world, pregnant with a message to every creature under heaven, Romanists have been strongly tempted to magnify the difficulty of understanding them fully. It is for the most part in relation to the system of Christian truth that this stumbling-block has been alleged to exist. The utterances of the Council of Trent, already quoted, assume that the doctrinal teaching of the Scriptures is, and must remain, obscure to the body of the people. Bellarmin said: "God did not ignore the fact, that many difficulties concerning the faith would arise in the Church, and therefore felt bound to provide a judge for her."[1] But even in recent times Romanists have not hesitated to charge the whole language and form in which they are written with obscurity. Cardinal Wiseman, for example, referred in this connection to the lyric poetry of the Bible—"a class of writing difficult to most readers in their own language, often almost unintelligible in the profane authors of antiquity, and still more so in the Scriptures, from the greater boldness of the figures and the greater conciseness of the speech"; to "the mysterious imagery of the prophets' visions, and the obscure language in which it is recorded"; to "those serious difficulties which prevent ordinary readers from understanding even the easier parts of Scripture." "It is sufficient," he said, "to look over the collections of commentators, to count the number of their volumes, and measure the bulk of matter written on almost every verse of Scripture, to satisfy yourselves that it is not so easy a book."[2]

Those amongst the Tractarian writers who approached nearest to the Church of Rome expressed the same opinions with still less reserve. While yet a member of the Anglican Church, Cardinal

[1] Cf. Hodge, *Syst. Theol.* vol. i. p. 107.
[2] *Lectures on the Catholic Church*, vol. i. pp. 47, 48.

Newman said: "While Scripture is written by inspired men with one and one only view of doctrine in their hearts and thoughts, even the truth which was from the beginning, yet being written not to instruct in doctrine, but for those who were already instructed in it, not with direct announcements, but with intimations and implications of the truth, the qualifications for apprehending it are so rare and high, that a prudent man, to say nothing of piety, will not risk his salvation on the chance of his having them."[1] Another writer went still further in the same direction: "If Scripture contains any system at all, it must contain it covertly and teach it obscurely, because it is altogether most unmethodical and irregular in its structure."[2]

Now even on a first view, this is a charge that seems hard to be made good. On their very face, the Scriptures carry features that it appears impossible to reconcile with the idea of obscurity as to the meaning of their language or their main drift and purpose.

How utterly foreign to the presence of such a stumbling-block, for example, is the fact that the Scriptures are the work and gift of God. It will not be denied that He who is the Creator of man, and the Author of his faculty of thought and speech, can frame a revelation of Himself and His will that shall be perfectly intelligible to His creatures. If it were otherwise, He could not be the living God or the object of man's worship. He had also every reason to make the whole strain of His communications to men as clear as possible. A king that wished to train his subjects to obedience would see to it that the whole tenor of the laws of his country should be unmistakable. A teacher that wished to attract a large number of disciples to his feet would spare no pains to make his whole course of instruction perfectly adapted to their general capacity. These are the very purposes God has in view in dealing with men through His word: His great aim is to win them over to become His obedient and intelligent servants. Is it conceivable that He should have knowingly and willingly suffered the revelation of His will to be presented in such a way as to frustrate the very design He had at heart in giving it? It was the very same love that prompted the Father to send His Son for the salvation of men, and His Spirit for their sanctification and equipment for service, that led Him also to give the Scriptures as an abiding source of instruction; and it is inconceivable that with the resources He had for presenting this testimony to the world aright, He should not have taken care to have it couched in a form perfectly fitted for its end.

This preliminary objection to the view that there is an inevitable obscurity in Scripture is confirmed by the agency through which God gave the revelation to the world. The Scriptures were written by men in the free exercise of their own faculties of thought and speech, and under a keen sense of responsibility for the way in which they

[1] *The Via Media* (Pickering, 1877), vol. i. p. 158; cf. *Development of Doctrine*, p. 71.
[2] *Tracts for the Times*, No. 85, p. 35.

discharged their task. They had all the means needed for securing simplicity and clearness in their productions. Those who were to write history had the traditions and documents that had been preserved from the beginning. Those who were to compile a book of prophecy had the addresses they delivered to the people. Those who were to write an account of the ministry of Christ were either themselves eye-witnesses of His life, or had access to the recollections of others who were. The apostles who wrote letters to the Churches had the circumstances of each community directly in view. Since these writers, as well as those that may have revised and edited their books, were also well aware that they were each one composing a part of that written Revelation on which their own future destiny and that of the world was to hinge, it is evident that they had every possible incentive to aim at thorough perspicuity alike in the special statements and the main current of their contributions.

The same conviction is forced upon us when we think of the circles for which the Scriptures were at first intended, or to which they were directly addressed. These included all ranks and classes of the people. Every sacred document was written with the popular use full in view. The Old Testament Scriptures were read in the synagogue every Sabbath day. Through them, the prophets, for example, still addressed the people as a whole : "Hear, O heavens, and give ear, O earth" ; "Hear, O Israel" ; "Hearken, O ye people." The Gospels of the New Testament were spoken or circulated amongst all classes that came to join in the service of the Church. The Epistles, occupied as they were with expositions of evangelic doctrine that require thought and discernment, were addressed not only to the elders and deacons, but also to the men, women and children of the Christian communities. It is inconceivable that all this should have been done apart from the feeling that the people, under the promised teaching of the Spirit and with due care and diligence, would readily understand what was thus expressly written for their instruction and admonition.

But we are able to do much more than raise these primary barriers against the imputation of obscurity in the Scriptures. With the sacred books in our hands, we can adduce various additional facts that when duly weighed effectually dispose of the charge.

The first of these assumes the form of an admission. There need be no hesitation in granting that the Scriptures as a whole are not presented in the shape of an exposition of doctrine. The different books of which they are composed do not claim to be contributions to systematic theology. A very large portion of them is occupied with historical records.

But is it any disadvantage to have doctrinal teaching ministered in this form? Surely not. The world of nature around us does not exhibit the various objects of which it is made up in the shape of rigidly classified departments. The very commixture of its elements and parts both constitutes its highest charm and presents the strongest incentive to men to go forth into the world and by patient study and observation form a scheme of classification for themselves. In like manner, the fact that doctrine is intermingled with the records of events connected with the unfolding of the divine purpose of love, is no real obstacle to the study of it. This combination only secures that in the history, there shall always be presented the starting-point of the doctrine and the key to its real meaning. Having history and doctrine woven into one web, men are stirred up to scrutinise the texture of the material more closely and so ascertain the real nature of the threads of which it is composed.

Yet again : there should be no reluctance to admit that there are passages and portions of the Scriptures that are not easily understood ; that are difficult to all ordinary readers, difficult in many instances even to those who are specially equipped for the study of them. This is a simple matter of experience. It seems to have been felt in the earliest times as well as now. Writing to his brethren on the subject of the Second Advent, the Apostle Peter was led to mention the letters of Paul as containing valuable statements upon it. But even he took the opportunity of saying in a parenthesis that there are in them "some things hard to be understood." It is quite safe for us to sympathise with Peter here. Nay : we may venture with truth to enlarge his admission and say that there are many statements in the Scriptures, even whole books, that are hard to be understood : not because the medium of revelation is obscure, but just because, in many cases, a certain measure of obscurity is inherent in the subjects with which they deal. Yet who shall dare to say that the Bible is less worthy of confidence on this account? If it presents difficulties to the reader or the learned student, it is only in the same position as the works of God in nature and providence. Are there not many points in the origin and development of plant and animal life on the face of the earth, that lie beyond the ken of the man of science? Are there not also many features of the progress of human life on the earth, such as its geographical distribution, the scourges that overtake it, the manifold ways in which it is destroyed and the obstacles it has to contend with in the struggle towards light and order that have never yet been explained? Yet such hard problems have not prevented men of all grades of culture from studying the laws of nature and providence and ascertaining them to an extent that has conferred the highest benefits on the race. Why then should difficulties connected with the endeavour to fit some statements or books of certain Biblical writers into a definite system of truth be held as sufficient to deter men from direct investigation of the Scriptures? The marvel would have been that such difficulties should not have occurred in books, written by so many men in such diverse circumstances and with such varied parts to play in the service of God. As a matter of fact, these unsolved problems do not have the effect of crippling the work of unprejudiced students of the Scriptures. When men have mastered what is easy to be understood, they are prepared to deal with what is difficult in a spirit of faith and patience and perseverance that sooner or later finds a rich reward. The past progress of the Church in the study of the Scriptures gives us every reason to expect that many statements hard to cope with in their relation to Christian doctrine will be found in the long-run to yield a perfectly intelligible meaning.

This hope is justified by the higher truth, which is ever to be remembered, namely, that the richest source of a true interpretation of Scripture is Scripture itself. Passages not easily understood meet the student at every turn. But there are no statements in Scripture on any theme which are really obscure, that are not to be balanced by other clearer statements on the same points found elsewhere in the sacred books. Such is the divinely-ordained structure of the Bible; and it is well fitted to inspire a spirit of hopefulness. With such an instrument of interpretation, we should never despair of being able to solve even the toughest problems in a way that shall commend itself to the mind and conscience of every reader.

This principle of seeking an explanation of less clear statements of Scripture in other more explicit statements of the same or different writers dealing with the same topic, is of supreme importance for binding the various branches of the Church together in a spirit of sympathy. It was adopted by all the Reformers and found expression in all the best Protestant symbols. It is stated very clearly in the second Helvetic Confession in terms similar to those just indicated. From this source, it found its way into the first Scottish as well as the later Westminster Confessions. The language used in the former is well worth noting : " When controversy then happens for the right place or understanding of any place or sentence of Scripture or for the reformation of any abuse within the Kirk of God, we ought not so much to look what men before us have said or done, as unto that which the Holy Ghost uniformly speaks within the body of the Scriptures and unto that which Christ Jesus Himself did and commanded to be done. For this is a thing uniformly granted, that the Spirit of God, which is the Spirit of unity, is in nothing contrary unto Himself. . . . For we dare not receive or admit any interpretation which is repugnant to any principal point of our faith or to any other plain text of Scripture or yet unto the rule of charity."[1]

When we recognise this great principle, we are set free to insist with all the greater emphasis on what is the main point to be maintained here, namely, that, however difficult it may be to fit certain statements or passages of Scripture into the system of divine truth, there is found in them ready to hand a representation of the whole scheme of evangelic doctrine sufficiently intelligible and varied to meet at once the needs of all classes of readers. This was

[1] Schaff, vol. iii, p. 464.

practically the position that Luther had in view when he proclaimed that the chief thing in the Bible for the soul of man was the word of God. For besides being themselves in a real sense the word or revelation of God, the Scriptures also contain this word in the narrower meaning of the gospel or message of salvation to the world as a whole, "the word of the truth of the gospel." This glad tidings is so vividly stamped on so many pages and indeed in so many single verses of the Scriptures that no reader of ordinary intelligence can fail to be brought face to face with every essential feature and condition of the divine covenant of mercy offered to men. The remembrance of this fact enables us to state the Protestant position with the utmost precision. There are truths that may be said to be fundamental to Christian doctrine, others not fundamental, though still strictly belonging to it. The latter have been defined as truths that have to be believed because they have been revealed: the former as truths that have been revealed, because they are essential to salvation. The contention of Protestantism accordingly is that these fundamental or essential truths are revealed in Scripture so clearly that any reader by the use of the ordinary means may reach a settled conviction as to what is the message of salvation. Scripture can make men wise in many things, if they have the capacity and learning required. But their main aim is to make men wise unto salvation; and this attainment they place within the reach of all. As the Westminster Confession says, "All things in Scripture are not alike plain in themselves, nor alike clear unto all; yet those things which are necessary to be known, believed and observed for salvation, are so clearly propounded and opened in some place of Scripture or other, that not only the learned, but the unlearned in a due use of the ordinary means, may attain unto a sufficient understanding of them."[1]

How fully these arguments for the perspicuity of Scripture are supported by the sacred books themselves, has already been so far seen. For every statement that enjoins on men the duty of searching the Scriptures and of coming to an intelligent decision respecting them, implies that their language as a whole and the main currents of their teaching may be readily understood. But there are also special utterances touching this very point, which show that students of the word of God from the earliest days of revelation found it easily apprehended and enjoyed. Did not one of the Psalmists say: "The testimony of the Lord is sure, making wise the simple";[2] and another: "Thy word is a lamp unto my feet and a light unto my path";[3] "The opening of Thy words giveth light; it giveth understanding to the simple"? Even the prophets wished their testimony to be so plain that, "he may run that readeth it."[4] The same thing is expressed in the oft-repeated admonitions of the Gospels: "Take heed how ye hear"; "Let him that readeth understand";[5] and also

---

[1] Ch. i. § 7.   [2] Ps. xix. 7.   [3] Ps. cxix. 105, 130.
[4] Hab. ii. 2.   [5] Luke viii. 18; Matt. xxiv. 15.

in the warning of the Book of Revelation: "He that hath ears to hear, let him hear what the Spirit saith unto the Churches."[1]

What is thus claimed by Scripture for itself is also confirmed by the large measure of agreement on the fundamental truths of Christianity that is found in the Confessions of the Protestant Evangelical Churches. Each of these formularies was composed after special and independent study of the Scriptures by bodies of the wisest men of the age to which they belonged. Yet drawing their statements from this one source, they arrive at substantially the same conclusions. This result shows that, amidst the inevitable variations of opinion respecting separate texts, the tenor of Scripture is unmistakably clear. As a distinguished Anglican theologian said, "This unanimity and consensus among different communions is certainly a tribute to the obviousness of that meaning of Scripture in which they agree. And when we find on the other hand that the matter of belief upon which they disagree is such as, being non-essential, Scripture is under no obligation to express, the evidence becomes strong for the acquittal of Scripture as an obscure book ; for a book is not an obscure book because it omits certain subjects which do not come within its necessary scope, if it is adequately clear and open upon those subjects which do."[2]

If any additional confirmation of this view were wanted, it is found in the simple matter of fact that numberless cases occur in every branch of the Church, in which men and women of humble education, though of earnest spirit, are seen to be thoroughly conversant, not only with the general meaning and purpose of the books of Scripture, but also with the details of the whole evangelic system as set forth there. The bold figurative language of the lyric and prophetic writings, instead of being a stumbling-block, as Cardinal Wiseman imagined, are felt to be a real help to the understanding of them. The striking metaphors and similes are found to leave a correct impression on the mind and heart, even when the precise shade of meaning may not be discerned. The prayerful reader is thus led into the knowledge of the truth. A wise Scottish theologian, writing in the middle of this century said that he had often met with pious men and women whose studies of the Bible had made them wiser than any of the ancient Fathers he had ever read. This statement will be endorsed by every pastor. Nor would anyone hesitate to echo these trenchant words which he also used : "To talk of the hopeless obscurity of the Scriptures, if they be not interpreted by creeds, seems to me the mere cant of sacerdotal assumption. That book which Timothy whilst but a child could know, so as to be made wise thereby unto salvation—that book which it forms part of the business of every pious parent to expound to his household around the domestic hearth—that book over whose choicest treasures thousands of the poor, the illiterate, the despised are rejoicing not only

[1] Rev. ii. 7 ; Isa. vi. 10 ; Heb. v. 12 ; Col. ii. 2 ; 1 Cor. ii. 12, 14.
[2] Mozley, *Lectures and Papers*, p. 65.

in this country but in lands which but a few years ago were covered with the gross darkness of heathenism—that book whose most hidden depths have been explored and expounded by men on whose minds the light of tradition never dawned—that book can be 'hopelessly obscure' only to those who are either too idle to study it or too proud to learn what it inculcates."[1]

[1] Dr. W. L. Alexander, *Anglo-Catholicism*, p. 120.

CHAPTER V

THE PERFECTION OF SCRIPTURE

NOT content with assailing the perspicuity of the Bible, Romanists have tried to undermine its sufficiency or perfection. Of itself, they say, it is not sufficient as a guide of belief and conduct. To fulfil this purpose, it requires to be supplemented by additions from the utterances and decisions of the Church that have been given in the course of her past history and will continue to be delivered in the days that are to come. To use the common form of expression, it is not the Bible alone, that is the rule of faith and practice, but the Bible and Tradition.

On this point, testimonies of the highest rank are available. In the preface to the Catechism of the Council of Trent, it is said that "the account of every doctrine which is to be delivered to the faithful, is contained in the word of God, which is divided into Scripture and Tradition."[1] The decrees of the Council are still more explicit: "Perceiving that this truth and discipline are contained in the written books and the unwritten traditions which, received by the apostles from the mouth of Christ Himself, at the dictation of the Holy Spirit, have come down even to us, delivered as it were from hand to hand, (the Synod), following the examples of the orthodox Fathers, receives and venerates with an equal affection of piety and reverence all the books both of the Old and of the New Testament, since one God is the author of both, as likewise these same traditions, as well those appertaining to faith as to morals, as having been dictated either orally by Christ or by the Holy Spirit and preserved in the Catholic Church by continuous succession."[2]

It is very worthy of notice that the distinguished Romanist theologian to whom we have so often referred, does not seem to be in full sympathy with the teaching of his Church here. Writing of the Church as "Teacher and Instructress," J. A. Möhler says: "Scripture is God's unerring word: but, however much the predicate of inerrability may belong *to it*, *we* at least are not free from error: rather do we become so, only when we have without error received into our hearts the word which is inerrable in itself. But in this reception, a human activity which may go astray is plainly neces-

[1] Q. 12.   [2] Sess. IV.

sary; and, therefore, in order that in the transition of the divine contents of the Holy Scriptures into our human possession no serious deception nor indeed any entire misrepresentation may find place, this principle is laid down: The divine Spirit to whom are entrusted the leading and quickening of the Church, becomes in His association with the Spirit of man, a special Christian tact, a deep sure-guiding feeling which, as it stands in the truth, also in turn leads into all truth."[1] Tradition is thus, in Möhler's view, twofold in its character, primarily subjective, but also objective. On the subjective side, "It is the special Christian sense present in the Church and perpetuating itself by ecclesiastical culture: which, however, is not to be thought of apart from its contents, but rather as having formed itself in and by its contents in such a way that it is to be called a realised sense. Tradition is the living word perpetuated in the hearts of believers." On the objective side, "Tradition is the collective faith of the Church through all centuries, presented in external historical testimonies."[2] This is a position that on the face of it does not need to be criticised in detail. From the prominence it gives to the unerring written word as governing the Christian consciousness of the Church, it is not truly Romanist in its tendency and affords a striking proof of the way in which Möhler's whole exposition was influenced by the Protestant literature of his day. To get at the real doctrine of the Church of Rome, we have to turn to the writings of her older apologists.

Here there is no lack of information as to what is meant by the tradition referred to in the decree. In his treatise, *On the Word of God*, Cardinal Bellarmin divides traditions into three classes, divine, apostolic and ecclesiastical: "Those are called divine which were received from Christ Himself as He taught the apostles and which are nowhere found in the divine Scriptures. Those traditions are properly called apostolic, which were taught by the apostles, not, however, without the assistance of the Holy Spirit, but nevertheless are not found written in their Epistles. Those traditions are properly called ecclesiastical, which are certain ancient customs initiated either by the bishops or by the people and which gradually obtained the force of law by the tacit consent of the people. And indeed divine traditions have the same force as the divine precepts or the divine doctrine written in the Gospels. And similarly unwritten apostolic traditions have the same force as the written apostolic traditions. . . . Ecclesiastical traditions moreover have the same force as decrees and written ecclesiastical constitutions."[3]

With respect to traditions that are spoken of as "unwritten," we have the highest authority for saying that this description does not necessarily imply that they are nowhere to be found committed to writing. They are so called because they were, in the first instance, simply spoken and intended to be delivered to others by word of mouth. Hence Cardinal Wiseman said: "By the term unwritten

[1] *Symbolik*, ss. 354, 355.   [2] *Ut sup.* ss. 356, 357.   [3] *De Verbo Dei*, iv. 1.

word, it is not to be understood that these articles of faith or traditions are nowhere recorded. Because, on the contrary, suppose a difficulty to arise regarding any doctrine so that men should differ and not know precisely what to believe and that the Church thought it prudent or necessary to define what is to be held, the method pursued would be to examine most accurately the writings of the Fathers of the Church, to ascertain what in different countries and in different ages, was by them held; and then collecting the suffrages of all the world and of all times, not indeed to create new articles of faith, but to define what had always been the faith of the Catholic Church."[1]

But what necessity was there for any such additions to the word of God as contained in the Scriptures? Wherein lies the defect in Scripture that they are intended to supply? In answer, it is alleged that there are not a few doctrines which Christians are under obligation to receive that are not fully declared in Scripture, that there are others which are only indistinctly hinted at, and that there are others equally valid which are not found there at all.

What the particular doctrines that the Church is alleged to owe to tradition are, we shall see in the course of the discussion. It is not needful to know them in detail to be even at this stage led to a general conclusion altogether unfavourable to the claims of tradition. On their own statement of it, the Romanists' rule of faith stands exposed at once to several insuperable objections.

1. For, in the first place, is it not singularly indefinite in character and extent? Since the great events on which the Christian religion is based have taken place and the testimony of its founders has long since been developed, it might not unnaturally be expected that any rule of faith which God provided for His Church would be speedily manifest and strictly limited. Indefiniteness or vagueness as to the terms or extent of any instructions He may give to men is the last feature that God's past dealings with His people would lead us to anticipate. These, however, are just the very features that are stamped on the rule of faith as constituted by the Church of Rome. Not only do Romanists add to the Hebrew Canon the unauthorised books of the Apocrypha, but to the New Testament they add the so-called oral traditions, and therewith the Acts and Decrees of the Church, including the Bulls of the Popes, the Decretals, the Acts of the Councils, the Acts of the Saints and the writings of the Greek and Latin Fathers. A more heterogeneous collection of authoritative documents could not well be conceived. When we remember that, from the nature of the case, it is bound to grow with the advance of time, we cannot but regard it as, not by the will of God but by the caprice of men, simply unlimited.

2. Further: these additions to the Scriptures are made in a spirit that takes no account of the wants of the Church as a whole. The Bible is a rule of faith that, translated into the language of every

[1] *Lectures on the Catholic Church*, vol. i. p. 61.

country, all members of the Church can carry about with them and read for themselves. As now circulated, it is a single portable volume, the lack of which even by the poor, may well be regarded as inexcusable. But, as the bare mention of it proves, the Romish rule of faith is such as can be accessible only to the clergy and to a very few even of these. This obstacle makes the exercise of individual judgment on matters of faith and duty quite impossible for the laity. As Cardinal Wiseman said, when a difficulty arose regarding any doctrine, the method pursued would be to examine all the traditional documents : "the investigation is conducted as a matter of historical inquiry and all human prudence is used to arrive at a judicious decision." In such inquiries, however, vital as they are to the faith and peace of every soul, only a very small minority can take part and the members of the Church have no alternative but submission to the dictates of others of whose motives they know nothing. Such a position could be acceptable only to those who were otherwise prepared to adopt a religion based wholly on human authority.

3. Again : is not the addition to the Scriptures of such other records as Rome accepts tantamount to a mingling of the human with the divine? No more solemn warnings are to be found in Scripture than just those that forbid unwarranted additions to the Bible as the word of God. One of the prophets says : "Every word of God is tried : He is a shield unto them that trust in Him. Add thou not unto His words, lest He reprove thee, and thou be found a liar."[1] The last book of the New Testament yields a testimony equally emphatic : "If any man shall add unto these things, God shall add unto him the plagues that are written in this book."[2] In the face of these utterances, how perilous is the addition of the Apocrypha. The contents of these books as a whole are not such as to commend them to the mind and conscience of readers who seek the teaching of the Spirit. Alongside of much that may be edifying, there is to be found still more that is false and fabulous. Many of their statements of truth are open to grave objection ; and the whole strain of several of the books is opposed to the teaching of the Scriptures. Hence the Apocrypha never formed any part of the Hebrew Bible as accepted by the Jews. Not one of the books is quoted by Christ Himself. Nor were they admitted into the Canon of the collected Scriptures during the first four centuries of the Christian Church. It was the third Council of Carthage held in 397 that first gave them ecclesiastical sanction ; and even this was done only on the understanding that other Churches should be consulted on the subject. Yet the Council of Trent gave them all a place in the list of sacred books and so tried to blot out the distinction betwixt what is human and what is divine.

The reception of tradition is only a flagrant example of the same reckless spirit. The Church of Rome admits that the Scriptures are the word of God, since He is the author of them. She also holds

[1] Prov. xxx. 5, 6.   [2] Rev. xxii. 18.

that tradition is the word of God and of equal authority. But she has never attempted to prove that tradition can be called the word of God on the same grounds, in the same sense and to the same extent as the Scriptures. The Romanists' collocation of the different elements in this rule of faith is purely arbitrary. Though they attempt to cover it with the authority of the Church, the assumption cannot be stripped of impiety in the eyes of those who recognise the exclusive right of Scripture to be called the word of God.

4. A further confirmation of the Protestant position is found in the sentence pronounced by the Lord Jesus on a method of dealing with the Old Testament by the Jewish teachers of His time, similar to the Church of Rome's treatment of the whole Bible. When after the return from the Exile and the establishment of synagogues over all the country, the Jews began to make the study of the Scriptures the most important of religious duties, there sprang up an order of officials who, from being copyists of the sacred books, speedily assumed the functions of interpreters of their meaning. These scribes, as they were called, framed a long series of comments on the Scriptures which, growing in course of time to huge dimensions, were handed down from one generation to another and gradually took the place of an authoritative exposition of the divine law.

But how did the Lord Jesus view such additions to the Scriptures? His sentence was one of unsparing condemnation. A principal part of His first great manifesto on the kingdom of heaven was devoted to reasserting the fulness and sufficiency of the divine law and clearing away the glosses that had been attached to its great precepts by the teaching of the elders. When at a later date, some of the scribes and Pharisees came to Him, asking plainly why He suffered His disciples to transgress the tradition of the elders in not washing their hands before meat, He asked them in return why they transgressed the commandment of God by their tradition. "Thus have ye made the commandment of God of none effect by your tradition."[1] Towards the close of His ministry, when all hope of winning His adversaries by gentler means had to be abandoned, He denounced these very parties for thus blinding the heart and conscience of men by their multitudinous maxims. "Woe unto you, lawyers, for ye have taken away the key of knowledge (that is, of the kingdom of heaven). Ye entered not in yourselves and them that were entering in ye hindered."[2] The reckless conduct of the Church of Rome in setting her traditions on a level with the written word cannot escape the same condemnation.

As has been already indicated, the usual method of replying to such preliminary objections which Romanists adopt is, first of all, to allege that there have been handed down within their Church from Christ and His apostles doctrines and practices which they have preserved ; and that in virtue of the source whence they have come, these traditions are binding on all believers. The New Testament

[1] Matt. xv. 6. [2] Luke xi. 52.

itself, it is said, has not a few indications that both Jesus and His apostles gave much in the shape of instruction that has not been recorded in the apostolical writings. The evangelist Luke professes to give nothing but the outline of what Jesus "began to do and teach." John says : " There are also many other things which Jesus did, which, if they should be written every one, I suppose that even the world itself could not contain the books that should be written."[1] The Apostle Paul himself quotes a saying of Jesus that is nowhere found in the written Gospels.[2]

In view of such testimonies, it is contended, we should be prepared to believe that there are many points of faith and practice, not recorded in the Scriptures which the Church of the apostolic times would preserve with the utmost care and hand down to the following generation ; and that this in turn, considering the source whence this traditional teaching came, would with equal reverence and accuracy transmit it to its successor. This process would make each generation the custodier of the precious heritage for those that were to follow, throughout the whole history of the Church. For the precise knowledge of these traditions we are referred to the writings of each succeeding age. The teachers of the Church were the most appropriate channel for such information ; and in their writings they would be sure to refer more or less fully to every important item in the original form of the traditions. In this way, it is alleged, the best guarantee is afforded that only genuine Christian and apostolic traditions would find recognition in the doctrine and practice of the Church of later centuries.

In dealing with this plausible form of defence, we have to admit at the outset that, if any doctrine or practice of the Church can be proved by adequate evidence to have proceeded from the Lord Jesus or His apostles, it would be binding on us to receive it, even though it were not recorded in the New Testament. As the founders of the Christian Church, the apostles were acquainted with the mind of Christ and acted under His infallible guidance. Everything that they said and did in the discharge of apostolic functions bore the stamp of His authority, and could not be disregarded by His people in any generation without sin.

But is there in point of fact any such evidence as is requisite, producible in behalf of the characteristic tenets of the Church of Rome? Can she adduce in support of the special forms of doctrine or practice which were authorised by the Council of Trent in opposition to Protestantism, a chain of historic testimony that reaches up to the apostolic age? Believing as they do that the Scriptures are in themselves perfectly sufficient as the guide of the Christian life, Protestants are not responsible for showing in any case that the doctrine or practice was otherwise originated. The burden of proof lies upon those that profess to believe in the apostolic origin of the tenets; and, if sufficient evidence is not forthcoming, Protestants are entitled

---

[1] John xxi. 25.   [2] Acts xx. 35.

to conclude that they have no Christian or apostolic sanction. Romanists and many of their followers in the Anglican Church pretend that they are able to meet this demand. They do not indeed profess that they find in the writers of the age that immediately followed the apostolic, all their special doctrines and practices, because the writers of that time were comparatively few and the special themes they chose did not readily permit them to allude to every element of tradition. But they nevertheless hold that these traditions must have been observed continually; for, when, as they say, we come to a period when Christian literature began to multiply, we find a general consent amongst the Fathers of the Church altogether in favour of the present tenets of the Church of Rome. This period is usually fixed at the close of the fourth and the beginning of the fifth centuries. Then first, it is maintained, do we see presented in permanent form the oral teaching which came down from the apostles and was duly observed in the whole intervening period. What has thus been continuously and universally taught and practised in the Church from the beginning must be the rule of faith and practice for all ages: or, as Vincentius of Lerinum put it, Catholic doctrine consists of all "quod semper, ubique et ab omnibus creditum est."

Several details in this statement, especially the allegation on the accuracy of oral tradition, will fall to be noticed in the sequel of this chapter. Here it has to be said at once that the whole substance of it is but a tissue of assumptions. As many eminent writers on this subject have abundantly shown, no honest student of patristic literature can for one moment admit that any such consent as is claimed can be found there. To use the words of Principal W. Cunningham, "There is not any one point of faith and practice not sanctioned and authorised by Scripture in regard to which Papists and Tractarians have ever been able to produce anything like sufficient or satisfactory evidence that it really proceeded from the apostles and has been accurately handed down by oral tradition. . . . Indeed almost the only tradition to which the rule 'quod semper, quod ubique, quod ab omnibus' really applies, the only point connected with or involved in these controversies on which the Fathers were unanimous or nearly so, was just the sufficiency and perfection of the written word as the only divine rule of faith, and the right and duty of all men to read and study it for their own guidance. The Fathers do indeed sometimes refer to oral tradition for certain purposes, but never to the exclusion or disparagement of the written word; and it has been proved conclusively that most of the passages in which the Fathers speak of tradition, the evangelical tradition as they often call it, and which are commonly adduced by Papists and Tractarians as testimony in favour of unwritten tradition, do really in the intention of the Fathers apply to the written word."[1]

The futility of the attempt to make tradition rather than Scripture

[1] *Theological Lectures*, p. 490.

the basis of belief and practice becomes only more manifest when we inquire into the special doctrines which, as the Romanists allege, would never have been known, had we been left to Scripture apart from tradition, as our only source of information. The Church of Rome has never presented any definite list of the doctrines which are alleged to be derived only from tradition. But when we examine the instances given by her theologians, we have no difficulty in characterising the kind of doctrines they have in view. Every one of them is found to be marked by some one or more features that render it incompetent to be adduced as a valid proof in this connection.

One of the first instances usually referred to is the canonical authority of the Scriptures. Apart from the traditional testimony of the Church, it is contended, it would be impossible for us to be assured of the right of the books of Scripture to occupy the place assigned to them in the records of revelation. This statement is not based on fact. As C. I. Nitzsch said, "The Church has not made the Scriptures genuine by her acknowledgment of them, but the Scriptures have proved themselves to her and they now make the Church genuine."[1] But on other grounds also the contention is invalid as adduced in behalf of tradition against the Scriptures. For it does not fall within the circle of the kind of doctrine with which we have here to do. We are at present occupied solely with truths which we as Protestants, on the one hand, maintain are to be found in Scripture, and which Romanists, on the other, assert are not to be found in Scripture at all, but only in the traditional teaching of the Church. The question of the canonical authority of the Scriptures is not one of these truths, but is a strictly preliminary question, which, as we have already seen, has to be settled by considerations that belong strictly to its own province. Whatever corroborative testimony may be derived from the writings of the Fathers we as Protestants are quite prepared to receive; but it is only a part, and that a minor one, of the evidence available on this subject; and, in any case, it is not relevant here as a proof of the value of tradition in opposition to the perfection of Scripture.

Specimens of other doctrines which are said to be due to tradition only, are the consubstantiality of the Son with the Father, the divinity and procession of the Holy Spirit, and the Trinity of persons in the Godhead. These are truths which we are as much concerned to retain in the testimony of the gospel as the Church of Rome. But we affirm that every one of them is, if not by express statement, at least by manifest implication, contained in the Scriptures. The Christian Church has been left by the Lord Jesus to exercise her mind on His own teaching and that of His apostles; and she is authorised to hold as scriptural, doctrines which, though they are not taught there in so many words, can be drawn from the language of Scripture by direct and valid consequence. It is a remarkable fact

[1] *System der Christlichen Lehre*, Sechste Aufl. s. 97.

that, when we turn to the writings of the Fathers, from which Romanists profess to draw their doctrines, we find them in turn basing their whole position on the statements of Scripture. Nothing could more effectually show the one-sidedness of the favourite assertion of Romanists that, "Tradition teaches and Scripture proves." If we could limit the idea of tradition to the results obtained by the Christian mind in the study of the Scriptures, the strictly logical way of putting the case would be : " Scripture teaches and proves : tradition summarises and formulates."

As examples of yet another class of doctrines which are alleged to be found only in the traditional teaching of the Church, there may be mentioned, regeneration by baptism, a state intermediate between heaven and hell, the commemorative sacrifice of the Eucharist and the adoration of the Virgin Mary. With respect to these, it can only be said that some statements of the later Fathers may be held to look in the direction of these tenets. Protestants have no interest whatever in denying this. But it affords no real aid to the Romanist position. For we deny that these doctrines of the Church of Rome are true, or can be proved to be true, by any kind of competent evidence whatever. With our views of the infallible authority of the Scriptures as the word of God, we refuse to accept any doctrine that is plainly contradicted by statements found there ; and that is the case with every one of such errors as those just mentioned.

On the whole, then, the side of tradition has nothing to gain from its representation of the matters of belief or practice of which it is said to be the sole support. The face of every one of them is marred by some defect. Either they do not belong to the class of doctrines in question ; or they are really taught in Scripture ; or they cannot be established as true by valid evidence of any kind. With respect to any doctrines derived from tradition that cannot be referred to these divisions, it may be safely said that they do not deal with points vital to Christian doctrine.

With these facts on the futility of the Romanist view before us, the two leading arguments in support of the Protestant position may now be set forth with greater distinctness and emphasis.

In the first place, we affirm that tradition, rooted in oral teaching, is utterly unfit to be made the vehicle of permanent instruction in divine truth. This result is due to the limitations of the faculties of man. To report any statement accurately requires power of attention and perception, a strong memory for forms of expression and a delicate appreciation of the force of words. Such gifts are especially requisite when the subject of tradition is connected with religion. For here an additional disturbing force comes into play. By nature, men are averse to divine truth. The mind is darkened, the moral perception blunted, and the heart alienated from it. In spite of every precaution on the part of those who teach, there is the greatest risk of perversion of truths that have to be transmitted by this channel. In short, it is simply impossible for one generation to transmit religious truths to another, without subjecting them to changes that well-nigh obliterate their original form.

The great lesson taught by experience and observation on this matter, therefore, is that the only safe channel for the transmission of divine truth from one generation to another is that of written documents. The introduction of oral tradition, even though it should at a later period be committed to writing, vitiates the confidence of men in the accuracy and worth of its contents. It is true that the Romish Church alleges that in the case of her traditions, it is not the unaided faculties of man alone that have been at work. She claims that they have been handed down by a Church rendered infallible in this work by the special intervention of the Holy Spirit. Since of such special divine aid, however, Romanists are enabled to adduce either a single promise of Scripture or a single proof from history, the assertion must be left to fall to the ground. The Christian Church must here be guided by the principles that govern the transmission of other facts. No sane man would attach the slightest confidence to utterances of Luther or any of the other great Reformers for which there was no better foundation than oral tradition. We are satisfied with nothing short of contemporary documentary evidence. When the fitting time arrived, it pleased God to lead His servants to commit to writing the records of His revelations. With these alone in preference to all traditions, the Church of every age is to carry on her work in the world.

All the more readily may this be done, that, as we now formally assert in the second place, the Scriptures are in themselves a perfectly sufficient rule of faith and practice. The prior considerations that might suggest this conclusion have already been adverted to. In view of the divine authorship of the Scriptures, the supreme object God had in view in giving them, and the instrumentalities He selected for the purpose of recording and preserving them, we are entitled to expect that the Scriptures would be altogether sufficient for the function they had to discharge. The main weight of our assurance on this point, however, must rest on the testimony of Scripture itself. This is found on examination to be quite adequate. Many of the texts already quoted in support of the right of private judgment and the perspicuity of the Scriptures are available here also. But we have others that are still more to the point. It was an injunction to Israel repeated again and again that they were to make no addition to the word of God given or subtractions from it.[1] In view of the manifest intention of having His word committed to writing, the Lord could not more solemnly intimate the perfection of those early communications to His people. When others came to use them at a later day, they proclaimed their sufficiency without reserve. "The law of the Lord is perfect, converting the soul: the testimony of the Lord is sure, making wise the simple. The statutes of the Lord are right, rejoicing the heart: the commandment of the Lord is pure,

[1] Deut. vi. 1, 2, xii. 32.

enlightening the eyes."[1] These words of the psalmist are echoed in the still stronger utterance of Isaiah in favour of the written word as the standard by which the worth of all human teaching was to be tested : " To the law and to the testimony : if they speak not according to this word, verily there is no morning for them."[2] In harmony with this same spirit, the Apostle John testified that, apart altogether from what might have been recorded of the words and deeds of Jesus, enough was presented in His own narrative and by consequence in those of others, to furnish the basis of a sure hope for eternity.[3] It was the habit of pious hearers of the apostles, like the Bereans, to bring all their utterances to the test of Scripture as the ultimate standard of appeal. Well might they do so : for, as Paul himself asserts, the Scriptures then in circulation were not only the vehicles of the Divine Spirit and so profitable for the inner life, but were also sufficient for the perfect equipment of a man of God who was preparing for Christian service.[4] That which makes perfect must, in the real sense of the word, be itself perfect ; and, if this maxim holds good of the Old Testament, it must be still more manifestly true of the New.

[1] Ps. xix. 7, 8.
[2] Isa. viii. 20.
[3] John xx. 30, 31.
[4] 2 Tim. iii. 17.

CHAPTER VI

THE PERFECTION OF SCRIPTURE—TRADITION (*continuation*)

IN view of the preliminary objections and main counter-arguments stated in the preceding chapter, the Romanist theory of tradition must be regarded as hopeless. But valid as these contentions are, they are not the only reasons that may be urged against it. There are other considerations that in some respects go yet more directly to the root of the question and show that the Romish doctrine is altogether untenable. Since the whole discussion is one of paramount importance, it will not be out of place to devote another chapter to a brief résumé of these additional points.

1. The first is the real origin of tradition. As has already been indicated in the chapter on the function of the Bible, it is to be traced back in the last resort to the erroneous principles of interpretation that prevailed in the early Christian Church, just as these in turn sprang from the influence of pagan philosophy on Christian thought. The allegorical method of interpreting ancient writings prevailed long before it was applied to the Scriptures. It was indeed the only way in which the myths of Greece and the East could be made to yield any solid grains of truth at all. Accustomed to wield such an instrument, men like Origen, who had been trained in the schools of pagan speculation, were under the strongest temptation to use it in setting forth the philosophical or practical teachings of the Scriptures, especially of the Old Testament. But from its very nature this style of exposition could be cultivated only by a very few. The laity became more and more dependent on the ingenuity of certain prominent teachers, while these in turn, like the philosophers of the schools, were led to claim, first for their masters and then for themselves, a deference to the authority of men of position and learning that put the ordinary readers of the Scriptures at a still greater disadvantage.

Thus, in course of time, the chief consideration came to be not what the Scriptures themselves were seen to teach, but the opinions held by men who had attained to influence in the Church. When these met in Synods or Councils and promulgated their views in definite statements with the intention of excluding errors, their decisions were looked on as possessing an authority to which the laity as a whole could only yield unquestioning submission. In this fashion the way was prepared for a condition of thought and feeling in which the Scriptures came to be regarded as less necessary for the nourishment of the spiritual life and a knowledge of the traditional teaching of the Church as the one thing that could not be dispensed with. The result as seen in Romanism is still tainted by the corruption at its source. It is the glory of Protestantism that it starts with principles of interpretation that are demanded by common sense and are consonant with the real nature of the Scriptures; and the issue, as is fitting, is, that not the opinions of men but the word of the living God is the only rule of faith and practice.

2. While this is the historic origin of tradition, it is an additional point against it that its introduction as an authority co-ordinate with the Scriptures was an afterthought and one of a very late period. It was only after the Reformation had begun its work that even the Church of Rome ever dreamt of putting it on a level with the Scriptures. The tendency toward an undue deference to the opinions of men showed itself at a very early stage. But it would be doing a grave wrong to many of the most eminent Fathers even of the first centuries to say that they had no convictions of the paramount authority of the Scriptures. On the contrary, they frequently expressed their mind on this point with unwavering certitude. The creeds and decisions of the Church were regarded by them at first as simply ecclesiastical and therefore subordinate aids to the promulgation and defence of the truth. In the course of centuries, the traditional teaching of the Church became loaded with many tenets and practices that were contrary to the Scriptures. Yet even when Luther and his friends proclaimed the first principles of the gospel, they never imagined that they had another authority to deal with besides the word of God as contained in the Bible. It was not as an authority competing for a place co-ordinate with that held by the Scriptures that Luther combated tradition. Both he and his opponents were at first prepared to fight the battle on the field of Scripture. When Luther opposed tradition, it was chiefly because it seemed to present a method of settling the problem of the salvation of men different from that sanctioned by the gospel. On this great theme, he would have no guidance but from the Bible; and every tenet or custom of the Church that appeared to be in conflict with the Biblical gospel, he opposed to the uttermost. This position not only gave him a deep insight into the meaning of the Bible, but also enabled him to wield its utterances with marvellous power. Very speedily his opponents saw that on this field it was impossible to meet him successfully; and, as we see in the disputation with Eck at Leipzig, they wished to tie him down to the decisions of the later Councils. Luther refused to be satisfied with any human authority whatever. When all hope of reconciliation betwixt the two parties had to be abandoned and the Reformed Churches set about a separate organisation, the Church of Rome saw that, if there was to be any

foundation at all left for her system, it could be obtained only by formally recognising the authority of tradition and making it coordinate with that of the Scriptures. Accordingly, this was done for the first time at the Council of Trent. Hence it is only in the Protestant confessions made after the date of that Council that the relations of Scripture are carefully defined. This adoption of tradition as a late controversial expedient is of itself enough to exhibit the radical weakness of the Romish position.

3. We are the more entitled to point out this unworthy specimen of the tactics pursued by the Church of Rome, that it lays bare a characteristic of her whole method of dealing with the teaching of the Scriptures in relation to tradition. We have seen that the authority to which Romanists turn for support of their doctrine and practice is the decrees and canons of the Church. No doubt seems to be entertained of *their* sufficiency. Many of the less scrupulous of the Romish theologians indeed would not hesitate to say that tradition may stand alone without the aid of the Scriptures. Some might even be found to assert that when tradition seems to be in conflict with the Bible, it should prevail. But as the case stands, most Romanists are very eager to find support for their tenets in the Scriptures. Not a few might even be prepared to fall in with the Tractarians and say that "tradition teaches but Scripture proves." In doing this, however, how manifestly are they governed by a false motive. From the way in which Romish theologians quote and appeal to the Scriptures, unwary readers are tempted to imagine that it was from the special study of the Scriptures that Romanists were led to form the views they hold in opposition to Protestants: that it was only because certain texts were first thought by them to bear a certain meaning that they were led to formulate the statements found in the decrees of their Councils. This would be a huge mistake. In point of historic fact, it is far otherwise. The characteristic tenets of the Church of Rome have their root in the erroneous views on many topics so acceptable to the natural man. These first took shape in various innovations. Because they were seen to suit the propensities of the people and the needs of the clergy, they gradually found their way into the writings of some of their divines. These in turn, reading the Scriptures under the influence of prejudices in favour of the novelties, found what they imagined to be utterances in favour of the new ideas. Then, though often in the face of the strongest opposition from the better educated and more conscientious of her theologians, they were introduced into the decrees of Councils and made a part of the Canon Law of the Church. Such a flagrant reversal of the respect due to the authority of God's word as compared with the opinions of men is an inexcusable blot on the whole creed of Rome.

4. Another argument of great force against the Romish use of tradition is found in the fact that, apart from it, there is in the common consent of the Church on the teaching of Scripture, a tie

sufficiently strong to bind all her branches in unity and sympathy. The stress laid by Romanists on the harmony of the Fathers in favour of their doctrines, has already been referred to. It is what has been believed "everywhere, always and by all" that they profess to accept. This consent is a mere fiction. A careful examination of patristic literature shows that it does not really exist. Yet it should not be supposed that there is no real counterpart to the devout imagination. In the writers that contributed to the records of divine revelation, there is a very manifest agreement on every point of doctrine that concerns the source, method and nature of salvation. This harmony is continued and reflected amongst all believing students of the Scriptures still. The Lord Jesus promised that by His Spirit disciples of every age should be led into all the truth. What all true believers, relying on this promise, have everywhere throughout the past centuries recognised to be the teaching of Scripture on the essential elements of the Christian gospel, must therefore be true : otherwise the promise of Christ can never have been fulfilled. It is in this way that the Christian Church has never ceased to accept such doctrines as the incarnation of the Son of God, His atoning death, His resurrection and ascension to heaven, His mission of the Holy Spirit, the Trinity, the regeneration and sanctification of the soul by the Spirit and the resurrection of the saints to life everlasting at Christ's second advent. Such consent of the Church as this is of the highest value : it is all that is needed to lay the basis of sympathy and co-operation amongst all her branches. The alleged common tradition of the Church of Rome, introducing as it does the disputable opinions of men, has proved only a source of alienation and schism. The secret of harmony in Christendom lies in making the Scriptures alone the source of information on doctrine and in cleaving only to what true believers of every age have taken to be its teaching on the essential elements of saving truth. As we see in his *Conference with Fisher*, even Archbishop Laud clung to this principle. "Sure Christ our Lord," said the Jesuit, "hath provided some rule, some judge to procure unity and certainty of belief." " I believe so too," said Laud, "for He hath left an infallible rule, the Scripture. Scripture, by the manifest places in it which need no dispute, no external judge, is able to settle unity and certainty of belief in necessaries to salvation. . . . The Romanists dare not deny but the rule of Scripture is 'certain'; and that it is sufficiently 'known' in the manifest places thereof and such as are necessary for salvation, none of the ancients did ever deny ; so there is an infallible rule."[1]

With these facts before us, we are now in a position to dispose of certain minor arguments in behalf of the Romish view that are often urged with great persistence, and so to close the discussion.

i. One plea for the necessity of tradition, for example, is drawn from what is called "the occasional character" of many of the

[1] Laud's *Relation of a Conference with Fisher* (Oxford, 1839), p. 163.

writings that compose the Scriptures. Not a few of the prophecies of the Old Testament were spoken and written to meet the special circumstances of the people at the time. The same feature characterises more than one of the Gospels and nearly all of the Epistles. These books accordingly are not regarded as possessing the form requisite for authoritative decisions on matters of faith and practice ; and tradition is thought to be necessary to supplement their deficiencies in this respect. This contention is void of all real force. It is no defect of the Biblical writings that they bear so many traces of the events and circumstances in the life of those by whom or for whom they were composed. For though the precise condition of things that called them forth has passed away and can never return, the great principles underlying the instructions then imparted are perfectly explicit and can never change. It was the habit of the apostles just to seize upon transitory circumstances as a starting-point for the exposition and illustration of great principles. The result is a permanent advantage. The historic condition imparts reality and interest to the statement of the truth, while on the other hand the truth illumines and explains the outward situation.

It is very interesting to find that on this point we can quote J. A. Möhler in opposition to the views of his co-religionists. In full sympathy with that reverence for the Scriptures which we have seen expressed in his *Symbolism*, he says in another work : "Without the holy Scriptures as the oldest embodiment of the gospel, Christian doctrine would not have been preserved in its purity and simplicity ; and it certainly exhibits a great want of the honour due to God to maintain that they are accidental, because they appear to us to have sprung out of purely accidental occasions. What a representation of the superintendence of the Holy Spirit in the Church ! Without the Scriptures, moreover, there would be lacking the first link in the series of her witnesses. Without the holy Scriptures, the Church herself would be left without a proper beginning and therefore unintelligible, confused and chaotic." [1]

ii. Another argument in behalf of tradition is that the New Testament itself sends us to this source for information on Christian doctrine. In this connection such statements as these are referred to : "Therefore, brethren, stand fast and hold the traditions which ye have been taught, whether by word or our epistle." [2] "Now we command you, brethren, in the name of our Lord Jesus Christ, that ye withdraw yourselves from every brother that walketh disorderly and not after the tradition which he received of us." [3] Here the word "tradition" is used in a wider sense than has become attached to it in the Protestant controversy. As Paul expressly indicates, it includes both written and oral instruction. This conjunction was very natural here, for his letter to the Thessalonians was one of the first he wrote and was sent not very long after he had preached

---

[1] *Die Einheit in der Kirche* (Tübingen, 1843), s. 54.
[2] 2 Thess. ii. 15.
[3] Ch. iii. 6.

the gospel to them. But evidently it was the written instruction alone that was to be regarded as of abiding value and authority for all time to come. The oral instructions given by the Lord and repeated by His apostles were of course binding on all that heard them. But, as we have seen, they could not be preserved intact from human error through successive generations. From the very nature of the case, it was the written word alone that could remain ; and we must be content that the unrecorded instructions should simply pass away with the occasions that gave birth to them. As Dr. Charles Hodge put it, "These unrecorded instructions were not intended to constitute a permanent rule of faith to the Church. They were designed for the men of that generation. The showers which fell a thousand years ago watered the earth and rendered it fruitful for men then living. They cannot now be gathered up and made available for us. They did not constitute a reservoir for the supply of future generations. In like manner, the unrecorded teachings of Christ and His apostles did their work. They were not designed for our instruction. It is as impossible to learn what they were, as it is to gather up the leaves which adorned and enriched the earth, when Christ walked in the garden of Gethsemane." [1]

iii. A third argument adduced in favour of tradition as a necessary and integral element of the rule of faith is that the Scriptures contain no formal summary of Christian truth, while tradition supplies this need. This contention takes it for granted that such a formulated exposition is indispensable for conveying an accurate idea of the contents of the gospel, that without it in fact, a full knowledge of Christian doctrine can never be obtained ; and it draws from this assumption the inference that, since the apostles did not in their writings bequeath to the Church any such joint confession, a plain indication is given that they did not intend the Scriptures to be regarded as a complete rule of faith. The so-called Apostles' Creed, which they are said to have dictated is held to be but one isolated token of what they might have given but did not. But are we entitled thus to assume that such summaries are in any sense so indispensable in Christian instruction ? Assuredly not. There are in the Scriptures many statements of the way of life far more concise, as well as interesting and forcible than any bare summary man could imagine. We have no right even indirectly to prescribe the method in which God shall give instruction in the religion of His Son. It is the duty of the Church to give full and free scope in all her service to the word of the living God. When the Scriptures have been used in this spirit, they have always been found, as in the case of Timothy, able to make men wise unto salvation. The Lord of the Church has left us at liberty to apply our faculties and gifts to the elucidation and expression of what we believe to be the teaching of Scripture. But the fact that no

[1] *Systematic Theology*, vol. i. p. 121.

summary of the kind that men have adopted as a vehicle of instruction is found in the Bible itself, can never be adduced as a valid objection to its perfection and sufficiency. Every doctrine we are required to believe for salvation is in the Bible in fact. The work of collecting and arranging its statements is one that God has left to us, to arouse us to diligence and energy in the duty of searching the divine records themselves. No more salutary exercise could be prescribed.

iv. The only other argument that need be noticed here is one based on the fancied analogy betwixt tradition and the unwritten or common law of a country. It is essentially Romanist in conception and spirit but has received its most earnest enforcement amongst the theologians of the Anglo-Catholic school. Keble, for example, put it in this way: "If a maxim or custom can be traced back to a time whereof the memory of man runneth not to the contrary; if it pervade all the different courts, established in different provinces for the administration of justice; and thirdly, if it be generally acknowledged in such sort that contrary decisions have been disallowed and held invalid: then, whatever the exceptions to it may be, it is presumed to be part and parcel of our common law. On principles exactly analogous, the Church practices and rules above mentioned and several others, ought, we contend, apart from all Scripture evidence, to be received as traditionary or common laws ecclesiastical."[1] This is certainly a very specious argument. We cannot deny the main fact on which it is based. If an advocate can show a judge that any legal principle has been accepted by the people of a country, even though it has not been formally engrossed amongst the statutes of the realm, he is certain to win assent for it: because this is tantamount to proving that it formed part of the law of the land before its legislation was committed to writing. But is the unwritten tradition of the Church exactly analogous to the common law of a country? Far from it. The common law was made by the people for themselves, anteriorly to the written, and that in matters that fell within their cognisance and authority. But these so-called ecclesiastical laws were made by the Church for herself on matters with which she is not entitled to interfere and after the divine law which constitutes her only and all-sufficient foundation had been enacted and promulgated. The very fact that such practices and rules are only matters of ecclesiastical tradition is enough to strip them of all binding force. Their very existence only brings into full relief the paramount authority of the code originally delivered by the divine Lord of the Church and committed to writing for the guidance of her ministers in every age of the world's history.

[1] Sermon on *Primitive Tradition recognised in Holy Scripture*, p. 33.

CHAPTER VII

THE DOCTRINAL STUDY OF SCRIPTURE—THE THEORY OF DEVELOPMENT

IN the views of Scripture set forth in the preceding pages, it has always been assumed and often asserted that it contains many statements that are fitted to take rank as fundamental truths or doctrines of the Christian religion. Many of them bear this character on their very face. They are given for the express purpose of being regarded as necessary principles of Christianity. Yet these are not all stated in express terms. There are many that are found to be no less momentous, which have not been so directly delivered. Some are only embodied in the facts of sacred history: others are only distinctly implied in statements made to serve incidental ends: others again are presented merely in the form of personal convictions. Yet all of these truths are such as from their simplicity and essential importance and ready recognition have come to wield a strong influence on the progress of Christian life and thought and thus cannot be denied the place of doctrines.

It has also been taken for granted that it is the duty of the members of the Church to make a special study of the doctrines delivered in the Scriptures. This is an exercise that on many grounds is found to be indispensable. The human mind has an instinctive desire to arrive at the principles that underlie the facts it may gather in any province. In the various branches of natural science, for example, a thoughtful man is never content with simply observing the phenomena that meet the eye: he ponders them until he discerns the laws that govern their action and results. So it should be in dealing with the contents of the Scriptures. The Bible itself invites this kind of investigation. In the sacred writings, there is presented not only a history of redemption, but also a course of instruction on the great truths that have influenced its progress,— truths also that are capable of a more precise statement than they receive at the hands of the Biblical writers. It is an essential part of the Church's duty to examine these facts and principles in all their relations and to present the results in the form and order that are fitted to make them most intelligible and impressive. By this means, the truths of Scripture are by the Divine Spirit implanted more readily and deeply in the heart of Christian disciples and are so made to tell more powerfully on the sanctification of their character and the direction of their service.

The knowledge of the system of Christian truth which the Church as a whole now enjoys has only been very gradually attained. At first, it must have been very meagre. At the close of the apostolic age, when the gift of full inspiration in the communication of divine truth ceased amongst men, the Christian communities scattered over the world had little more to start with than the first principles of the gospel. Doubtless these were firmly grasped, and through the grace of the Holy Spirit, the apprehension of them became a very potent means of grace to the followers of the Lord. For they were lodged in the soul as fruitful germs which, as life took on more serious aspects and the responsibilities of Christian service grew heavier, continually sent forth new light into the mind, a holier love into the heart, and a fuller energy into the will. Yet as regards the full conscious possession of the truth and the power of expressing it and applying it to the varying circumstances of the Church, there must have been a very wide gulf betwixt the apostles and even the most intelligent teachers they left behind. Both time and experience were required to enable the Church to make progress in the knowledge of God's salvation. As everyone who has traced the course of the Church's history knows, it has only been by many a sharp conflict with error and after many a long interval of sluggishness and indifference that the Church has been stirred up to lay hold of all the grace of the gospel and to discern the obligations which this grace entails.

The Reformation of the sixteenth century with which we are here specially concerned is just an instance in point. The most striking feature of the whole movement was the new grasp which men were enabled to take of the apostolic method of salvation. No one who reads the literature of the early Christian Church can doubt that the blessing of justification by faith was known and preached from the beginning. Yet the whole course of the Church's action shows that the doctrine itself had never yet come into her consciousness as a distinctive element of the Christian faith. In spite of the fact that it was never wholly forgotten by some of the best doctors of the Romish communion in the Middle Ages, the Church as a whole had never seen its full significance as the starting-point of all definite Christian experience. It was only after slumbering in indifference for a whole millennium that the Church was at length by the trumpet tones of Luther awakened to grasp what the apostles taught at the very outset of the gospel.

It would be a mistake, however, to suppose that, slow as the movement in this direction has been, there has not been a real and measurable advance. On many questions of the highest moment, the Church has been enabled to attain to answers that may be regarded as both accurate and complete. This is especially manifest in connection with the great subjects of the constitution of the Godhead and the person of Christ. The decisions reached by the early Councils of the Church after so much strife and debate have stood the test of the keenest scrutiny for many centuries and are still received as the Catholic doctrines of Christendom. Indeed it is plain now that there has been a substantial growth or development of doctrine in the Church. Not only has one fundamental truth after another been elucidated from the Scriptures and set in its recognised place alongside other truths, but the vital and logical connexion of these truths has now been fully ascertained. It is seen that one doctrine, when duly received by the Church, has gradually educated the Christian mind into a state of preparation for another : so that we have not a set of separate and independent truths, but the truth of Scripture in the shape of an organic growth with branches, distinct indeed, yet proceeding from the same trunk and fed from the same root. It is thus also no exaggeration to speak of Christian doctrine under the old figure of "a body of divinity." Feeble enough in its infancy, the evangelic system has grown from childhood to youth and youth to early manhood. It may still but imperfectly reflect the perfect man delineated in the apostolic teaching. But if the Church be faithful, through the grace of the Spirit, the knowledge may yet reach the measure of the stature of the fulness of Christ. In the present concentration of thought on Christ's oneness with His people by incarnation and their oneness with Him in glory by faith and the consequent deepening interest in the doctrines of sanctification, adoption and consecration, we see tokens of coming attainments that cannot fail to enrich her experience and strengthen her energies for new conquests.

But to come now again to the point at which the Romish and Protestant Churches diverge, what has been the secret and the safeguard of this progress in the knowledge of Christian doctrine? What is it that has rendered any real advance possible and has stamped it when attained as of real value? Simply that it has been all along conducted only on the lines marked out for it in the word of God. With the views they held on the perspicuity and sufficiency of the Scriptures, the Reformers could not possibly recognise any other authority. To their mind, there was no need of any doctrine beyond what was set forth in Scripture, and they made no attempt to pass the limit. It was from the suggestions given in the word of God that they drew their teaching ; and, after they had been enabled to exhibit the results of their study in exact and orderly statements of truth, they taught the people to regard them as nothing more than a help to the closer examination and better understanding of the Scriptures. This has been practically the evangelical Protestant position all along. It is the Scriptures that furnish the starting-point of all doctrinal study : by them all statements of doctrine are to be tried : on the fuller knowledge of them must all attainments in doctrine be made to converge. Any development of doctrine that is to be truly Protestant therefore must always be within the circle of Scriptural influence. At no stage can it be independent of the word of God. As an eminent Scottish theologian has so well pointed out, what Protestantism aims at is "a development up to the Scriptures : and the Scriptures are always above it, as the perfect standard never reached. There is ample room for it, just because the Scriptures, on grounds already stated, are so much more and deeper than all that man teaches out of them. Thus room is made for whatever of genuine growth and movement the history of mankind requires. Yet the perfection and sufficiency of Scripture remain."[1]

Of those who have shown the strongest opposition to these principles, the first to enter the field were the theologians of the rationalistic school founded under the influence of the German philosopher, Immanuel Kant. Ammon, Bretschneider, Wegscheider, and Röhr may be named as prominent members of it. A leading feature in their method of teaching was a review of the history of doctrine from the earliest periods of Chistian literature. In this survey they professed to find many unmistakable tokens of progress and interdependence. The system of Christian doctrine held by the modern Church seemed to them a great advance beyond what had been received in the first age of Christianity. To use their own mode of expression, it was a development of truth attained by the reasoning faculty in man acting under the aid of Divine Providence. But in their view, this was the origin of all religion. It had no specially supernatural element about it. The Bible itself was just the fruit of human thought on the higher relations of the soul of man at the hands of writers who had been placed by Providence in circumstances highly favourable to progress in this department. Dogmatic ideas, therefore, could not but vary from age to age. In every case, they were the fruitage of contemporary thought and were handed down to succeeding generations for emendation and enlargement. Hence there was not only a subjective development of Christian doctrine in the minds of men, but also a right on the part of Christian thinkers in each age to form their own opinions on past doctrinal results and to issue them afresh from the mint of their own spirit in shapes more adapted to the needs of the time.

At first sight it seems very strange that defenders of Romanism should ever be associated with a theory which sprang from Kantian Rationalism. Yet this in fact is what has come to pass. The view of the history of Christian doctrine which Rationalism adopted has been seized upon by Romanism ; and baptized by a new name, it has been fashioned into a weapon of defence in behalf of its distinctive positions. The point of affinity betwixt the two parties lies in the fact that the Romish Church in particular is confronted in her own system with the same wide divergence of her present doctrine and practice from that which the study of early Christian

[1] Rainy, *The Delivery and Development of Christian Doctrine*, p. 226.

doctrine has brought into such full relief. Recent historical investigations have made the differences betwixt modern Romanism and the faith of the primitive Church so palpable that they cannot be ignored. Hitherto the explanation has always been—and this is the view that still prevails in the Church as a whole—that all the special features of the present Romish system were handed down by tradition from the apostles. Where the link of connection in literary documents could not always be made plain, the gap was said to be due to the *disciplina arcani*, or the principle alleged to be observed by ancient writers of keeping back articles of belief or points of practice for which the times were not ripe. The modern study of Church history, however, has shaken the faith of not a few Romish theologians in the possibility of their justifying the apostolic origin of the doctrines and practices of their Church; and, if not as a direct substitute for tradition at least as a co-ordinate help in defence, they have resorted to the theory that these divergences from primitive Christian doctrines are due to the Church herself, which, in the exercise of an infallible developing authority, has evolved these doctrines from germinal principles in the apostolic teaching.

The first adherents of Rome to make this use of the rationalistic theory were De Maistre and J. A. Möhler. The latter especially comes out here in his unique combination of Romanist, evangelical mystic, and philosophic rationalist. As we have seen, he begins his exposition of the Romish view of tradition by presenting a theory of it which would practically identify it with the contents of Scripture as held in the mind and consciousness of the Church. Even this view stands exposed to the objection of leaving open a loophole by which the Church can introduce changes she may deem necessary for the complete articulation of her system. But Möhler does not stop at this point. He acknowledges the entire validity of tradition as the rule of faith which has grown in the course of past centuries and is now preserved in the historic testimonies of the Church of Rome. But how has this body of doctrine with its marked differences from the original divine deposit come into existence? He explains it by a process of development in this way: "After the divine word had become human faith, it had to enter into all purely human destiny. It must be continually received by the energies of the human mind and also be embraced by them. The preservation and reproduction of the word were in like manner bound up with a human method." This he says is seen in the very composition of the Gospels and yet more fully in the apostolic Epistles. "Everything received by the mind of man from without, which is to be truly its own property and in which it is to see thoroughly its own way, must be first reproduced by the mind itself. At the same time, the original truth, as the human mind had repeatedly wrought it out, presented itself in a form that had undergone a great variety of changes: it remained always indeed the original truth and yet it was not: it was like itself in essence, but different from itself in respect of form. In the process of the development of the divine word, during the apostolic time, we may set the divine guidance of the disciples of Christ as high and extend it as wide as we choose, yet without men themselves, without the special activity of men, it would certainly never have gone forward as it did."[1]

Möhler then goes on to say: "It could not be otherwise, even after the death of the apostles, even after the Gospels and the Epistles had been written.... When in the manner just indicated, the Church explains and establishes the doctrine of faith against misrepresentations, even the apostolic expression necessarily changes into another, which is the most appropriate for thoroughly exhibiting and at the same time warding off special contemporary errors. As little as the apostles themselves in the course of their polemical teaching could preserve the form in which the Saviour delivered the divine doctrine, could the Church retain that which she had received from them.... Finally, as the truths of salvation come into view in the apostolic writings with greater clearness and in their organic interdependence, so also in the teaching of the Church, does the doctrine of Scripture come out to us in ever multiplying aspects. Foolish as it is accordingly to find any other distinction betwixt the doctrine of Jesus and that of the apostles than what is formal, it is just as thoughtless to discover any other opposition betwixt the earlier and the later tradition of the Church."[2]

It is in vain that Möhler thus tries to make tradition represent truly the contents of the Scriptures. The apostles' gospel was indeed an advance on that of Christ, simply because Christ came to be the gospel, and, after He went to heaven, developed Himself the evangelic message in their minds. But we deny to the uttermost the analogy here drawn betwixt the apostolic teaching in relation to Christ's and the teaching of the Church in relation to that of the apostles. The difference betwixt the primitive apostolic teaching and the later teaching of the Church is far more than formal. If that had been so, no such elaborate theory as this would have been necessary to defend it. The present system of Rome is full of substantive additions to the apostolic doctrine and practice that are really foreign to their spirit. Its whole scheme is due to the arbitrary action of the Church in yielding to the mere suggestions of men in each passing age, while yet she poses as "a living visible authority which in every conflict unerringly discerns the truth and separates it from error."

While Möhler may thus be said to have been the first to show how this theory could be utilised by Rome, the theologian who has most fully expounded and applied it is Dr. J. H. Newman. It was elaborated by him while he was still a minister of the Anglican Church, and it became the stepping-stone on which he passed into the communion of Rome. The first definition he gives of it is "that the increase and expansion of the Christian Creed and Ritual and the variations which have attended the process in the case of individual

[1] *Symbolik*, § 40, ss. 369, 370, 371.   [2] *Symbolik*, ss. 369, 370, 371, 372.

writers and Churches, are the necessary attendants on any philosophy or polity which takes possession of the intellect and heart and has had any wide or extended dominion; that, from the nature of the human mind, time is necessary for the full comprehension and perfection of great ideas; and that the highest and most wonderful truths, though communicated to the world once for all by inspired teachers, could not be comprehended all at once by the recipients, but, as being received and transmitted by minds not inspired and through media which were human, have required only the longer time and deeper thought for their full elucidation. This may be called the Theory of Development of Doctrine." [1]

At first sight this does not seem to be a very pernicious conception. In many respects it may be said to be only in accordance with the principles laid down in the beginning of this chapter, which are found to be quite compatible with a belief in the perfection and sufficiency of Scripture. This seeming harmony, however, has arisen from the fact that at this point of the exposition, Dr. Newman is really inconsistent with himself. He leaves out of view the distinction which Wegscheider, for example, is so careful to draw, namely, that which obtains betwixt a subjective and an objective development of ideas. Apparently he is arguing for a subjective development of the leading ideas of New Testament Christianity in the minds of the members of the Church, while that which he seeks to introduce and establish is really an objective extension and enlargement of them in forms adapted to what seem to be the changing needs of the times.

That this is really his aim is manifest from statements made at a subsequent stage of the argument.

Speaking, for example, of the Romish doctrine that Baptism is intended for the pardon of sins committed before it and not after it, he says : "As far as the letter goes of the inspired message, every one who holds that Scripture is the rule of faith, as all Protestants do, must allow that 'there is not one of us but has exceeded by transgression its revealed Ritual and finds himself in consequence thrown upon those infinite sources of Divine Love which are stored in Christ, but have not been drawn out into form in the appointments of the gospel.' Since then Scripture needs completion, the question is brought to this issue, whether defect or inchoateness in its doctrines be or be not an antecedent probability in favour of a development of them." [2]

So again, referring to the intermediate state between death and the resurrection, he says : "As Scripture contemplates Christians, not as backsliders, but as saints, so does it apparently represent the Day of Judgment as immediate and the interval of expectation as evanescent. It leaves on our minds the general impression that Christ was returning on earth at once, 'the time short,' worldly engagements superseded by 'the present distress,' persecutors urgent,

[1] *An Essay*, etc. pop. ed. pp. 29, 30.   [2] *Essay*, etc. pp. 61, 62.

Christians as a body, sinless and expectant, without home, without plan for the future, looking up to heaven. But outward circumstances have changed, and with the change, a different application of the revealed word has of necessity been demanded, that is, a development. When the nations were converted and offences abounded, then the Church came out to view, on the one hand as a temporal establishment, on the other as a remedial system, and passages of Scripture aided and directed the development which were before of inferior account. Hence the doctrine of Penance as the complement of Baptism and of Purgatory as the explanation of the Intermediate State."

Such statements as these set it beyond doubt that what Dr. Newman was aiming at and trying to commend was not a fuller explicit apprehension of divine Biblical ideas by the mind of the Church, but real additions to the teaching of Scripture and ecclesiastical applications of it, to suit the altered needs of each succeeding generation. So far is it from being necessary that this development should go forward in subordination to Scripture that it is really an independent continuation of it. Hence he adds: "While it is certain that developments of Revelation proceeded all through the Old Dispensation, down to the very end of our Lord's ministry, on the other hand, if we turn our attention to the beginning of apostolical teaching after His ascension, we shall find ourselves unable to fix an historical point at which the growth of doctrine ceased and the rule of faith was once for all settled. Not on the day of Pentecost, for St. Peter had still to learn at Joppa that he was to baptize Cornelius; not at Joppa and Cæsarea, for St. Paul had to write his Epistles; not on the death of the last apostle, for St. Ignatius had to establish the doctrine of Episcopacy; not then nor for centuries after, for the Canon of the New Testament was still undetermined."[1]

If anything further were required to exhibit the real nature and pretensions of the theory, such statements as the following would probably be sufficient: "If the developments which have above been called moral, are to take place to any great extent, and without them it is difficult to see how Christianity can exist at all, if only its relations towards civil government have to be ascertained, or the qualifications for the profession of it have to be defined, surely an authority is necessary to impart decision to what is vague, and confidence to what is empirical, to ratify the successive steps of so elaborate a process, and to secure the validity of inferences which are to be made the premises of more remote investigations. . . . This is the doctrine of the infallibility of the Church; for by infallibility I suppose is meant the power of deciding whether this, that, or a third, and any number of theological or ethical statements are true."[2]

As to the way in which the distinctive doctrines of Romanism would fall into order under the influence of this theory, the following

[1] *Essay*, etc. pp. 67, 68.   [2] *Essay*, etc. pp. 77, 78.

naïve and, as from a controversial standpoint we might well call it indiscreet illustration will give some idea: "These doctrines are members of one family and suggestive or correlative or confirmatory or illustrative of each other. One furnishes evidence to another, and all to each of them; if this is proved, that becomes probable; if this and that are both probable, but for different reasons, each adds to the other its own probability. The Incarnation is the antecedent of the doctrine of Mediation, and the archetype both of the sacramental principle and of the merits of the saints. From the doctrine of Mediation follow the Atonement, the Mass, the merits of Martyrs and Saints, their invocation and *cultus*. From the sacramental principle come the Sacraments properly so called; the unity of the Church, and the Holy See as its type and centre; the authority of Councils; the sanctity of rights; the veneration of holy places, shrines, images, vessels, furniture and vestments. Of the sacraments, Baptism is developed into Confirmation on the one hand; into Penance, Purgatory, and Indulgences on the other; and the Eucharist into the Real Presence, adoration of the Host, Resurrection of the body, and the virtue of relics. Again the doctrine of the Sacraments leads to the doctrine of Justification; Justification to that of Original Sin; Original Sin to the merit of Celibacy. Nor do these separate developments stand independent of each other, but by cross relations they are connected, and grow together, while they grow from one. The Mass and Real Presence are parts of one; the veneration of Saints and their relics are parts of one; their intercessory power and the Purgatorial State, and again the Mass and that State are correlative; Celibacy is the characteristic mark of Monachism and of the Priesthood. You must accept the whole or reject the whole; attenuation does but enfeeble and amputations mutilate."[1]

The remaining portion of Newman's treatise is occupied chiefly with a statement of various "notes" by which true developments are to be distinguished from false, and with their applications to the developments just indicated. Into the detailed criticism of these or the illustrations connected with them, beyond what has been given in earlier chapters of this exposition or may yet be given, we cannot now enter. Enough has been presented to exhibit the real nature and tendencies of the theory. All that remains now is to recapitulate the main grounds on which it cannot be entertained.

1. The first argument against it is that it is entirely opposed to the perfection and sufficiency of Scripture. This doctrine has been already established on grounds that Romanists have never succeeded in overthrowing. To development in subjection to the only divine rule of faith and practice, Protestantism can offer no objection. The statements made in the beginning of this chapter have shown that there can be development of doctrine which is in no respect sub-

[1] *An Essay*, etc. pp. 93, 94.

versive of the authority and sufficiency of the Scriptures. But this is not the object of Newman's Essay. As Dr. W. Cunningham well said at its first appearance, "There is a subjective development of Christian doctrine both in individuals and in churches, whereby men grow in the knowledge of God's revealed will and whereby theological science is extended and improved. But the result of this development is merely to enable individuals and Churches to understand more fully and accurately, and to realise more thoroughly, *what is actually contained in or deducible from, the statements of the written word, and can be shown to be so*. This, however, is essentially different from, nay, it is in a certain sense the reverse of, an objective development, which changes and enlarges or diminishes the external revelation, the standard or system of faith."[1] To a process of dealing with the elements of Biblical doctrine such as this, respect for the Scriptures as the word of God bids us show the strongest opposition.

2. The second main argument against this theory is that it postulates in behalf of the Church a function that she is not entitled or called on to exercise. As Dr. Newman expressly states, if there is to be a process of development, there must also be an infallible developing authority. "The common sense of mankind," he says, "feels that the very idea of revelation implies a present informant and guide, and that an infallible one; not a mere abstract declaration of truths unknown before to man, or a record of history, or the result of an antiquarian research, but a message and a lesson speaking to this man and that. . . . In proportion then, as we find, in matter of fact, that the inspired Volume is not adapted or intended to subserve that purpose, are we forced to revert to that living and present Guide, who, at the era of our rejection of her, had been so long recognised as the dispenser of Scripture, according to times and circumstances, and the arbiter of all true doctrine and holy practice to her children. We feel a need, and she alone of all things under heaven supplies it. . . . The Church undertakes that office; she does what none else can do, and this is the secret of her power."[2]

This is a position with which we have still to deal in detail. Here it can only be said, as will yet be shown on indisputable grounds, that neither Christ, the Head of the Church, nor His inspired apostles ever ascribed to the Church on earth any such power or authority; that no particular branch of the Church, such as the Church of Rome, can adduce any valid claim to it; and that there exists not the slightest necessity for any Church to make this claim, in order to afford stable grounds for the faith of men, seeing that already by the grace of God, we have a divine judge of controversies, in the Comforter which is the Holy Ghost. As the Westminster Confession says, with adequate scriptural support for the assertion, "The Supreme Judge, by which all controversies of

[1] *Discussions on Church Principles*, p. 56.
[2] *An Essay*, etc. pp. 87, 88.

religion are to be determined and all decrees of Councils, opinions of ancient writers, doctrines of men and private spirits, are to be examined and in whose sentence we are to rest, can be no other but the Holy Spirit speaking in the Scriptures."[1]

3. The last insuperable objection to this theory is that it is essentially a new device derived from a questionable source for explaining in a way fitted to cover the Romish position, facts in their system of doctrine and practice that can only be accounted for on a different principle. The real origin of the theory in the school of Kant has already been adverted to. It still retains its rationalistic spirit in the new application: because, though used by the Church and professedly in defence of the faith, it nevertheless abandons the authority of Scripture and gives full scope to the independent action of human reason in determining what is best for her doctrine and practice. As used in behalf of Romanism, it is a novel expedient. As a matter of fact, though looked upon with favour by many Romanist theologians, it has never yet been embraced by the Church of Rome in any authoritative way. When called on to explain the wide divergence of their present system from that of primitive Christianity, the majority of Romish divines have always contended that they retain nothing but what has been handed down to them by tradition from the apostles; and they do not hesitate to attempt proving in a fashion that the present elements of her belief and practice can be justified by that method. On the part of others, however, confidence in the validity of this claim has been rudely shaken by modern investigations of the history of doctrine. Dr. Newman himself evidently lost faith in it. "For three hundred years," he says, "the documents and the facts of Christianity have been exposed to a jealous scrutiny; works have been judged spurious which once were received without a question; facts have been discarded or modified which were once first principles in argument; new facts and new principles have been brought to light; philosophical views and polemical discussions of various tendencies have been maintained with more or less success. . . . The assailants of dogmatic truth have got the start of its adherents of whatever creed; philosophy is completing what criticism has begun; and apprehensions are not unreasonably excited lest we should have a new world to conquer before we have weapons for the warfare. . . . An argument is needed, unless Christianity is to abandon the province of argument; and those who find fault with the explanation here offered of its historical phenomena will find it their duty to provide one for themselves."[2] Here the real motive of the theory comes out. It is an attempt to explain the difficulties arising from the Romish variations on primitive Christianity in a way that shall make the Church independent of the old shattered argument from apostolic tradition.

[1] Ch. i. § 10. Cf. Matt. xxii. 19, 31; Eph. ii. 20; Acts xxviii. 25.
[2] *An Essay*, etc. pp. 30, 31.

But, as has been shown again and again, all the facts of the case which caused Newman so much anxiety can be explained on a simpler and more trustworthy principle. This is the Protestant view that all these divergences from the apostolic doctrine and practice are corruptions having their origin in the heart of man as depraved by sin and blinded by the god of this world. This has been the prolific source of error from the dawn of human history.

> "Faults in the life breed errors in the brain,
> And these reciprocally those again;
> The mind and conduct mutually imprint,
> And stamp their image in each other's mint."

Such was the origin of the varied forms of ancient Paganism, of Jewish Traditionalism, of Oriental Philosophy and the later Gnosticism. The primitive Church was surrounded by these influences from many quarters; and when, leaving the simplicity of the apostolic teaching, the clergy began to exalt their own functions as the means of regenerating society, a tide of corruption began to flow in upon the Church that never ceased till it reached its height in the sixteenth century. Under the bondage of those errors the Church of Rome still lies. The shackles will never be broken till from within her own pale reforming forces shall arise sufficiently strong to turn her back to the Scriptures as the only divine rule of faith and practice.

PART III

THE POLITY OF PROTESTANTISM

DIFFERENCES CONCERNING THE ECCLESIASTICAL EMBODIMENT OF THE TRUTH — THE SOCIAL PRINCIPLE

CHAP.	PAGE
I. The Nature of the Church	159
II. The Ministry of the Church	170
III. The Worship of the Church	178
IV. The Sacraments of the Church — Their Nature and Number	187
V. The Sacraments of the Church—Baptism	195
VI. The Sacraments of the Church—The Lord's Supper—The Mass	200
VII. The Constitution of the Church—The Roman Primacy	210
VIII. The Teaching of the Church—Papal Infallibility	219
IX. The Authority of the Church—Papal Supremacy	228
X. The Church in Relation to the Unseen World — The Saints—The Mother of our Lord	237

CHAPTER I

THE NATURE OF THE CHURCH

FROM the divergent views of Romanism and Protestantism on the application of the truth to the individual soul and on the divine records in which it is found, we turn now to its bearings on the social life of believers.

In the theological teaching of the Middle Ages, the topic of the Church was not set in the forefront. No question had then arisen that seemed to affect seriously the unity or authority of the Church of Rome; and her leading divines were content to let this point rest as a matter beyond dispute. Even after the Reformation had begun, this was the feeling that prevailed. For when in the Council of Trent, a Franciscan theologian proposed that before establishing Scripture and tradition as the foundations of the faith, they should deal with the subject of the Church, which was the chief foundation of all, others contended that this was a point that did not admit of discussion. It had been assumed all along that by the Church was to be understood the ecclesiastical orders, especially the Council and the Pope; and if the subject were opened at that stage, many might be tempted to think that there were difficulties upon it or at least that it was a truth but newly cleared up and one that had not always been believed in the Christian Church. This was the view adopted in the Council. In vain do we search its decrees and canons for any formal statements or definitions of the nature and constitution of the Church.

While the Council of Trent was not prepared to discuss this topic in open debate, we are not left without full information as to the views held by the great majority of its members. This we owe to the Catechism of the Council. For treating of the ninth article of the Apostles' Creed, "I believe in the Holy Catholic Church," it presents to us a complete exposition of all the leading points connected with the nature and attributes of the Church.[1] With this aid, read in the light of explanations given by leading Romanist divines, we have no difficulty in ascertaining the whole doctrine of the Church of Rome on this subject.

The Catechism begins its exposition with the origin of the Latin

[1] Ch. x. q. 1-25.

word for "church" and the various applications it has in the New Testament. Here its statements are simple and accurate. "The word, *ecclesia*, means a calling forth : but writers afterwards used it to signify a council or assembly." It is derived from the Greek and gained its concrete meaning from the fact that the Athenian assembly (ἐκκλησία from ἐκ-καλέω) which gave rise to the name was convened by the voice of heralds. Hence we find the word applied to gatherings that have no connection with religious worship. It is used in the statement of the town clerk of Ephesus that, if there was to be an inquiry into the conduct of Paul and Silas, it should be settled "in the regular assembly." It is even used by Luke himself in saying that when this official had thus spoken, he dismissed the multitude (*lit.* the assembly). In the Septuagint, it is even applied to the gathering of evildoers.[1] "In the ordinary application of Holy Scripture, however, the word was subsequently used to designate the Christian commonwealth and the congregation of the faithful."

In this connection also, the word has various applications. Sometimes it is used to describe the believers gathering together in a single house, as is the case of Gaius and Philemon. At other times, it embraces the Christian congregation of a city or province, as "the Church of Rome,"[2] of Corinth, Ephesus, Colossæ, Galatia, Asia, Macedonia. At other times, we have to add, it is taken by many to include the whole body of professing Christians throughout the world. As instances of this last kind, such statements as the following are adduced : "And great fear came upon the whole Church and upon all that heard these things." "But Saul laid waste the Church,"[3] "Gaius mine host and of the whole Church." "Give no occasion of stumbling either to Jews or Greeks or to the Church of God."[4]

After mentioning some of these facts, the Catechism, with a rather illogical sequence, proceeds to notice the two component parts of the Church, namely, the Church triumphant and the Church militant, the former being "the most glorious and happy assemblage of blessed spirits . . . who, now free and secure from the troubles of this life, enjoy everlasting bliss"; the latter, "the society of all the faithful that now dwell on the earth," called militant, "because it wages eternal war with the world, the devil and the flesh."[5] It is with this second part of the Church that pastoral instruction is chiefly concerned and on its nature and attributes accordingly the Catechism principally dwells.

The most important fact we have to learn about the Church militant is that in it "there are two classes of persons, the good and the bad ; and the bad profess the same faith and partake of the same sacraments, but differ in their lives and morals." "Nor does the Church include the good only but likewise the bad, as we learn from many parables contained in the gospel; as when the kingdom of

---

[1] Ps. xxvi, 5.   [2] Q. 9.   [3] Acts v. 11, viii. 3.
[4] Rom. xvi. 23 ; 1 Cor. x. 32 ; cf. *The Scripture Doctrine of the Church,* by Dr. D. Bannerman, p. 573.   [5] Q. 5.

THE NATURE OF THE CHURCH

heaven, that is, the Church militant, is compared to a net cast into the sea, to a field in which tares were sown, to a threshing-floor on which the grain is mixed up with the chaff, and to the ten virgins some of whom were wise and some foolish." " Hence only these classes are excluded from her pale : first, infidels, next heretics and schismatics, and lastly, the excommunicated."[1]

The Church thus composed is said to be marked by these special notes, namely, unity, sanctity, catholicity and apostolicity. The Church is *one*, because it has "one Lord, one faith and one baptism." "This Church has also one ruler and one governor, the invisible one Christ, whom the eternal Father hath made head over all the Church, which is His body ; but the visible one is he who, the legitimate successor of Peter, the Prince of the apostles, occupies the see of Rome."[2] " The Church is called *holy*, because she is consecrated and dedicated to God ; for so other things, such as under the old law vessels, vestments, altars, when appropriated and dedicated to the divine worship, although material, are called holy ; as in like manner, the firstborn who were dedicated to the Most High God were also called holy."[3] "The Church is called *catholic*, because unlike human republics or the conventicles of heretics, she is not circumscribed within the limits of one single kingdom, nor is she confined to one class of men, but embraces in the bosom of her love all mankind, whether they be barbarians or Scythians or slaves or freemen or males or females."[4] The Church is called *apostolic*, " from her origin which she derives under the revelation of grace from the apostles : for her doctrines are truths neither novel nor of recent origin, but delivered of old by the apostles and disseminated throughout the world." . . . " For the Holy Ghost who presides over the Church, governs her by no other than apostolic ministers ; and this Spirit was first imparted to the apostles and has by the supreme goodness of God, always remained in the Church."[5]

How fully these views have been adopted by leading Romanist divines may be seen, for example, in the statements of Bellarmin. According to him, the Church "is a society of men, united by a profession of the same Christian faith, and a participation of the same sacraments, under the government of lawful pastors and especially of the one vicar of Christ on earth, the Roman pontiff." " Of this definition," he adds, "there are three parts, the profession of the true faith, communion in the sacraments and subjection to the pastoral authority of the bishop of Rome." After mentioning the three classes thus excluded from membership, namely, the heathen or heretics, the excommunicated and schismatics, he makes this very significant statement. "All others, even impious and reprobate men are included in the definition ; for the Church is a society of men as visible and palpable as the Roman people, the kingdom of France, or the republic of Venice."[6]

[1] Q. 6-8.   [2] Q. 10-12.   [3] Q. 13.   [4] Q. 14.   [5] Q. 15.
[6] Winer, *The Confessions of Christendom* (Clark), pp. 331, 332.

Now that there are certain elements of truth in such descriptions of the Church cannot be denied. As a careful investigator has pointed out, several facts have been thus adduced, which Protestants must be prepared to accept at once.[1]

No Protestant, for example, has the slightest interest in denying that "the Christian life is essentially a social one." The aim of Christ was not merely to save individual souls, but to draw them into relations of fellowship with one another.

Hence the Church must always be so far visible. For the communion of Christian disciples must manifest itself before the eyes of men in the observance of social worship and the sacraments appointed by the Lord. Möhler has given very unfair representations of the Protestant view on this point. Dealing with certain isolated statements of Luther instead of going to the public Confessions of the Reformed Churches, he has attempted to identify Protestantism with a Church wholly invisible. This opinion we repudiate. As he himself has shown, the very historic fact of the Incarnation demands at least a visible Church as its sequel. There is no reason why any Protestant should hesitate to adopt his strong language when he says: "Without external bonds, there is no true spiritual connection, so that the idea of a mere invisible universal fellowship to which we are bound to adhere is a fruitless, needless fiction of the imagination and of perverted feeling, which remains void of influence on man."[2]

Moreover it is by the agency of the Church that the children of believers are to be brought into living union with the Saviour and those that are without are to be evangelised and led into the knowledge of the true God. Möhler in several passages has represented Protestantism as dispensing with the mediating work of the Church altogether: "Since every individual believer was looked upon as being inwardly taught by God alone and as being able to attain to Christian knowledge without any special assistance of men, in the first place an external Christian ministry could no longer be conceived: God was by means of the Holy Scriptures the only teacher."[3] Echoing this view, an eminent statesman of the Anglican Church also once said that, according to the Protestant theory, "The Church is not considered as intervening in anyway between the Saviour and the individual.... This salvation is conveyed direct by an operation exclusively internal.... Each man becomes to himself the arbiter of revealed truth and the sole witness of effectual grace; and the love shown to him does not according to his conceptions belong to all around him."[4] Such statements do a grave injustice to the spirit and method of the Reformers. All the best Reformed Confessions affirm in the most explicit way the necessity of aggressive effort on the part of the Church and the duty on the part of all to avail themselves of her ministry.

Hence, last of all, it is admitted on both sides that there is an

---
[1] Litton, *The Church of Christ* (1851), pp. 56 sq.   [2] *Symbolik*, s. 347.
[3] *Symbolik*, s. 404.   [4] Gladstone, *Church Principles*, p. 126.

aspect of the Church in which her life is invisible. The Romanist does not utterly deny this. The Catechism of the Council expressly says : " In the Church, they are called the good, who are linked together not only by the profession of the same faith and the communion of the same sacraments, but also by the spirit of grace and the bond of charity, of whom it is said : 'The Lord knoweth them that are His.'[1] Who they are that appertain to this class of pious men, men may also form some conjecture but cannot know with certainty."[2] " For although anyone by his reason and senses may ascertain the existence of the Church, that is, that there is a society of men on earth who are devoted and consecrated to Christ the Lord . . . Yet it is by the light of faith only and not by any process of reasoning that the mind can comprehend these mysteries which . . . are contained in the holy Church of God."[3]

On these four points then, the social character of the Christian life, the necessary visibility of the Church, her ministerial work and the element of invisibility in her life, both Romanists and Protestants may be said to agree. But, if this be so, wherein does the difference betwixt them lie? At what precise point do the two systems diverge? As an eminent Anglican writer has pointed out, the difference lies in the relative importance attached to the two aspects of the Church's life. "The Romanist, while admitting that there is or ought to be in the Church an interior life not cognisable by human eye, yet regards this as a separable accident and makes the essence of the Church to consist in what is external and visible ; the Protestant, on the contrary, while admitting that to be visible is an inseparable property of the Church, makes the essence thereof to consist in what is spiritual and unseen : namely, the work of the Holy Spirit in the hearts of Christians. The one defines the Church by its outward, the other by its inward characteristics."[4]

That this and nothing more or less is the real point of divergence on the nature of the Church, may be seen from the statements of Romanist theologians themselves. Bellarmin, for example, says : " This is the distinction between our view and that of the Protestants, that they, to constitute anyone a member of the Church, require internal virtues, and consequently make the true Church invisible : we, on the contrary, believe that all internal graces, faith, hope, charity and others, will be found in the Church, but we deny that to constitute a man a member of the true Church, any internal virtue is requisite but only an external profession of the faith and that participation of the sacraments which is perceptible by the senses."[5] With this statement Möhler entirely coincides : " The differences betwixt the Catholic and Lutheran modes of regarding the Church may be reduced to a short, precise and definite expression. The Catholics teach : the visible Church is first, then comes the invisible ;

[1] 2 Tim. ii. 19.   [2] Q. 6.   [3] Q. 18.
[4] Litton, *The Church of Christ* (1851), p. 70.
[5] Winer, *The Confessions of Christendom* (Clark), p. 332.

the former gives rise to the latter. On the other hand, the Lutherans say the reverse : out of the invisible Church proceeds the visible and the former is the ground of the latter. In this apparently most insignificant opposition an immense difference is declared." [1]

Such being a fair statement of the Romanist doctrine, we are now in a position to test its validity by the written word. Does the essential element in the Church consist primarily and chiefly in its outward visible organisation or in its internal spiritual life?

1. In upholding the latter view, we are led to remark at the outset that the Romanist position is evidently based on a wrong conception of the real nature of Christianity as springing out of Judaism. That the Christian Church is genetically related to the Mosaic is a simple historic fact. That it is a higher, nobler and more spiritual form of religion is also admitted on all hands : it stands to Judaism as the flower and fruit to the bud wrapped up in its capsule or as the full-grown man to the little child. What the Romanist does not sufficiently recognise is that Christianity, while higher and nobler than Judaism differs also from it specially in its whole method of operation. Judaism was a system of law designed to drill men into the culture of the religious life by positive ordinances. It was an external institute for the promotion of spiritual religion and thereby embraced in its pale all who belonged to the nation, with any others that were prepared to accept the initiatory rites. It was an inflexible method of operating on the spirit of man from without inwards. Christianity is conceived by the Romanist to be an institute of a more spiritual form indeed but essentially of the same kind. It is a new law, designed to drill men into the habits of the religious life ; and the Christian Church is therefore an external institute or organisation which carries out this discipline in all its details.

Against this whole conception of Christianity and the Christian Church, the Reformers entered the strongest protest. "The law was given by Moses, but grace and truth came by Jesus Christ." [2] The primary instrument of Christianity is not the law but the gospel. The Christian Church is not an institute, wielding a system of ordinances for making men Christians by profession. It is primarily a community of believing souls, who, quickened by the grace of God which they received through faith, become in turn witnesses for Him in the gospel of His Son and press on the acceptance of men salvation in His name, while at the same time in their own life and worship and service they exhibit what God requires of those that are called out of the world to be His people. It is not an external organisation for establishing a connection of souls with the hope of salvation : but a society of those who, having believed in Christ as a Saviour, have also received His Spirit into their hearts and, on the ground of this spiritual union with the Lord, abide in the fellowship of life and love with one another and endeavour to extend it over the whole world.

[1] *Symbolik*, s. 419.   [2] John i. 17.

2. It is only in accordance with their failure to discern the spirituality of the Christian dispensation that the Romanists do not do justice to an aspect of the Church which in the New Testament receives marked prominence. The various applications of the word "Church" to larger or smaller Christian societies have been already noticed. In the Tridentine Catechism the chief stress is laid on those passages where it is used to designate the whole community of professing Christians throughout the world. But there are other statements that manifestly take in a higher range of ideas and in which the merely local or historical aspects of the Church, as man discerns it, give place to one that, being heavenly and divine, can be observed only by the eye of faith. The key to these utterances is found in the words of Jesus to the disciples: "On this rock I will build My Church and the gates of hell shall not prevail against it."[1] Here evidently the Lord has in view a society that, while it is to have a visible manifestation, has already a place in the divine purpose towards the world and is to be reared throughout the ages under the eye of God. This idea has been most fully developed by the Apostle Paul. Speaking to the elders of Ephesus from the same lofty standpoint, he charges them to "feed the Church of the Lord which He purchased with His own blood."[2] Later on in writing to the Ephesians, he speaks of "the Church which is His body, the fulness (or plenary manifestation) of Him that filleth all in all";[3] of Christ's loving the Church and giving "Himself for it, that He . . . might present it to Himself a glorious Church."[4] Similarly to the Colossians he writes that Christ is "the Head of the body the Church";[5] and he gives directions to Timothy "how he ought to behave himself in the House of God, which is the Church of the living God."[6] The writer of the Epistle to the Hebrews identifies the Church with "Mount Zion, the city of the living God, the heavenly Jerusalem," and characterises it as "the general assembly and Church of the firstborn whose names are written in heaven."[7]

In these and similar passages we have in view a society that is plainly to be distinguished from the collection of Christian Churches scattered over the world. This is the one true Church of Christ gathered out of the race; and it is necessary to keep its special characteristics before us to understand the teaching of Scripture on the real nature of the Church and to set aside the views of Rome.

i. Only those that are true Christians belong to this great society. In the local Churches of the world, many are to be found who are not really children of God. They may profess to have faith in Christ, but by their works they show that they have never been united to Him. These it is found impossible to distinguish perfectly and separate from true believers. The Lord Jesus taught His disciples that such a mixture of good and bad, of souls saved and unsaved,

[1] Matt. xvi. 18.   [2] Acts xx. 28.   [3] Eph. i. 23.
[4] Ch. v. 25.   [5] Col. i. 18.   [6] 1 Tim. iii. 15.
[7] Heb. xii. 22.

would always be found in the Christian communities of the world.[1] The parables of the Tares, the Draw-net and the Ten Virgins were spoken for the very purpose of preparing His people for such facts. Many attempts have been made to form a perfectly pure Church. They have all ended in defeat : but there is a Church of which only the children of God are members and this is composed of those whom God has called into the fellowship of His Son and who have been knit to Him by the bonds of a living faith.

ii. All the members of this Church being thus united to Christ are also closely united to one another. Being every one permeated by the life of Christ, they cannot but be joined in one living community. This is the ground on which the Church is described as a body of which Christ is the Head. All the members of the human body derive life, sustenance, guidance and protection from the head, but they are also connected with one another and made to serve the growth of the whole system. So is it with Christ and those that are knit to Him by the Spirit. Receiving the fulness of His grace, they form with and under Him one vast spiritual society, the individual members of which manifest His glory and minister to their common welfare : so that we can speak of Christ as the Head "from whom all the body fitly framed and knit together through that which every joint supplieth, according to the working in due measure of each several part, maketh the increase of the body unto the building up of itself in love."[2] It is on the same principle that the Church is also called the temple of God, of which Christ is the corner-stone.[3]

iii. From the fact that the bond which unites Christians to the Lord and to one another, namely, the presence of Christ and His Spirit in their hearts through faith, is invisible, the true Church of Christ is also invisible. This is really all that is meant by the use of this term. It has been the practice of Romanist divines to represent Protestants as holding that the Church of Christ is in no sense visible. Möhler put himself to a large amount of needless pains to show that this extreme position is untenable.[4] As we have indicated, the Protestant Reformers never attempted to hold it. They had no interest whatever in ignoring the fact that the Church of Christ must have a visible manifestation, "a local habitation and a name" in the world. All that they contended for was that so far as the local historical Churches were true Churches, they were originated and sustained by the true members of the one invisible Church of Christ. This indeed is what Möhler himself, overmastered for the moment by the evangelical principles in his heart, has practically admitted. "Moreover," he says, "it is not to be doubted that Christ maintains His Church in victorious energy by means of those who live in His faith, belong to Him in spirit and disposition and rejoice in His second coming ; it is also not to be doubted that these are the bearers of His truth and that without them, it would soon be forgotten, pass

[1] Matt. xiii. 24-30, 47-50, xxv. 1-13. [2] Eph. iv. 16.
[3] Eph. ii. 20-22 ; 1 Pet. ii. 4. [4] *Symbolik*, ss. 419-424.

into open error or be transformed into a hollow empty form of words. Yes: it is certainly these, the invisible ones, who have been changed and beautified by God into the image of Christ that are the pillars of the visible Church : the wicked in the Church, the unbelievers, the hypocrites, the dead members in the body of Christ, would not be able even for one day to preserve the Church in her external character." The only point where the distinguished apologist comes short is in grasping the idea that these faithful regenerate souls are not to be identified with the mere visible institute of the Church on earth, but form with and under the glorified Son of God a spiritual invisible society which is therefore rightly designated "His body." As Bishop Taylor said, " The mere profession of Christianity makes no man a member of Christ ; neither circumcision nor uncircumcision availeth anything in Christ ; nothing but a new creature ; nothing but a faith working by love and keeping the commandments of God. Now they that do this are not known to be such by men. . . . That quality and excellence by which they are constituted Christ's members and distinguished from mere professors and outsiders of Christians is not visible. . . . But they are known only to God ; and therefore it is in a true sense the invisible Church."[1] The time will come when all that are not truly members of Christ will be separated from His Church as the tares from the wheat. The Lord who "knoweth those that are His"[2] will thoroughly purge His floor at His second coming. Then the righteous shall shine forth as the sun in the kingdom of the Father and the true Church of Christ will be manifested in glory. But till that crisis arrives, we must be content that in the reality of her corporate life and the fulness of her spiritual inheritance, she should remain invisible.

iv. Hence also this spiritual invisible Church is through all the changes of time one and indivisible. Speaking from the standpoint of history we may say that the Church of Christ was founded, when the Lord Jesus called the twelve apostles or more particularly when He poured forth His Spirit on the assembled disciples at Pentecost. But from the standpoint of the divine purpose we may affirm that the Church began to be founded, from the acceptance of the first promise of redemption in Eden. All the saints of pre-Christian times therefore join with all true Christians that have passed within the veil and all who are now living or shall live on earth, in constituting one Church of Christ, one Bride of the Lamb. In claiming for the visible Church on earth the prerogative of being the holy catholic Church, Romanist theologians stand chargeable with the inconsistency of blending into one and the same body the spirits of just men made perfect and those who here on earth are confessedly stained with sin. In affirming that believers only belong to the true Church of Christ, we maintain the idea of a common holy life flowing into the whole body of the redeemed from one supreme source. The Church

[1] *Dissuasive from Popery* (Clar. Press), p. 129. [2] 2 Tim. ii. 19.

triumphant is not separate from the true Church militant; they constitute one ransomed army. Those that are in heaven only enjoy in perfection that which the others have in process of growth and conflict.

3. The third main objection to the Romanist view of the Church accordingly is that it misapplies and misappropriates the "notes" or distinctive marks of the Church as these are used in Scripture. According to the epithets of the Nicene Creed, these are unity, sanctity, catholicity and apostolicity. Since the Church is alluded to here as an object of faith, we can have no difficulty in accepting these marks as characteristic of the invisible Church of Christ. This Church may be said to be apostolic, because in its distinctively Christian form it was built on the foundation of the apostles and makes progress by the proclamation of their gospel. It is catholic because it is prepared to embrace souls from every tribe and kindred and tongue under the whole heaven. It is one because it is united to the one Lord by the same faith, in connection with the same baptism, is pervaded by the one Spirit and serves the one God and Father of all. It is also holy, because the seed of an uncorruptible life has been implanted in the heart of every believer; and this, if duly nourished by the Word and Spirit will grow till the soul is presented without fault before the face of God.

But here comes in the unwarrantable assumption of the Church of Rome. In spite of the fact that these "notes" find a fitting subject only in the Church of true believers, she appropriates and applies them to herself alone as distinguished thereby from all other Christian communities. The Romanist theologians assume that their Church can justly lay claim to these characteristics, and they thereby uphold her claim to be regarded as the one community outside whose pale salvation cannot be obtained by any creature on earth.

Against this proud boast, the voices of the Reformed Churches rise with one accord. The claim cannot be sustained. As has been already shown, no Church has diverged more from the apostolic doctrine: it will yet be seen that no Church has altered more the apostolic type of worship and government. The Church of Rome is no more catholic than any other great Church in Christendom: there are immense communities alike in the old and new worlds that refuse to own her sway. Nor is she truly one. Save in the external uniformity secured by enforced subjection to one visible head at Rome, which instead of being her glory is her shame, the Church of Rome has nothing in the shape of union that is not more fully enjoyed by the Reformed Protestant Churches. As for the holiness she claims, that according to her own statement is also of an external kind. It is only the sanctity that belongs equally to things or buildings. Of holiness in heart and life, the Church of Rome for long centuries showed herself to be utterly regardless. There have been many holy men and women reared within her communion. But it cannot be said that their numbers are greater in proportion than in other Churches : while it may be confidently affirmed that it has not been by the distinctive features of the Romanist system but only by the grace and truth belonging to vital Christianity in every Church that these results have been achieved.

The motives of the Reformed Churches in resisting the claims of the Church of Rome are not to be misunderstood. This opposition does not spring from a desire to arrogate these notes specially for themselves. They belong to them only in so far as they represent the catholic invisible Church of Christ, and this must ever be to a very imperfect extent. The Protestant Churches are content to be regarded as faithful branches of the true visible Church on earth. This claim is established by their bearing the marks that may be legitimately regarded as characteristic of this Church.

According to almost all the Reformed Confessions, the first and chief of these is the preaching of the unadulterated apostolic gospel. Wherever the word of God is faithfully proclaimed, it may be assumed that there are souls in the community that have been born from above into the family of heaven. "Where thou findest the word," says Luther, "doubtless the Church is there."

Another presumptive token in favour of the presence of true believers and therefore of a true Church, is the right scriptural administration of the sacraments. The use of Baptism and the Lord's Supper is expressly enjoined by Christ and except where the sense of duty is blinded by ignorance or prejudice, these means of grace will always be administered.

A third mark of a true Church, though not perhaps so decisive as the first or second, is separation from the world and from those that fall into its open sins. Where the Church is not easily distinguishable from those that adopt the course of life moulded by the natural man and the carnal heart or where lapses into gross sin on the part of individual members are not marked by suspension from the privileges of communion, there is reason to fear that the numbers of God's children there are on the wane.

By these marks, the Protestant Churches hold, a worthy branch of the true historic Church of Christ can be discerned. Beyond such distinctions they decline to go. They will not pronounce on the claims of one Church rather than another to be the true Church. With them the question is not : *Which* is the true Church ? but rather : *Where* is the true Church ? The reply they give is that the one true invisible Church of Christ will always be found in such visible Churches as cherish the faithful preaching of the word of God, observe the sacraments, and cultivate separation from the world. By fellowship with such larger or smaller communities, Christians may have their souls prepared for holy service here and for heaven hereafter. In affording such provision a Church fulfils the great function assigned to her by the exalted Lord.

CHAPTER II

THE MINISTRY OF THE CHURCH

IF the Church is to retain the form of a visible society enjoying the ordinances appointed by Christ, it is indispensable that there should be chosen from among her members individuals to whom the necessary work may be entrusted. This is a principle that is evidently in accordance with the mind of God. The varied duties connected with the observance of religious worship and the advancement of His kingdom in the world, were never left undefined or without adequate provision being made for their due performance. This organisation is seen even in the very beginning of social worship on the earth. It is the most striking feature in the arrangements made for promoting the religious life of Israel. When the Lord Jesus set about founding the Christian Church, His first step was to attach to Himself a permanent college of disciples whom He might train for the work of ingathering men, and of setting some in every Christian community to maintain His ordinances in operation. This has been the practice of the Church in every age since.

On this point accordingly there is no dispute amongst the different branches of the Church. The divine appointment of a ministerial order is accepted by Romanist and Reformed Protestant alike. Nay, more: there is a very real sense in which these two parties may be said to agree on the perpetuation of the ministry. For they both hold that it belongs to those who are already placed in the ministry by the proper ecclesiastical authority to train and ordain or recognise others to take their place. The points on which the real divergence is manifest are the source in the Church from which the authority to appoint ministers in the last resort flows, and the relation to the members of the Church in which as appointed they stand.

The Romanist view, as it is set forth in the decrees of the Council of Trent, may be said to embrace these main elements.

1. It starts with the assumption that the Lord Jesus acted as a High Priest after the order of Melchisedek not in heaven only, but also on earth, and that not simply by offering up His life on the cross as a ransom for sinners, but very specially, even before the crucifixion, by presenting to God in the sacrament of the Supper a

sacrifice of Himself in the form of bread and wine. So the decree of the Council literally runs: " He therefore, our God and Lord, though He was about to offer Himself once on the altar of the cross to God the Father by means of His death, there to operate an eternal redemption; nevertheless because that His priesthood was not to be extinguished by His death, in the last Supper on the night in which He was betrayed—that He might leave to His own beloved spouse the Church, a visible sacrifice such as the nature of man requires, whereby that bloody sacrifice, once to be accomplished on the cross might be represented and the memory thereof remain unto the end of the world, and its salutary virtue be applied to the remission of those sins which we daily commit—declaring Himself constituted a Priest for ever according to the order of Melchisedek, He offered up to God the Father His own body and blood under the species of bread and wine."[1]

2. To this statement about Christ's action as a priest in the Supper, is subjoined another about the new office assigned to the twelve disciples then present. By the very delivery of the bread and wine into the hands of the apostles, they were, it is held, constituted priests and endowed with the same power of presenting Christ as a sacrifice that the Lord Himself exercised. " Under the symbols of these same things, He declared (His own body and blood) to be received by the apostles, whom He thus constituted priests of the New Testament, and by these words, ' Do this in remembrance of Me,' He commanded them and their successors in the priesthood to offer (them); even as the Catholic Church has always understood and taught."[2]

3. As to those whom the decree of the Council designates as successors of the apostles in the priesthood, there can be no doubt that in the first instance at least, it is the bishops or chief priests that are intended. For, in a later chapter, " The holy Synod declares that besides the other ecclesiastical degrees, bishops, who have succeeded to the place of the apostles, principally belong to this hierarchical order; that they are *placed*, so the same apostle says, *by the Holy Ghost, to rule the Church of God*; that they are superior to priests; administer the sacrament of confirmation; ordain the ministers of the Church; and that they can perform many other things: over which functions others of an inferior order have no power."[3] Yet the ordinary priesthood is itself regarded as a position of great dignity. This is secured to it by the authority which the priests have of offering the sacrifice of the Supper. Although he may not ordain other priests or confirm catechumens or suspend from the privileges of communion, yet so long as he is entitled to offer the sacrifice on which hangs all hope of pardon here and acceptance hereafter, the priest must be regarded by the people as occupying a place of high honour.

It is this sacrifice indeed that is regarded as constituting the very

[1] Sess. XXII. *On the Sacrifice of the Mass*, ch. i.
[2] *Ut sup.*   [3] Sess. XXIII. ch. iv.

basis of the priesthood. As the decree of Trent says, "Sacrifice and priesthood are by the ordinance of God in such wise conjoined, as that both have existed in every law. Whereas therefore in the New Testament the Catholic Church has received from the institution of Christ, the holy visible sacrifice of the Eucharist, it must needs be confessed that there is in that Church a new visible and external priesthood, into which the old has been *translated*."[1] The Church of Rome endeavours to enhance this prominence by placing the priest at the head of six other functionaries. "Whereas the ministry of so holy a priesthood is a divine thing, to the end that it might be exercised in a more worthy manner and with greater veneration, it was suitable that in the most well-ordered settlement of the Church, there should be several and diverse orders of ministers to minister to the priesthood by virtue of their office."[2] Six of these orders are mentioned, namely, the deacon, sub-deacon, acolyte, exorcist, lector, and doorkeeper, making with the priesthood the perfect number of seven.

4. With these facts before us, it becomes easier to understand how the Romish priest comes to be not only invested with ecclesiastical authority for the performance of his duties, but even regarded as stamped with a new disposition and put thereby in possession of a new sacred power. The special inward mark is held to be fixed in the act of ordination as performed by the bishop. The decree of Trent says that, "Forasmuch as in the sacrament of Order, as also in Baptism and Confirmation, a character is imprinted which can neither be effaced nor taken away, the holy Synod with reason condemns the opinion of those who assert that the priests of the New Testament have only a temporary power."[3] A special canon adds: "If anyone saith that by sacred ordination the Holy Ghost is not given, and that vainly therefore do the bishops say, 'Receive ye the Holy Ghost'; or that a character is not imprinted by this ordination; or that he who has once been a priest can again become a layman: let him," etc.[4] What this indelible character in itself is, is nowhere expressly stated. It is not described as an access of spiritual life or increase of the spiritual graces: it is rather a new disposition of the mental and moral faculties given with a view to the occupation of a new office. So at least the Catechism of Trent seems to teach. For it is there "denominated a spiritual character, because by a certain interior mark impressed on the soul, those who have received holy orders are distinguished from the rest of the faithful and devoted to the divine service."[5]

The chief endowment conferred in ordination, however, is said to be "a special power in reference to the most holy Eucharist, a power full and perfect in the priest, who alone can consecrate the body and blood of our Lord."[6] This, the Catechism explains, is imparted by

---
[1] Sess. XXIII. ch. i.   [2] *Ut sup.* ch. ii.
[3] *Ut sup.* ch. iv.   [4] Canon IV.
[5] Pt. ii. ch. vii. q. 31.   [6] *Ut sup.*

the bishop when, anointing the priest's hands with the sacred oil, he "presents to him a cup containing wine and a patten with a host saying : 'Receive power to offer sacrifice unto God and to celebrate masses as well for the living as for the dead.' By these ceremonies and words, he is constituted an interpreter and mediator between God and man, which must be deemed the principal function of the priesthood."[1] It is only a natural adjunct of this new divine power that the priest should also have authority to forgive and retain sins. For the Catechism adds : "Finally, again placing his hands on his head, the bishop says : 'Receive thou the Holy Ghost : whose sins thou shalt remit, they are remitted unto them, and whose thou shalt retain, they are retained'; thus bestowing on him that celestial power of remitting and retaining sins, which was conferred by our Lord on His disciples."[2]

After such a representation of the power conferred by the Church of Rome on her ministers, it does not surprise us to find the Catechism extolling their dignity in these terms : "For whereas priests and bishops are the interpreters and heralds of God, who are commissioned in His name to teach mankind the divine law and the precepts of life and are the representatives on earth of God Himself, it is plainly impossible therefore to conceive a function more exalted ; and justly therefore are they called not only angels, but also 'gods,' holding as they do amongst us the power and might of the immortal God."[3]

The divergence betwixt Romanism and Protestantism on the subject of the ministry is thus seen to merge in several related topics, such as the value of episcopal ordination, the nature of the Lord's Supper and the method of Church government. Leaving these to be discussed more fully under their proper heads in the course of the exposition, we confine ourselves here to the main question raised, namely, the real nature of the Christian ministry or the relations in which it stands to God and man.

How did the view that the ministry is a priesthood first take root in the Church? The Fathers of Trent evidently wished to convey the impression that it is a natural sequel of the doctrine that the Eucharist is a real propitiatory sacrifice. Since the Lord instituted a sacrifice, there must needs be a priesthood to offer it. It is now agreed on all hands that this representation is not in accordance with fact. It was not until the eighth century at the earliest that the idea of a sacrifice in the Supper took root in the Church, while it can be set beyond doubt that in the beginning of the third, the ministry was already designated as a priesthood. As a historian of the Council of Trent has said, "The Roman priesthood seems to us to have been fully constituted long before the mass was the mass. The uniform conjunction of priesthood and sacrifice in other religions is of small importance ; here it is not the priesthood that has been instituted for the sacrifice : it is the sacrifice that has been

[1] *Ut sup.* q. 24.   [2] *Ut sup.*   [3] Ch. vii. q. 2.

gradually introduced in order to complete and legitimise the priesthood."[1]

As to the causes that led to the formation of the priestly theory, some historians are inclined to give the chief place to the associations of paganism. It is manifest that the details of the different orders are borrowed from this source. The very name of Pontiff worn by the chief bishop of the Roman Church is derived from the title, 'Pontifex maximus' given to the head of the pagan hierarchy. But it seems probable that it was false views of the relation of Christianity to Judaism that had the strongest influence in this direction. While the canon of the New Testament was still in the course of formation, the older books were the main basis for Christian instruction and exhortation. After the death of the apostles, there were no teachers left in the Church with a sufficient grasp of the distinctive features of Christianity to enable them to decide with accuracy on what was transient and what was abiding in the earlier economy. While so many members of the Jewish Church were going over to Christianity and yet retaining their crude ideas about the external service of the Church, there was the strongest temptation to fall in with their sentiments and permit the application to the Christian ministry of titles and functions that strictly belonged only to the Jewish priesthood. That this temptation was first unconsciously yielded to and then willingly embraced, can be shown by specific references in the earliest Christian literature.

In the Apostolic Fathers, apart from some bold metaphors and illustrations based on the Levitical orders, there is nothing that can be regarded as tantamount to an assertion of the priestly theory. But when we come down to Tertullian in the beginning of the third century, it is already full-blown. He constantly applies the words "priest," "priesthood" and "priestly" to the Christian ministry. His whole mode of speech indeed is such as to suggest that these designations were already in current use in his time. "The right of giving baptism," he, for example, says, "is possessed by the chief priest, who is the bishop."[2] Hippolytus follows in the wake of Tertullian by designating bishops as successors of the apostles and partaking of the grace of high-priesthood. Origen indeed still speaks of a spiritual priesthood, yet he too applies sacerdotal terms to the Christian ministry. At last comes Cyprian, who not only applies the same language to ministers, but in the most pronounced way claims all the special authority and dignity which the titles to his mind imply. To use the language of Dr. Lightfoot, "As Cyprian crowned the edifice of the episcopal power, so also was he the first to put forward without relief or disguise these sacerdotal claims; and so uncompromising was the tone in which he asserted them

---

[1] Bungener, *History of the Council of Trent*, p. 375.
[2] Cf. Lightfoot, "The Christian Ministry," pp. 255-259 (in *Com. on Epistle to the Philippians*).

that nothing was left to his successors but to enforce his principles and reiterate his language." "For if Jesus Christ, our Lord and God," says he in one of his letters, "is the High Priest of the Father and first offered Himself a sacrifice to the Father, and commanded this to be done in remembrance of Him, so the priest really ministers in the room of Christ."[1] Ambrose in the fourth century only echoes Tertullian when he speaks of the bishop as having "the functions of Christ" and acting as "the Vicar of the Lord." The Catechism of Trent carries these principles to their logical issue in speaking of Christ and the priest as being "one priest." "As the victim is Jesus Christ, the priest also is the same Christ our Lord."[2]

How strongly these errors were opposed by the leaders of all the Reformed Churches, is manifest both in their writings and in the public confessions they framed. The very form in which the decrees and canons of Trent are cast is derived from the pointed statements drawn by the Reformers from the Scriptures. Modern investigation of the historic origin of the ministry and the whole strain of Biblical teaching on the subject have only strengthened the conviction that the whole Romish theory is destitute of any divine authority.

How contrary to truth, for example, is it to assert that the Lord Jesus offered Himself as a sacrifice to God at the institution of the Supper. Such an idea is not even suggested by the evangelic narrative. It would never have been mooted at all, had it not been demanded by the exigencies of a preconceived theory. It was an impossibility alike physical and moral for the Lord to offer Himself in any real sense before He died on the cross: for then He offered Himself "once for all." The words of institution refer to the Supper only as a divine gift to men: "Take, eat": "divide it among yourselves."[3] It assumed the Lord's offering up of Himself on the Cross as already accomplished in the divine counsel from before the foundation of the world and presents it in its spiritual fruits and effects in the souls of men. Moreover it was not as a priest after the order of Melchisedek that the Lord then acted. He entered on His glory in that order, only when He ascended into heaven, and sat down at the right hand of God.[4] The offering of bread and wine to Abraham by Melchisedek had no sacrificial element in it: it was simply an act of hospitality.[5] If it can be said to be in any sense fulfilled in Christ, it is in His now presenting Himself to men from heaven as the food of the soul, not merely in the Supper, but in the whole life of faith.

Equally void of foundation is the statement that in the Supper the Lord Jesus constituted the apostles priests. He gave them the symbols of bread and wine as tokens and channels of inward grace to their souls. When He said to them: "Do this in remembrance of Me,"[6] He simply commanded and authorised them to

---
[1] Cf. Jacob, *The Ecclesiastical Polity of the New Testament*, p. 103.
[2] Pt. ii. ch. iv. q. 74.   [3] Matt. xxvi. 26; Luke xxii. 17.
[4] Heb. vi. 20.   [5] Gen. xiv. 18.   [6] 1 Cor. xi. 25.

maintain for others the observance of the ordinance in His name, as He was then dispensing it to themselves.

In the light of these facts, it cannot with the slightest show of reason be affirmed that the apostles were then empowered to ordain priests in succession to themselves. Such a meaning has to be forced on the words without any point of attachment. The whole procedure of the apostles in constituting the Christian Church and the whole tenor of their instructions to ministers as well as Churches show that the idea of founding a priestly order never entered into their minds.

1. For, in the first place, the very perfection of the high-priesthood of Christ excluded the formation of any other priestly order. The Romish theory practically makes Christianity a mere continuation of Judaism. "The new law," as they call it, may be higher than the old, but its essential character is not changed. Such teaching is utterly discountenanced by the whole scope of the Epistle to the Hebrews. The precise object of the writer of that exposition is to show that in virtue of His perfect and everlasting sacrifice, Christ not only fulfilled the idea to which all the sacrifices of the old covenant pointed, but abolished the necessity for any further external sacrifice or mediator whatever. The external law was changed into one that was spiritual and internal; for "the priesthood being changed, there is made of necessity a change also of the law."[1] The sacrifices were abolished and with them the priests. Christ as our High Priest at God's right hand, ever presenting in Himself the one all-sufficient sacrifice of His blood, needs no mediatorial agent or representative on earth apart from His Holy Spirit.

2. Besides, the ministry of the Christian Church is evidently modelled, not on that of the Temple, but on that of the Synagogue. This institution existed for centuries before the Lord Jesus came. He Himself recognised it in His evangelistic tours in Palestine; and, after Pentecost, the apostles always made it the starting-point of their aggressive work. It was most natural, therefore, that, wherever the gospel was accepted, the organisation of the synagogue should be continued or reproduced. This is found to be so in fact. The names of the office-bearers in the Church, the method of worship, the place of meeting are all adopted from an institution which was regarded as being entirely distinct from the temple.

3. Hence also the ministers of the Christian Church never have priestly names or functions attributed to them in the New Testament. They are called "ministers," "servants," "stewards," "messengers," "preachers," but never "priests." The special official titles given to them are "overseer" and "presbyter." This last word indeed is etymologically the same as "priest" in our language, but it is the rendering of a totally different word from that which stands for "priest" in Greek. The former is "*presbuteros*": the latter is

[1] Heb. vii. 12.

"*hiereus.*" The New Testament "presbyter" is nowhere regarded as a "priest" in the sacerdotal sense of the term.[1] This silence cannot be regarded as other than positive proof that no priestly order was ever intended to exist in the Christian Church.

4. If any additional confirmation were required, that surely is supplied in the fact that all Christians are regarded as being priests unto God in Christ and so placed on a footing of perfect equality in His sight.[2] This is what Romanists do not practically admit. They may say after the Catechism of Trent that there is an internal priesthood, but, so long as in defiance of the proofs already adduced they claim the privilege of an additional external priesthood, they ignore and oppose the first principles of the gospel of Christ.[3] Through the Son of God in heaven all Christians have full access in one Spirit unto the Father. An external priesthood cannot be other than a barrier betwixt the Lord and the souls He came to redeem. It is the Church that is now the temple : Christ is its only High Priest : all Christians are priests in Him : ministers are only the servants of this priesthood for Jesus' sake.[4]

With the fiction of a mediatory priesthood there falls to the ground the law of celibacy which the Church of Rome in 1074 instituted for this and other orders of her communion, to exalt their influence over the people. If a minister of the Church is simply an office-bearer and a teacher, liberated by her authority from any secular calling that he may devote all his time and energies to the oversight of a flock, then there is no reason why he, like other servants of the Church, may not enter into the relation of marriage. The highest chastity may be cultivated in holy wedlock. Scripture gives no countenance to such a restriction. Peter was married.[5] So were "other apostles and brethren of the Lord." Paul claimed the liberty of leading about a believing wife.[6] Marriage is spoken of as "to be held honourable by all."[7] Elders are called on to govern their households well, keeping their children under wise restraint.[8] The enforcement of celibacy by the Roman Church is but another instance of her subjection to the superstitious spirit of ancient paganism. It was not heard of in the Early Church ; and it has been the source of unspeakable misery and corruption in every later century of her history.

[1] Cf. Lightfoot, *Com. on Epistle to the Philippians*, pp. 186, 264; but also Bannerman, *The Scripture Doctrine of the Church* (Clark), p. 577, where Lightfoot's qualifications are criticised.
[2] Rev. i. 5.   [3] Cat. pt. ii. ch. vii. q. 23.   [4] 2 Cor. iv. 5.
[5] Matt. viii. 14.   [6] 1 Cor. ix. 5.   [7] Heb. xiii. 4.   [8] 1 Tim. iii. 4.

CHAPTER III

THE WORSHIP OF THE CHURCH

THE first duty of the Christian ministry is the conduct of social worship. In the apostolic Church, this was of the simplest kind. Already in the services of the synagogue, the Jewish people had been accustomed to a form of worship in which praise, prayer, and the reading and exposition of the Old Testament were the leading parts. When the Christian Church was instituted it was natural for them to continue the same type of service. The only additions were the two Christian sacraments, Baptism and the Lord's Supper.

It seems beyond doubt that the apostles intended this simplicity to be maintained. Nowhere in their actions or writings is there to be found the slightest hint that the Church had authority to make any addition to the essential parts of worship. The whole system of service associated with the temple was to be done away. The synagogue furnished the model on which the Church was to be organised. Having begun on this understanding, the apostles cleaved to the original idea. The only point at which discretion could be granted to the Christian communities of different cities or countries was the circumstantial arrangement of the parts of worship. A certain divergence of view here was inevitable; and the Churches were to adopt and apply the great principle of doing everything "in decency and order." The arrangements for worship were to be such as to satisfy the great law of Christian love and to preserve that unity of action which befitted the life of the Christian society.[1]

It is very evident, however, that the dignified simplicity at which the apostles aimed was not long suffered to continue. It began to be infringed under the rule of their immediate successors. At that time a great multitude of converts flocked into the Church. Very many of these were Jews who not unnaturally clung to the ceremonial observances they had so long practised, especially to such as were susceptible of a Christian interpretation. Still more were converts from paganism, who had also been accustomed to certain rites and could not be persuaded to abandon at once everything in the shape of outward ceremony that Christianity did not require. Under the impression that they had a certain discretionary power in the way of

[1] 1 Cor. xiv.

adopting forms of Christian worship to suit the needs and tastes of such large accessions to the Church, the presbyters of the leading communities, or bishops, as they soon began to be called, permitted the introduction of certain rites which were speedily regarded not as mere arrangements for the conduct of worship, but essential elements or parts of it. Once the process of innovation was commenced, it was too congenial to human nature to be interrupted. The rulers of the Church seemed almost to vie with one another in the introduction of ceremonies that seemed fitted to impress the minds of the multitudes that then joined the ranks of the Church ; and since their reputation for zeal in such matters was at stake, the observance of them was all the more rigorously insisted on.

The result was that within the first four or five centuries of the Christian Church the germs of nearly all the innovations of which her worship is capable had been already sown in the mind or practice of the people. When the Church of Rome became the centre of Western Christendom, it was not to be expected that she should take any step to prevent these germs from coming to fruition. Too ignorant in many cases to discern the spirituality of the religion they professed, too much bent on self-aggrandisement to have any scruples respecting the limits of ecclesiastical power in the conduct of worship, too astute not to observe how much the minds of the rude tribes they had to convert were impressed with the splendour of outward ceremonial, her rulers and priests fastened upon every form of pagan ritual that seemed capable of being loaded with a Christian significance and gradually introduced them into the service of the Church.

At the era immediately before the Reformation, all these innovations on the primitive mode of worship were in full vogue. A careful observer of the Romanist ritual could not but be struck by the sharp contrast it presented with the simplicity of the apostolic service.

There had been, for example, a vast multiplication of the *times of worship*. The primitive Church was taught to be content with one day in seven as the period to be allotted to the public service of God according to His commandment : this was the first day of the week, the Lord's day. The Church of Rome instituted a huge number of religious holidays in the shape of fasts and feasts, to the observance of which the people were taught to attach greater importance than to that of the Christian Sabbath.

The very *parts of worship* had been increased in number. In addition to the Scriptures of the Old and New Testament, the apocryphal books had been introduced into the service of the Church. Instead of there being only two sacraments, namely Baptism and the Lord's Supper, there were now seven : the other five being, Confirmation, Matrimony, Extreme Unction, Orders, and Penance. Even the two primary sacraments were not left untouched. In connection with them, there had been introduced changes and additions in the symbolic elements used, the mode of administration, the functions assumed by the priests and the very garments in which they were arrayed, that tended to make these sacred ordinances as dissimilar as possible to the simple rites originally instituted by the Lord Jesus.

There had been what cannot be held to be other than substantive additions to the *objects of worship*. The primitive Church was called to worship the Three Persons of the Trinity. But the Church of Rome had placed alongside the Father, the Son, and the Holy Ghost, the Virgin Mary, the Apostles, Martyrs and Saints, along with relics, images, and pictures which were fitted to keep them ever before the worshipper's mind, and which themselves were permitted to be used in a fashion so closely akin to worship that no practical distinction could be drawn betwixt the veneration they received and that yielded to God.

Thus in truth, the whole *method of worship* had been changed. Originally it was instituted by the Lord as an exercise of the renewed spirit, a service fitted to call forth the noblest activity of mind, heart, conscience, and will. Now the word of God, the chief instrumentality in this devotion was thrust into the background ; and the worshippers' attention was fixed on a scenic display that could minister only to their superficial sensibilites and emotions.

How earnestly the Reformers set their faces against this system is manifest on almost every page of their writings. Luther indeed favoured the retention of some features of the Roman ritual. "Altars ornamented with candles and crucifixes as well as images were retained in the churches, not for adoration, but to excite and elevate devotion."[1] He was never fully prepared to cast off the last shreds of the old ceremonies to which he had been so long accustomed. The reason assigned was that thereby the breach betwixt the old and new religions was made less abrupt and an easier mode of transition left for those who were attracted by the evangelic preaching of the Reformers. This is an insufficient ground. Yet any danger involved in Luther's position was largely neutralised by his stern refusal to admit the slightest merit in the observance of any ceremony whatever. As he said in his *Table-Talk*, " It is of the devil himself that the Papists hold the final cause of instituting human traditions to be, that thereby God is truly worshipped and served, and that, therefore, they are necessary to salvation. 'Tis most monstrous : for though such human traditions were the best and most esteemed works of Christianity, which they are not, yet to say they are necessary to salvation or give God satisfaction for our sins, and so purchase grace, spoils all and makes the best of works to be utterly rejected of God."[2]

If Luther wavered, however, this cannot be said of Calvin. The great principle on which he fell back was the perfection or sufficiency of Scripture as the guide of the Church in every department of her life and service. As it is from the word of God she draws the

[1] Kurtz, *Church History*, vol. ii. p. 123 (Clark).
[2] *Table-Talk* (Bohn), p. 221.

materials of her teaching, so it is from this source she receives the directory of her worship. Here are to be found examples of the essential parts of worship and illustrations of the way in which they are to be rendered to God. Along with these are given special injunctions as to the time, manner and spirit in which worship is to be conducted. In addition to these precepts are many more general statements, whence the Church may draw the main principles that should govern her whole procedure in the matter of worship. With these facts before him, Calvin felt impelled to lay down the great law that the Church is not at liberty to introduce into her worship as an essential part of it, anything for which she cannot produce express warrant in the word of God.[1] It is not enough for the Church to show that what she holds to be a necessary feature of her service is not forbidden in the Scriptures: it must be such as is directly or by implication fully supported there. Such utterances as these are true for the New Covenant as for the Old: "What thing soever I command you, that shall ye observe to do: thou shalt not add thereto nor diminish from it";[2] "Add thou not unto His words, lest He reprove thee."[3]

Taking up this position, the Swiss Reformer was able to urge some very strong and pointed objections against the Romish system of innovations.

1. For did not the claim of power to institute such ceremonies on the part of the Church really undermine the supreme authority of Christ? It is not denied on either side that Christ is "the Head of the Church which is His Body," and is entitled to exercise the highest dominion there. But this royal prerogative extends also to the way in which the Church is to offer to God the worship that is due to His name. Every precept or example or principle given in the word of God regarding this duty comes from the Lord and bears the stamp of His authority. When He gave to the apostles their final commission, it was the gospel as He had taught it that they were to preach, and baptism as He had sanctioned it that they were to administer. But He also charged them to teach their disciples to observe all things whatsoever He had commanded them.[4] Only on this condition could His presence go with them. When therefore those who profess to be successors of the apostles lay upon the people ordinances which the Lord did not enjoin, they at once forfeit this blessing and incur His displeasure. Speaking to Israel by Isaiah, Jehovah said: "Forasmuch as this people draw nigh unto Me and with their mouth and with their lips do honour Me, but have removed their heart far from Me and their fear of Me is a commandment of men which hath been taught them: therefore the wisdom of their wise men shall perish and the understanding of their prudent men shall be hid."[5] Addressing the same class in His own day, the Lord Jesus appropriated and applied the prophet's words: "In vain do they worship Me, teaching

[1] *Institutes*, bk. IV. ch. x. vol. ii. p. 413 (Clark).   [2] Deut. xii. 32.
[3] Prov. xxx. 6.   [4] Matt. xxviii. 20.   [5] Isa. xxix. 13, 14.

as their doctrines the precepts of men."[1] So far as the worship of the Church is dictated or inspired by men, it is no true worship at all.

2. Again, did not the introduction of new ceremonies on the ground of mere ecclesiastical authority tend to mar the spirituality of worship? This is an interest for which the Church of the New Covenant is bound to care. Spirituality is set forth in the teaching of Christ and His apostles as one of her chief characteristics. Speaking of the new era He was to usher in, the Lord said that the worship of God was to be essentially a worship of the spirit and the understanding. The Church in Israel had a complete system of rites and ceremonies, the direct aim of which was to symbolise and teach spiritual truths. But after Christ came to fulfil these types and reveal the Father in the fulness of His grace and truth, such a system was no longer required. The material and symbolic is to give place to the spiritual. "The hour cometh and now is, when the true worshippers shall worship the Father in spirit and in truth : for such doth the Father seek to be His worshippers. God is spirit, and they that worship Him must worship in spirit and truth."[2] It was on this principle that the Gentiles on being received into the Christian Church were set free from the ordinances of the Mosaic law. "Now therefore," said Peter at the Council of Jerusalem, "why tempt ye God that ye should put a yoke upon the neck of the disciples which neither our fathers nor we were able to bear?"[3] When certain Judaisers tried to bring the Galatian Christians under the observance of old rites, Paul withstood them to the uttermost : "With freedom did Christ set us free : stand fast therefore and be not entangled in a yoke of bondage."[4] On this same principle, the Christian Church is to resist the introduction of new rites still, however much they may seem adapted to her present position. As an able teacher of ecclesiastical polity has said, "If the typology of a former Church, *divinely* appointed, is forbidden to be used as inconsistent with the spiritual nature of worship now, shall we say that a *human* typology of ecclesiastical rites, and ceremonies, mystical and significant, is to be accounted as lawfully standing in their place?"[5]

3. An equally strong objection against the introduction and use of new rites was that they tended to obscure and distort the evangelic method of salvation. The apostles taught that men are saved by grace through faith and that not of themselves : "it is the gift of God."[6] This is a law that cannot be changed. But all experience goes to show that, wherever men are taught to regard rites which they can perform themselves as essential parts of worship, they are tempted to think that the observance of them will help to set them right with God and constitute a ground of confidence before Him. Luther set his face against this tendency with all the energy of which he was capable. "As for ceremonies," he said, "they might go whither

---

[1] Matt. xv. 9.   [2] John iv. 23, 24.   [3] Acts xv. 10.   [4] Gal. v. 1.
[5] Bannerman, *The Church of Christ*, vol. ii. p. 374.   [6] Eph. ii. 8.

they would, for they are the touch-powder, giving occasion to superstition; people thinking that they are necessary to salvation and that their being omitted is sin."[1] All that history teaches us of human nature goes to support the conclusion that ritualism, in the full sense of the word, invariably tends to the depreciation of the gospel of the grace of God. It affords men materials of which they imagine they can boast: and this is a sentiment fatal to the faith by which alone a soul can be saved.

4. In this way the use of needless rites cannot but prove a hindrance to the religious life. By occupying the attention so much, they obscure the divine objects of worship. They prevent ready apprehension of the truth. They tend to make the service of God a weariness to the flesh. In connection especially with the observance of feasts and fasts they often interfere with the discharge of family, social and civil duties. As making the people continually dependent on ministrations of the clergy for which fees are exacted, they encourage priestly greed and the desire for ecclesiastical preferment and aggrandisement.

5. Hence the last and worst result of ritualism and therefore the strongest objection to it, is that it leads to tyranny on the part of the ecclesiastical authorities that sanction it. For what is the position in which those who wish to adhere to the primitive forms of the apostolic worship are placed? Where the rites or ceremonies introduced are made constituent elements of the service, they have no alternative but either to conform to the authorised practice or else be refused communion. In the case of those who are "weak" or have no great strength of conviction, this draws them into the acknowledgment of what they feel to be wrong. In the case of others who are strongly conscientious, there remains only the duty of refusal and suffering. History has often presented the amazing spectacle of the expulsion from the Church of men who were eminent for piety, while multitudes remained in the full enjoyment of ordinances whose life was in many respects in flagrant inconsistency with the law of Christ.

In the face of arguments like these, the pleas urged by Romanists at the Reformation and since are seen to be of no account.

It is vain, for example, to say that the rites they have introduced were derived by tradition from the apostles. For the apostles could not contradict the whole strain of the teaching handed down in their authentic writings: and this is directly opposed to any rites beyond those appointed by the Master. Besides, the historical research of modern times has enabled us to fix the precise date at which many of these ceremonies were first mentioned and introduced, long after the apostolic age.

Equally futile is it to contend that, since the Church has the fulness of the Spirit, these ceremonies were introduced under His guidance and have His authority. The Spirit of God has given a

[1] *Table-Talk, ut sup.* p. 222.

definite and final revelation of His will in the New Testament. He cannot guide into practices inconsistent with its teaching.

Nor is it a valid ground for supporting such practices that they are a help to the ignorant. The word of the truth of the gospel is so simple that a child can understand its meaning. In Baptism and the Lord's Supper, Jesus instituted two symbolic ordinances which give any additional help that may be required in the way of outward representation. Beyond these rites, no further symbol is required. The whole tendency of human additions to them is to obscure truth otherwise evident in its own light.

On the same principle, we are entitled to repel the plea that such rites are fitted to inspire men with humility. That seems to have been the very argument used by the Judaising party in the days of the apostles. Paul meets it by saying that the use of such ordinances is a retrograde movement. It is a return to a kind of discipline that may have been suitable enough in the first stages of redemption, but is now utterly out of place.[1] He admits that there may be a show of wisdom and humility in such observances.[2] But they are really "will-worship," which contributes no honour to God or man and ends only in satisfying the carnal heart.

Of the further plea that the use of such rites is justified by the obedience due to ecclesiastical superiors, it need only be said that it is quite of a piece with the despotic spirit in which they originated and inconsistent with the position of men who are not to be lords over God's heritage, but only ensamples of the flock.

When we survey the history of the Church, we find that it is chiefly amongst the Free Churches of Britain and America that Calvin's principles have been fully put into force. The position laid down in the Westminster Confession is indicated in the chapter on "Christian Liberty." "God alone is lord of the conscience and hath left it free from the doctrines and commandments of men which are in anything contrary to His word or beside it, in matters of faith and worship. So that to believe such doctrines or to obey such commandments out of conscience is to betray true liberty of conscience : and the requiring of an implicit faith and an absolute and blind obedience, is to destroy liberty of conscience, and reason also."[3] This is just the view of Calvin stated in a form adapted to modern controversy. No one who studies it in connection with other statements of the Confession can justly call it either narrow or sectarian. Ample room is left, for example, for the introduction of anything that may be necessary on the ground of "decency and order." Nothing is to be instituted as a part of worship that has not the sanction of the word of God.[4] "Nevertheless," says the Confession in another chapter, "there are some circumstances concerning the worship of God, and government of the Church, common to human actions and societies, which are to be ordered by the light of nature and Christian prudence according to the general rules of the word, which are always to be

[1] Gal. iv. 9.   [2] Col. ii. 23.   [3] Ch. xx. § 2.

observed."[1] Within this narrower sphere, the Church has power to legislate. As George Gillespie pointed out, when a proposed practice is "first, only a circumstance of divine worship and no substantial part of it—no sacred, significant and efficacious ceremony"; and second, "where it is such as is not determined by Scripture"; and third, where it is such as she is "able to give a sufficient reason and warrant"[2] for the appointment of it, the Church is at perfect liberty to prescribe laws for the people. In the face of such freedom, the charge of laying stress on minute points of worship is unworthy of consideration. The Church has a rule she is bound to adhere to. The objection of narrowness falls only on those who would urge her to depart from it for the sake of petty innovations on the essential parts of worship which she is not at liberty to entertain.

The Anglican Church, on the other hand, has reverted more to the view originally favoured by Luther, and thus stands midway betwixt the Calvinistic and Romanist positions. A modern Lutheran historian has said: "Catholic worship appeals only to the imagination and feelings; the worship of the Reformed Church satisfies merely the understanding; but Lutheran worship combining both these elements appeals to the heart. The first sensualises everything, the second spiritualises everything, while in the last all is harmonised in a well-balanced vital manner."[3] This also seems to be the Anglican ideal. Retaining the hierarchy, the Church of England aimed at retaining not a few of the Romish ceremonies, in form at least, if not in power. The law she has laid down for her guidance is that, "The Church hath power to decree rites or ceremonies: And yet it is not lawful for the Church to ordain anything that is contrary to God's word written."[4] This, it is to be observed, is something different from the direct sanction of God's word. This rule still leaves the Church of England free to introduce ceremonies like the wearing of white vestments, the consecration of buildings, the eastward position in prayer, kneeling at the reception of the Supper, and the sign of the cross in baptism, which, in the words of the Prayer-Book, she holds to be "such as be apt to stir up the dull mind of man to the remembrance of his duty to God by some notable and special signification whereby he might be edified."

It was against this position that, adopting the whole range of arguments we have already laid down, the Puritan party of the Church of England contended so earnestly. The course of the conflict forms one of the saddest pages of her history. When the ecclesiastical authorities enforced the observance of the unscriptural rites and ceremonies they had adopted, two thousand of the flower of the Anglican ministers left their benefices and seceded from their communion. No intelligent observer of the life and work of the Anglican Church will refuse to admit that she is now reaping the fruit of this

[1] Ch. i. 6.
[2] Gillespie, *English Popish Ceremonies*, pt. iii. ch. vii. pp. 5-7.
[3] Kurtz, *ut sup.* p. 122.   [4] Art. XX.

bygone tyranny. One of the most honoured amongst her dignitaries does not hesitate to say that if the ritualistic movement within her pale goes on at the present rate, the great majority of the Churches will speedily be Romanist in everything but the name.[1]

A characteristic illustration of the Romanising tendency in the Anglican Church is seen in the widely prevalent custom of praying for the believing dead.[2] That such a practice should be maintained in the Church of Rome, especially in connection with the celebration of the Mass, is not to be wondered at.[3] Like so many other Romish customs, it was early imported from paganism; and as it helped to originate the idea of a Purgatory, so is it now regarded as a direct outgrowth of that doctrine. With the overthrow of this superstition accordingly, it too must fall. For even the Council of Trent says nothing more in its support than that it is "agreeable to tradition."[4] But it is marvellous that in any Church which expressly rejects the idea of a Purgatory, this practice should be welcomed and clung to. As the Jesuit professor we have already quoted remarks, "it is inexplicable except on some view equivalent to that held by Catholics."[5] To say that such prayers for the dead are only a part of intercession for the consummation of God's kingdom is to give a disingenuous description of their real nature. If praying for the dead that have died in faith has any meaning at all, it must imply that petitions are offered up for their deliverance from sin and suffering. No such duty, however, is either suggested or inculcated in Scripture. It is true that Paul prayed for Onesiphorus that he might find "mercy of the Lord in that day."[6] But though he is mentioned apart from his family, it is by no means certain that Onesiphorus was dead at the time; and even if he had been, such an utterance is here used only as a pious ejaculation, a passing expression of intense affection for a fellow-disciple. The whole tendency of anything like deliberate intercession for the dead is to strip the present life and its crisis in death of the overmastering solemnity everywhere attached to them in the word of God. We pray for our friends on earth because they are with us and we can give effect to our intercession in sympathy and help. For the dead we may not pray, because their time of probation is past: they are outside the sphere of our present existence and in the hands of God alone. It was under the influence of these convictions that praying for the dead was rejected by all the Reformers. For Protestants to tamper with the practice is to play with fire.

[1] Dean Farrar. [2] Littledale, *Prayers for the Dead*, p. 2.
[3] Shipley, *Purgatory: Tracts for the Times*, pp. 29-46.
[4] Sess. XXII. ch. xxii. Sess. XXV. *On Purgatory.*
[5] Hunter, *Outlines of Dog. Theol.* iii. p. 443. [6] 2 Tim. i. 18.

CHAPTER IV

THE SACRAMENTS OF THE CHURCH—THEIR NATURE AND NUMBER

A VERY prominent feature in the worship of the Christian Church is the administration of the sacraments. As this duty has always been held to belong to the ministry, it is at this stage that these ordinances fall to be considered. Herein the method of Protestantism is seen to differ from that of Romanism. Believing as they did that the sacraments are the main channel by which righteousness is imparted to the sinner, the theologians of the Council of Trent discussed them immediately after the topic of justification. "For the completion of the salutary doctrine on justification, it hath seemed suitable to treat of the most holy sacraments of the Church, through which all true justice either begins or being begun is increased or being lost is repaired."[1] By pursuing this order, they seemed to gain a certain advantage. The sacraments present the point at which the work of the Church comes into vital contact with the spiritual life. If men can be persuaded to take the Romanist view of these ordinances, it is inevitable that they should be predisposed to accept their view also of the ministry and the Church. Hence it is that Möhler, for example, following the Tridentine order, discusses the sacraments before either the Church or the ministry.

With Protestant theologians, on the other hand, the sacraments can be discussed rightly only after an independent consideration of these two topics. Holding that Scripture presents ample materials for settling the real nature of the Christian society and the relations and functions of those who are to conduct its worship, Protestantism treats of these topics first, and then proceeds to consider the sacraments in the light of the special teaching of Scripture about them. As the object of this exposition is to exhibit the distinctive principles of Protestantism, we feel bound to follow this order.

The Romish doctrine of the sacraments finds its first expression in the view of what it is that really constitutes a sacrament. The Council of Trent did not venture on any formal statement on this point, but the compilers of its Catechism did not feel themselves under the same constraint and have given what practically amounts to a definition. This is seen to be carefully adjusted, so as to meet

[1] Sess. VII. Proëm.

the views which have been gradually developed in the Church up to the time of the Reformation. Using very general terms, Augustine had said that "a sacrament is a sign of a sacred thing." Most of the scholastic theologians expounded this by saying that it is "a visible sign of an invisible grace instituted for our justification."[1] The Tridentine Catechism sets its seal to this description by remarking that "a sacrament is clearly to be numbered amongst those things that have been instituted as signs; for it makes known to us by a certain appearance and resemblance that which God by His invisible power accomplishes in our souls."[2] Finally, it adds that to explain more fully the nature of a sacrament, the pastor must teach that "it is a thing subject to the senses, and possessing by the divine institution the power at once of signifying and accomplishing sanctity and righteousness."[3]

When we proceed to examine the form of the sacraments, we are struck at the outset by the great stress laid on the material elements in them. Amongst the reasons assigned for their institution by the Tridentine Catechism, "the first is the weakness of the human mind: for we see it so constituted by nature, that no one can aspire to matters of mental and intellectual knowledge, unless through the medium of things that are perceived by some sense."[4] But it is not held sufficient to say that they are used because they are in themselves fitted to suggest the spiritual truths they are made to teach. The employment of the symbolic elements of the sacraments is indispensable to the whole nature of man as at present constituted; and as sanctified and used by the Church, they have a direct bearing on his restoration to a higher life. For it is added: "To the end therefore that we might more easily understand the hidden effects of His divine power, the Sovereign Creator of the universe has most wisely and of His tender kindness towards us, ordained that that same power be manifested to us through the intervention of certain sensible signs."[5] Later on it is even said that "the sacraments subdue and repress the pride of the human heart, and exercise us in humility from the fact that in them we are obliged to subject ourselves to sensible elements in obedience to God from whom we had before impiously revolted, to serve the elements of the world."[6]

These utterances of the Catechism are substantially reproduced in the teaching of modern Romanist theologians. Möhler, for example, says that, "man as a being belonging himself also in part to the world of sense, needs a type drawn from the same region to become conscious of and hold fast that which passes in his supersensual part":[7] and further, that, "symbolical signs bring the higher world near to sense and at the same time communicate from this world the capacity for receiving its influence."[8]

In conceptions like these a manifest basis is laid for the large

---

[1] Cat. pt. ii. ch. i. q. 3.   [2] *Ut sup.* q. 5.   [3] Q. 8.
[4] Q. 9.   [5] *Ut sup.*   [6] *Ut sup.*
[7] *Symbolik*, s. 254.   [8] *Ut sup.* s. 266.

number of sacraments which the Church of Rome claims to enjoy. The Catechism acknowledges the principle that, "the greater the number of aids unto salvation and a life of bliss which the people shall understand to have been provided by the divine goodness, the greater must be the piety with which they direct all the powers of their souls to praise and proclaim the singular beneficence of God toward us."[1] Hence it adds that "the sacraments of the Catholic Church are seven as is proved from Scripture, handed down to us by the tradition of the Fathers and testified by the authority of Councils." The first canon of the Council's decree says : "If any one saith that the sacraments of the New Law were not all instituted by Jesus Christ our Lord ; or that they are more or less than seven, to wit, Baptism, Confirmation, the Eucharist, Penance, Extreme Unction, Orders and Matrimony ; or even that any of these seven is not truly and properly a sacrament : let him," etc.[2]

The chief Biblical evidence adduced in behalf of the number of sacraments claimed by Rome is neither more nor less than the prevalence of the number "seven" in the Scriptures. Seven is a sacred number : it is the symbol of symmetry or perfection. There are seven days in the week : every seventh year was a Sabbath : every seven times seventh year was a jubilee : there are seven golden candlesticks, seven stars in Christ's right hand and seven spirits before the throne. Hence it is said to be fitting that there should be seven sacraments.

The evidence from tradition is simply to the effect that for several centuries before the Reformation, the schoolmen had agreed that there were to be seven sacraments. In earlier centuries, there had been much difference of opinion as to the precise number. Some fixed them at three, others at six, others at twelve. Peter Lombard, a schoolman of the twelfth century, hit upon the number seven ; and, no special objection to this definition having been raised in the succeeding Councils of Lyons and Florence, the Fathers of Trent formally decreed in the terms already quoted that this number should be retained.[3]

One feature of this number of seven that seemed to commend it to the mediæval theologians, was the way it represented the sacraments as falling in with the course of human life. Thomas Aquinas was one of the first to exhibit this analogy. Man is born : he needs to be strengthened : he requires nourishment : when he falls into sickness, he must be restored : he has to provide for the continued existence of his species : he must live in the recognition of legitimate authority : when life comes to an end in this world, he has to be specially prepared for that which is to come. The seven sacraments of the Church correspond to all these stages on their spiritual side. In Baptism man is born again : in Confirmation, he receives strength for the conflict with sin : in the Holy Supper, he is

[1] Q. 14. [2] Sess. VII. i.
[3] Herzog, *Real-Encyclopædie*, art. "Sakrament," vol. xiii. s. 241.

supplied with spiritual nourishment : in Penance he is restored and healed : in Matrimony he is united in a heavenly alliance with one of his fellow-creatures for the propagation of the race : in Orders, he is supplied with an infallible spiritual ruler and guide : in Extreme Unction, he receives a parting preparation for entering into the unseen world at death.[1]

By these seven ordinances, the Church thus claims to meet all man's deepest needs. This is the view adopted by the Catechism of Trent and elaborated by modern apologists. Möhler uses it as apparently the strongest argument for the number of the sacraments with which he is acquainted. "On the other hand it becomes evident how the Catholic who does not, for example, contemplate the believer from the onesided point of view of a man who for Christ's sake has obtained remission of sins, but regards him as a living believer redeemed from sin and in spirit and sense consecrated to God, needs a circle of sacraments, which so embraces all the momentous crises of his life that in everyone of them this mode of conceiving his whole earthly pilgrimage is constantly presented, which expresses also the higher relation of every separate stage of his career to the redemption that is in Christ, and at the same time secures and really imparts the divine power that is requisite for its beginning and progress."[2]

It is only in accordance with the fundamental ideas of the whole system that the sacraments should be held to operate with unvarying certitude in the bestowal of the blessings they signify. The Council of Trent pronounces sentence against anyone who says "that the sacraments of the New Law do not contain the grace which they signify, or that they do not confer that grace on those who do not place an obstacle thereunto":[3] so also on any one who says "that by the said sacraments of the New Law, grace is not conferred through the act performed, but that faith alone in the divine promise suffices for the obtaining of grace."[4] The Roman Catechism interprets this utterance to mean that, "unless the recipients themselves wish to defraud themselves of so great a good and to resist the Holy Ghost, nothing can prevent their receiving (through the sacraments) the fruit of grace."[5] Möhler emphasises this doctrine by asserting that, "the religious energies of the human soul are set in a new motion by the sacrament, inasmuch as its divine contents fertilise the soul of man, quicken it anew, draw it into the deepest fellowship with God and operate in all men who show themselves capable of receiving its blessing, or, as the Council expresses its view, do not place any hindrance in the way."[6]

High Church Anglicanism takes up essentially the same position. Newman, even while still in the Church of England, said : "The two sacraments are the primary instruments of justification, faith is the secondary, subordinate, or representative instrument. . . . Faith,

[1] *Summa*, pt. iii. q. 65.   [2] *Symbolik*, s. 263.   [3] Canon 6.
[4] Canon 8.   [5] Pt. ii. ch. i. q. 19.   [6] *Symbolik*, s. 256.

then, being the appointed representative of Baptism derives its authority and virtue from that which it represents. . . . Baptism is the primary instrument and causes faith to be what it is and otherwise is not."[1]

To these statements only one proviso has to be attached. The priest administering the sacrament must have a sincere "intention" of actually making it valid. The Council gives prominence to this condition by inveighing against any one who says "that in ministers when they effect and confer the sacraments, there is not required the intention at least of doing what the Church does."[2] If he observes all the essentials of the sacrament itself, his own moral condition does not affect its validity.

Last of all, the reception of these sacraments by the members of the Church is as a rule absolutely indispensable. The Church of Rome does not indeed say that they are all equally necessary or all necessary for salvation. But the decrees and canons of Trent as well as the Catechism set it beyond doubt that each is necessary for attaining the special grace associated with it. Baptism, for example, is indispensable for salvation : so also is Penance for the forgiveness of post-baptismal sins. It is true that, chiefly to avoid the terrible issues of this principle, certain exceptions are made in favour of those who simply desire to partake of the sacraments without being able actually to partake ; and certain restrictions are relaxed as to the persons by whom they are to be administered. But of the general principle of this necessity, there can be no modification. The necessity is one of means for obtaining the grace and is thus also based on divine right.

Now that in these views there is much which is fitted to attract and fascinate the mind, no one will doubt. It is quite conceivable that those who have a spiritual life nourished on higher truths might use these sacraments without immediate conscious or visible deterioration, though even in such the sense of freedom must inevitably suffer. Yet the influence of this circle of rites on the Christian life as a whole is evidently hurtful. For face to face with the harvest it yielded, the noblest spirits of the Church at the Reformation turned to the primitive use of the sacraments with a feeling of unspeakable relief. Luther, indeed, did not at once abjure the whole Romish sacramental system. Some of the old prejudices adhered to him to the last. He contented himself with throwing off the outer yoke and restoring Baptism and the Lord's Supper to their rightful position. But the Reformed Churches were not content with any such half measures. Nothing would satisfy Calvin and his followers but to take the only two sacraments instituted by Christ and assign to them no higher position or influence than could be justified by the teaching of Scripture. The keen and prolonged discussion of this topic into which the Protestant theologians were drawn gave rise to very careful statements in the Confessions of the Reformed Churches ;

[1] *Lectures on Justification*, pop. ed. pp. 226, 227.   [2] Canon 11.

and these leave us in no doubt of the way in which they regard the tenets of Rome.

The first point of difference turns on the explanation given of what constitutes a sacrament. The error of the Romanists lies in making their definition too general. It is wide enough to include every symbol that has been at any time used in the worship of God. The only reasonable method of arriving at the truth is to fall back on the two ordinances which all branches of the Christian Church agree in regarding as veritable sacraments, namely, Baptism and the Lord's Supper, and to gather up what seem to be their essential features. Adopting this principle, the Westminster Assembly gave this simple, comprehensive definition: "A sacrament is an holy ordinance instituted by Christ, wherein by sensible signs Christ and the benefits of the New Covenant are represented, sealed, and applied to believers."[1] From this statement, the marks of a true sacrament may be easily deduced. In the first place, it must have been instituted by the Lord Jesus Himself, in the course of His earthly ministry and for the service of the Christian life. In every true sacrament also, use is made of a certain material element chosen by the Lord on account of its fitness to suggest certain truths or facts: in the case of Baptism, water; in the Lord's Supper, bread and wine. The element adopted is to be used in the manner indicated by Christ and in connection with the mode He employed to explain its meaning. The whole ordinance thus instituted is not a mere symbol of spiritual truth, nor even a mere badge of the Christian profession, but becomes at once a channel by which the Lord dispenses His grace to the soul and an abiding seal to the disciples of vital union and communion with Him.[2]

In view of this description, it is a manifest error to attach such value to the material elements employed as the Church of Rome does. It is true that human nature is made up of body as well as soul and spirit; and it is on this ground that God has condescended at all to introduce any outward forms or elements into our religious service. But in this method no humiliation is necessarily implied. Since God has so constituted us that we are accessible to the ideas suggested by material things around us, it is only a gracious accommodation to the present state of human nature, that, in at least two of the ordinances of the Christian Church, physical elements should be employed. From the Christward bent that all nature has received, it is inevitable that certain material elements should become appropriate symbols of the life of His kingdom. But the mere use of these things in this connection has no saving power. It is the word of the Lord that wields the influence. Without that word which in the Spirit's hands is the seed of life, the symbol is dead. It is the word of Christ that is the vital force of the sacraments.

When these principles are grasped, it becomes comparatively

[1] Sh. Cat. q. 92.   [2] Cf. Ch. of Eng., Art. xxv.

easy to dispose of the other points of difference betwixt the Romanist and Protestant doctrines.

This is the case with *the number* of the sacraments. If we are not to have an unlimited number, we must take the criteria supplied by the two universally accepted sacraments of Baptism and the Lord's Supper. Tested by these, the five ordinances added by the Church of Rome are seen to be not worthy of the name. Confirmation, for example, cannot be shown to have been instituted by Christ, and least of all, as a sensible sign of His own grace. This is true also of Penance, Matrimony, Orders and Extreme Unction. The Lord called on men to repent and the apostles urged their followers to confess their sins one to another. But, as has been shown, this is a duty totally different in spirit, motive and method from auricular confession of sins to a priest authorised by the Church to act as a judge. Matrimony was instituted by God Himself before ever sin stained the world. Christ simply gave it His benediction. Though the Apostle Paul compares the union betwixt Christ and the Church to that which exists between husband and wife, he does not call matrimony itself a sacrament, but only declares that the spiritual analogy he has suggested is a great mystery: that is, a special truth, which fruitful as it is of rich spiritual ideas could have been made known only in the days of the new covenant. A form of Orders or a certain outward method of conferring ordination was also practised by the apostles. But the laying on of hands cannot be regarded as "a sensible sign" in the same meaning as the water of Baptism or the bread and wine of the Supper. The apostles also sanctioned the anointing of the sick with oil in connection with the exercise of the miraculous gift of healing. But there is no indication that they ever intended this form to be retained and used after miraculous gifts had been withdrawn; and in any case it is a very different thing from providing a safe passport for the unseen world. Thus the additional five so-called sacraments of Rome are shown to be only forms of invention, which even as such the Council of Trent had no warrant for adding to the simple and all-sufficient, because divinely-instituted ritual of the Christian sacramental service.

The Romanist doctrine on the operation of the sacraments is thus also seen to be a manifest error. The sacraments do not contain the grace which they signify, nor do they impart that grace by the mere act of their reception. As we have already partly seen and shall show yet more distinctly, when we study Baptism and the Lord's Supper in detail, faith is everywhere in the Scriptures set down as the act of the soul on which its salvation turns; and it is only as faith is maintained and the power of the indwelling Spirit thereby received, that a sacrament can impart any benefit. The Westminster Catechism simply reproduces the teaching of the Reformed Churches, when it says: "The sacraments become effectual means of salvation, not from any virtue in them or in him that doth administer them, but only by the blessing of Christ and the working of His Spirit in them that by faith receive them."[1] On this point Luther unfortunately diverged to some extent from the Reformed teaching. Led astray by attaching a onesided meaning to the Lord's statement on the agency at work in the new birth, he supposed that the water of baptism was absolutely essential to regeneration, and that it must have, though only through the word, a certain virtue for the communication of blessing. He extended this principle to the Lord's Supper. Herein, we believe, Luther erred. It is only through the Spirit that even the word can quicken and bless the soul. So must it be with the sacraments, which, as an eminent Scottish theologian said, do not present anything different from what we have in the word, but simply offer it to us through a different and in some respects more impressive channel.[2] The Lutheran view, however, is largely neutralised by the feature in it, that it invariably holds the absolute necessity of faith on the part of those who would enjoy the blessing of the sacraments.

As to the necessity of the sacraments, since they held that the soul resting by faith on the Son of God offered in the gospel and through Him on the Father, could receive through the Spirit all the blessings of salvation, the Reformed Churches could not admit that the sacraments were absolutely necessary as means of salvation, either in its beginning or its progress. But this view did not prevent their acknowledging the obligation to use the sacraments that lay on all believers. They contended, and on their principles rightly, that the necessity of receiving the sacraments was not that of means but only of precept.

[1] Q. 91.   [2] Robert Bruce, *Sermons*, pp. 49, 50 (Wodrow edition).

CHAPTER V

THE SACRAMENTS—BAPTISM

IN view of the ideas that have moulded the Romish doctrine of the sacraments, it does not surprise us to find the first sacrament of Baptism assuming the form it now has in the worship of the Church. For while water is the "matter" or element used and sprinkling with it the central action, the Roman Church has added ceremonies of her own, alike before the administration of the rite, at the font itself and after baptism is performed. In the first place, the water to be used in baptism is to be specially prepared, the baptismal font being consecrated and the oil of mystic unction added. Then, waiting those to be baptized at the door of the church, the priest breathes three times in their face, applies salt to the mouth, makes the sign of the cross on the forehead, eyes, breast, shoulders and ears, and finally anoints the nostrils and ears with spittle. After the performance of these ceremonies, the persons to be baptized are brought to the baptismal font, and after being called on to renounce Satan are sprinkled with the water. The baptism being thus performed, the priest anoints the crown of their head with chrism, puts on a white garment and sets a lighted candle in the hand. So the baptism is completed.[1]

The changes which the Church claims to effect by baptism have been already alluded to. The Catechism of Trent mentions them in detail. The faithful are to be taught in the first place that by this sacrament, sin is remitted and pardoned, whether it be original or actual and however great may be its heinousness. Concupiscence does indeed remain; but, as the Council taught, in those that are baptized, it has not the nature of sin. Nor is it only sin in its guilt that is remitted: all the punishments due to sins and crimes are cancelled, even the punishments due to original sin after the course of this life is ended. Moreover the soul of the baptized person is replenished with grace which, besides remission of sins is held to include "a divine quality inherent in the soul, and, as it were a certain splendour and light that effaces all the stains of our souls and renders the souls themselves brighter and more beautiful." Hence the soul has infused into it all the virtues that flow from the grace of

[1] Cat. pt. ii. ch. ii. q. 59-74.

God. It is also incorporated with Christ and with the whole Church which is His body. Thereby it receives not only a special character or seal that can never be erased, but also all the gifts that are needed for Christian service in the world.

It is in the light of these blessings communicated by baptism that the rites added by the Church acquire their meaning.[1] For the most part, they set forth certain other specific results that Baptism secures. The breathing in the face, for example, denotes the expulsion of the devil and the restoration of the new life. The sign of the cross on eyes and ears sets forth the dedication of the physical energies to God's service, the spittle on the nostrils and ears the opening of man's faculties for the influence of the heavenly kingdom, the anointing of the head the consecration of the life, the white garment the beauty of the holiness imparted and the burning light in the hand the new light of life kindled in the soul.

All of these blessings the Church in baptism pledges herself to impart. For, as administered by the Church, baptism is said to operate with all the certitude of a natural law. What the Council of Trent in its decree affirmed of all the sacraments is specially true of Baptism : it confers grace "through the act performed." Let the priest or others who in an emergency may be permitted to act in his behalf, only have the sincere intention of making the sacrament and use the requisite element and proper form of words, and, as surely as the rite is completed, all the blessing attached to it is inevitably conferred.

Hence also the reception of baptism is regarded as absolutely indispensable to salvation. The Council expressly anathematises any one who says "that baptism is free, that is, is not necessary unto salvation."[2] According to the Catechism, "the Law of Baptism is presented by our Lord to all, insomuch that they, unless they be regenerated unto God through the grace of baptism, whether their parents be Christian or infidel, are born to eternal misery and perdition."[3]

The way in which the Reformed Churches regard this doctrine has been indicated in a preceding chapter on the Method of Christianity. But in view of the momentous part Baptism plays in the Romanist system, the grounds on which they so emphatically dissent from such tenets, may be more completely summarised.

The first point in this delineation to which the Protestant apologist adverts is the number of additional rites with which the Church of Rome has surrounded the primitive ordinance. There is no indication in the New Testament that the disciples of Christ used any other element in baptism than water or that they adopted any other ceremony than simple sprinkling with it. In so doing they had the sanction of the Lord : for when He was on the earth, they baptized under His eye : after He went to heaven, they maintained the original

---

[1] Cat. pt. ii. ch. ii. q. 41-53.
[2] Sess. VII. *On Baptism*, Canon 5.   [3] *Ut sup.* q. 30.

method. On principles already explained, this apostolic practice must be a rule for all time. Christ alone has the right to dictate in what way the worship of the Church is to be conducted. For men to add ceremonies which may be pleasing in their own eyes is not only to go in the face of the spirituality of the New Covenant but to invade the supreme authority of the Lord.

The next feature in the Romish doctrine against which the Protestant mind chiefly revolts is the great spiritual changes which Baptism is alleged to effect. This is a topic that has been discussed in every century since the Reformation and the Protestant position has become thoroughly definite. That there are certain statements in the New Testament which by their mere literal form seem to lend support to the view of Rome, is very manifest. No one need deny that in the apostolic writings, Baptism is associated with the principal blessings conferred by the gospel. It is connected, for example, with the forgiveness of sins : " Be baptized and wash away thy sins, calling on the name of the Lord"; [1] with regeneration : "He saved us through the laver of regeneration and the renewing of the Holy Ghost"; [2] with salvation : "He that believeth and is baptized shall be saved"; [3] with deliverance from sin and entrance on a new life : "We were buried with Him by baptism into death, that we should walk in newness of life"; [4] "Buried with Him in baptism, wherein also ye were raised together with Him." [5] But while all this is so, the Romish doctrine is not thereby established. It still remains to be shown that the connection betwixt Baptism and these blessings is either invariable or causal. Against this view the following strong considerations are to be adduced.

1. The blessings of the gospel said to be conferred by Baptism are still more distinctly and frequently associated with faith. Faith is the only thing in man himself that is asked as a condition of being saved : " Believe ye that I am able to do this?" [6] "Thy faith hath saved thee"; [7] " Through this man is preached unto you the forgiveness of sins and in Him all that believe are justified from all things"; [8] " Being justified by faith, let us have peace with God"; [9] " By grace are ye saved through faith." [10] No language could more clearly indicate that it is faith which, above all and in a sense true of nothing else in man, unites to Christ and receives the blessings of redemption.

2. This point is confirmed by the fact that in the order of spiritual life and experience faith is set before Baptism as being the act of the soul on which the outward observance turns. Disciples were first to be made, which could only be done by faith in the person and teaching of the divine Master, and *then* they were to be baptized in token of their faith. "The Pharisees heard that Jesus

---

[1] Acts xxii. 16.　　　[2] Tit. iii. 5.　　　[3] Mark xvi. 16.
[4] Rom. vi. 4.　　　[5] Col. ii. 12.　　　[6] Matt. ix. 28.
[7] Luke vii. 50.　　　[8] Acts xiii. 39.　　　[9] Rom. v. 1.
[10] Eph. ii. 8.

made and baptized more disciples than John, though Jesus baptized not but His disciples";[1] "Go ye into all the world and make disciples of all nations, baptizing them";[2] "He that believeth and is baptized shall be saved";[3] "Lydia, whose heart the Lord opened ... and when she was baptized and her household"; "Believe in the Lord Jesus and thou shalt be saved"; "He was baptized and all his ... believing in God with all his house."[4]

3. In those passages where there is an apparent emphasis on baptism instead of faith, a simple and sufficient explanation of the change can be given. This is the principle that a symbol may be put for that which it symbolizes. In the ratification of a legal transaction, it is customary for the parties concerned to attach their seal to the document in which its terms are set forth. The seal is but the symbol of their moral consent: but we still say that the deed has been sealed as frequently as agreed to or ratified. Baptism is the outward expression of faith; and it is only yielding to the same natural mental impulse to substitute the one for the other.

In this case, the transposition is less to be wondered at that for the vast majority of the members of the Churches to whom the apostles wrote, the acceptance of Baptism had been the accompaniment of a real divinely implanted faith. The work of evangelisation in their day was so owned by the Spirit of God that the apostles could assume that a very large proportion of those to whom they wrote were true believers. To speak of such therefore as having been baptized into Christ, was only to remind them in a very graphic way of the fact that they had sealed their faith by their baptism. The reference to the outward form might quicken their sense of responsibility for all that it implied in the way of consistency and courage. This consideration along with the others should be enough to exhibit the futility of appealing to the prominence given to Baptism in proof of the Romish doctrine.

These arguments should also be a sufficient refutation of the statement that Baptism confers salvation by the mere performance of the act itself. In the New Testament, this virtue is not even claimed for faith. Faith saves only as it is the instrumental grace which receives the salvation achieved by Christ and imparted by the Spirit. As the expression of faith and subsequent to it, Baptism can become a means of grace, not by any virtue in itself, or in him that administers it, but only by the blessing of Christ and the working of His Spirit in them that by faith receive it.

On the same ground, we object to the Romish doctrine of the necessity of Baptism. As a sacrament instituted by Christ, it is to be observed by all that believe in His name and profess to be His people. But this necessity is nowhere set forth as absolute: it is only ordained. It is the necessity of precept, not of means. It is true the Lord said: "He that believeth and is baptized shall be

---

[1] John iv. 1.
[2] Matt. xxviii. 19.
[3] Mark xvi. 16.
[4] Acts xvi. 14, 31, 33.

saved." But in the second member of the same statement where, if anywhere, the absolute necessity of Baptism would have been insisted on, it is not mentioned. The Lord simply adds : " He that believeth not shall be damned."

Hitherto we have discussed this difference betwixt Romanism and Protestantism in its bearing on adult baptism. This order is due to the fact that it is in connection with adult baptism that the ordinance is alluded to in the New Testament. Infant baptism is practised in the great majority of Protestant Churches as regularly as in the Church of Rome. But, except amongst the ritualists of the Greek and Anglican Churches, not one is found prepared to hold that Baptism is in itself the means of regeneration and salvation to those to whom the Church administers it in infancy by the hands of the minister ; or that this result is secured by the mere performance of the rite ; or that it is necessary to salvation. The Reformed Churches that practise pædo-baptism frankly acknowledge the indirect character of the evidence which is drawn from Scripture in its behalf. It is chiefly from the analogy presented by circumcision that the privilege of receiving the infants of Christian believers into the membership of the Church is claimed. Apart from tradition, the Church of Rome itself has no higher ground to urge. But if this be so, then it is impossible to uphold the doctrine of baptismal regeneration. For circumcision did nothing but seal a promise of God and confirm an obligation ; and on the ground of this very analogy, all that Baptism can be held to perform is, on the one hand, to seal to the infant baptized the divine promise that, if it turn to God in repentance and receive His Son in faith, He on His part will receive it as His own child ; and on the other, to lay on the infant a special obligation to realise its baptism in fact, and accept the Lord as its only Saviour.

Such a promise thus sealed is a great spiritual blessing. So also is the obligation which out of love for His people, and in the exercise of His sovereign grace, God lays upon their children. If rightly used, the mingled grace and duty may become a mighty lever for lifting the soul in due time into union with Christ. It is conceivable also that in response to the faith and prayer of the parents, God, if it seem good to Him, may impart the seed of the new life even by and in baptism. But this is in His own sovereign hands. All that Baptism does is to seal the promise and impose the obligation. For baptized infants, the great law still holds that " we are all the children of God by faith in Christ Jesus."[1]

[1] Gal. iii. 26.

CHAPTER VI

THE SACRAMENTS—THE LORD'S SUPPER—THE MASS

WHEN we turn to the Romish administration of the Lord's Supper, we find the same prominence given to outward form as in the case of Baptism. An altar is provided for the display of the elements of bread and wine. Besides the paten and the cup, there are a crucifix, a jar of water, a pot of incense, and a bell to indicate the great stages of the observance. The priests stand in full view of the congregation, clothed in vestments suggestive of different incidents of the crucifixion. Water is mingled with wine in the cup to set forth the fact that from the wounded side of Christ, there flowed forth blood and water. Then the rite itself is introduced and carried out in connection with a series of very varied actions and prayers by the priests.

There can be no doubt that the whole scene on the altar is arranged with a view to dramatic effect. It is intended to furnish an appropriate setting for the new divine Presence which is alleged to be infused into the elements. This is said to be effected by the priest's use of the words of consecration: "This is My body"; "This is My blood." For the Council of Trent put it in the front of their decree on the Supper, that, "in the august sacrament of the Holy Eucharist after the consecration of the bread and wine, our Lord Jesus Christ, true God and man, is truly, really and substantially contained under the species of these sensible things";[1] or, as it is given more fully in a later chapter, "that, immediately after the consecration, the veritable Body and His veritable Blood, together with His soul and divinity are under the species of bread and wine; but the Body indeed under the species of bread and the Blood under the species of wine, by the force of the words; but the Body itself under the species of wine and the Blood under the species of bread and the soul under both, by the force of that natural connection and concomitancy whereby the parts of Christ our Lord who hath now risen from the dead to die no more, are united together; and the divinity, furthermore, on account of the admirable hypostatical union thereof with His body and soul."[2] Lest this very precise language should be misunderstood, the Catechism explains it to mean that,

[1] Sess. XIII. ch. i.   [2] *Ut sup.* ch. iii.

"the real body of Christ, the same that was born of the Virgin,"[1] or, as it is also said, "the Bones, Sinews and all the things appertaining to the Perfection of man, are here truly present together with Divinity."[2]

This doctrine of the Real Presence, however, is but the first link to which another of yet deeper significance and more commanding influence is attached. If the veritable body and blood of the Lord Jesus enter into the bread and wine on the priest's utterance of the words of consecration, what effect does this divine possession of the elements have on their substance? The Council of Trent declared that the result was the most marvellous which it is possible to conceive : "Because that Christ our Redeemer, declared that which He offered under the species of bread to be truly His own body, therefore has it ever been a firm belief in the Church of God, and this holy Synod doth now declare it anew, that by the consecration of the bread and of the wine, a conversion is made of the whole substance of the bread into the substance of the body of Christ our Lord, and of the whole substance of the wine into the substance of His blood; which conversion is by the holy Catholic Church suitably and properly called Transubstantiation."[3] To root out the least appearance of dubiety on this point, a canon of the same session adds : "If anyone saith that in the sacred and holy sacrament of the Eucharist, the substance of the bread and wine remains conjointly with the body and blood of our Lord Jesus Christ, and denieth that wonderful and singular conversion of the whole substance of the bread into the Body, and of the whole substance of the wine into the Blood—the species only of the bread and wine remaining— which conversion the holy Catholic Church most aptly calls Transubstantiation : let him," etc.[4] Evidently, therefore, the Catechism only expresses what was in the mind of the Fathers, when it calls on the pastors to teach that "however remote from and alien to the senses it may seem, no substance of the elements remains therein," and also "that the accidents which are beheld by the eyes or perceived by the other senses exist in a wonderful, ineffable manner without a subject. All the accidents of bread and wine we indeed may see; they, however, inhere in no substance, but exist by themselves; whereas the substance of the bread and wine is so changed into the body and blood of our Lord, that the substance of bread and wine altogether ceases to exist."[5]

From this dogma two very important practical consequences are drawn.

The *first* is that the worshippers present when the Supper is dispensed are called on to worship the consecrated elements as divine. "There is no room left for doubt," says the Council, "that all the faithful of Christ may, according to the custom ever received in the Catholic Church, render in veneration the worship of *latria*,

[1] Part ii. ch. iv. q. 26.   [2] *Ut sup.* q. 31.   [3] *Ut sup.* ch. iv.
[4] Canon 2.   [5] Q. 26, cf. q. 35.

which is due to the true God, to this most holy sacrament. . . . For we believe that same God to be present therein, of whom the eternal Father, when introducing Him into the world, says : "And let all the angels of God adore Him."[1]

The *second* inference is that no deprivation of grace is entailed although only one element of the Supper be partaken of. For from the very nature of Christ's real presence in the sacrament, it is held "to be most true, that as much is contained under either species as under both ; for Christ whole and entire is under the species of bread and under any part whatsoever of that species ; likewise the whole (Christ) is under the species of wine and under the parts thereof. . . . Therefore, as regards the fruit thereof, they who receive one species alone, are not defrauded of any grace necessary to salvation."[2]

When the communicant is duly exercised in the spirit of contrition, the Supper thus consecrated and prepared is held to confer the highest benefits on his soul. On the guilt of sins indeed it is not supposed to wield the greatest influence. "That by the Eucharist are remitted and pardoned lighter sins, commonly called venial, should not be matter of doubt. . . . But these things are to be understood of those sins of which the mind has no strong perception and in which it has no prevailing delight."[3] But apart from this benefit, which, as we shall see, is provided for more largely in another use of the Supper, there is no grace the soul can desire that this ordinance does not bestow. "For," to use the language of the Tridentine Catechism, "the Holy Eucharist is truly and necessarily to be called the fountain of all graces, containing as it does after an admirable manner the Fountain itself of celestial gifts and graces and the Author of all the sacraments, Christ our Lord." The soul is refreshed and "increased" by this spiritual food: it is also preserved from temptation and other deadly evil : it is a token of our unity with the Church ; and "is most efficacious towards the attainment of eternal glory."[4]

Up to this point, however, we have presented only one aspect of the Romanist doctrine of the Supper. This ordinance is capable of another use, which makes it the most characteristic and prominent function of the whole system of Romanism. By the priest's repetition of the words of consecration, "This is My body," the Supper is made a heavenly Feast for the soul. But the Lord Jesus is held to have used words which point to another and, if possible, higher application of the elements. He also said to the disciples : "Do this in remembrance of Me" ; and in uttering this injunction, He is said to have indicated what He meant by offering the consecrated, transubstantiated bread and wine as *a sacrifice* to the Father. Thereby the Lord declared Himself constituted a priest for ever after the order of Melchisedek : thereby He instituted "a visible

---

[1] Sess. XIII. ch. v.   [2] Sess. XIII. ch. iii., XXI. ch. iv.
[3] Cat. *ut sup.* q. 50. Cf. Hunter, *Dog. Theol.* vol. iii. pp. 263, 265.
[4] Q. 45-52.

sacrifice such as the nature of man requires, whereby that bloody sacrifice, once to be accomplished on the cross, might be represented and the memory thereof remain unto the end of the world, and its salutary virtue be applied to the remission of those sins which we daily commit." Thereby also, as we have seen, He constituted His apostles "priests of the New Testament," to offer the same sacrifice as He then presented.[1]

Thus, as the Catechism of Trent points out, between the Eucharist as a *sacrament* and as a *sacrifice*, "the difference is very great: for as a sacrament it is perfected by *consecration*: as a sacrifice, all its force consists in its *oblation*." Hence "as a sacrifice, it is not only a source of merit, but also of satisfaction; for as in His Passion Christ the Lord merited and satisfied for us, so also those who offer this sacrifice by which they communicate with us, merit the fruit of His Passion and satisfy for sin."[2]

In this last statement, we evidently reach the core of the new function. It is offered not merely as a sacrifice of praise and thanksgiving, nor even as a scenic representation of the crucifixion of Christ, but as a sacrifice that in itself atones for sin. This result is secured by the fact that, as is alleged, Christ, the crucified Saviour, is physically present in the elements. "Forasmuch as in this divine sacrifice which is celebrated in the Mass that same Christ is contained and immolated in an unbloody manner, who once offered Himself in a bloody manner on the cross, the holy Synod teaches that this sacrifice is truly propitiatory. . . . For the Lord, appeased by the oblation thereof and granting the graces and gift of penitence forgives even heinous crimes and sins." Since, according to the theory of the Roman Church, there is no breach made betwixt the living and the dead as regards either standing or communion, the eucharistic sacrifice is available for all alike. "Wherefore not only for the sins, punishments, satisfactions and other necessities of the faithful who are living, but also for those who are departed in Christ and who are not as yet fully purified, is it rightly offered, agreeably to a tradition of the apostles."[3]

In making this oblation, the Church, according to Möhler, only vindicates her rightful claim to be, "when regarded in one aspect, a kind of living portraiture of Christ, appearing and working through all the ages, whose atoning and redeeming activities, therefore, it eternally repeats and continues in unbroken succession. . . . If Christ hidden beneath an earthly veil develops to the end of the world His whole activity begun on earth, He of necessity offers Himself eternally to the Father as a sacrifice for men; and the real abiding presentation thereof can never cease in the Church, if the historic Christ is to celebrate in her life His whole imperishable existence."[4]

In dealing with this central dogma of the Roman Church, it is not

[1] Council, Sess. XXII, ch. i.   [2] *Ut sup.* q. 63.
[3] Council, Sess. XIII, ch. ii.   [4] *Symbolik*, s. 300.

needful to dwell on the inanity of the ceremonies with which she has surrounded the celebration of the Supper. On the principles already laid down and illustrated in the parallel case of Baptism, such additions are utterly unwarranted. A spiritual mind at once discerns that the beauty of the Supper as an ordinance lies in the simplicity of its ritual. It is "when unadorned, adorned the most." What demands attention are the very significant doctrines associated with the Supper: doctrines which, though they arise in this connection, are bound to exercise a dominant influence on the whole life and polity of the Church. Even of these the discussion need not now be so prolonged. One special aspect of them has been already dealt with in the chapter on the ministry. Here we have to examine only that other side of them which looks to the nature and effects of the sacrament itself.

1. The first point then to which we advert is the alleged presence of Christ in the elements of bread and wine. Against this view in the Romish sense of the term, the Reformers were unanimous in setting their face. Luther alone did not take up such a distinct attitude of opposition as could have been wished. Under the influence of the strong mystical element in his nature, he had long been inclined to lay stress on the words of Christ in instituting the Supper: "This is My body"; "This is My blood"; and when he saw the apparently bare significance which, as he thought, Zwingli was inclined to attach to the ordinance, he adopted tenets that certainly approximated to the Romish view. For he held that, when the Supper was dispensed, the gracious power of God was so exercised that the Lord Jesus was present "in, with and under" the elements, and was spiritually but really partaken of in the fulness of His personality as the God-man, alike by believers and unbelievers: by the former to their spiritual benefit, by the latter to loss and judgment. This doctrine of Consubstantiation, as it was called, was supposed to be rendered more probable by the concurrent doctrine of the ubiquity of Christ's human nature, which Luther also held.

Calvin, on the other hand, was very decided in his rejection of the Romish view. He held that the prayer of consecration with which the administration of the ordinance was introduced, did indeed separate the elements from a common to a sacred use and made them sanctified organs for communicating the grace of God. But they were mere bread and wine before their use, and, after it, mere bread and wine they remained. Hence the presence of Christ vouchsafed in the Supper could only be at most a fuller measure of that very same spiritual presence in the heart which the believer receives by faith in the Lord and by the operation of the Holy Spirit. That this presence was real, Calvin ever taught. It was not a devout imagination, but a direct, powerful, vitalising communication of the grace that is in Christ Jesus.

Calvin was led to develop this view with the greater precision that it seemed to be not only in accordance with Scripture, but also fitted to reconcile the followers of Luther and Zwingli. This hope was largely fulfilled. While Luther lived, the unhappy controversy continued; though even then some of his followers exhibited leanings towards the Calvinistic view. After he died, many of them, including Melanchthon, gave in their adherence to the mediating doctrine. To this day, the movement in this direction is maintained. While Luther's original view is adhered to by those who profess to be his strict followers, not a few portions of the Church that bears his name, retain the Calvinistic view. It is now felt that much of the sharpness of the original disputation was due to mutual misunderstanding of the language in which the divergent views were expressed.

2. The best proof of this agreement is found in the fact that Lutherans and Calvinists alike reject utterly the Romish dogma of Transubstantiation. The Reformers inveighed against it in their controversial writings, and the Churches embodied earnest protest against it in their public Confessions. The grounds on which they based their opposition are immovable.

i. First of all, there is not the slightest indication in the institution of the Supper that any such change was either desired or expected. The bread and wine that were used had already formed part of the paschal feast. The fact that the Lord set them apart for the Supper by the prayer of thanksgiving could not effect any change. No more would the simple statement that the elements were to be the symbols of His body and blood. This is all that the words, "This is My body," "This is My blood" can be held to imply. The Lord would not use any word for "is" in Aramaic, and the whole past training of the disciples in the use of figurative or symbolic language would be against their imagining for a moment that the bread and wine could by such an utterance be identified there and then with the living body of the Lord before them.

ii. Besides, such a change as the Church of Rome requires her members to accept is opposed to the nature of the Christian redemption. When the Lord Jesus rose from the dead, His body was transformed. It was no longer the natural body that was born of the Virgin and was subject to the laws or modes of earthly existence, but a spiritual body, governed by the laws of the heavenly world. To aver therefore that the glorified person of Christ can in any intelligible sense of the words be eaten by men on earth as they would eat bread and wine is to contradict the fact of the Ascension of Christ and His session at God's right hand.

iii. This theory is also opposed to the spirituality of the relation that exists betwixt Christ and His people. In the addresses at the synagogue of Capernaum, He did indeed speak of men's eating His flesh and drinking His blood.[1] But it cannot be proved that these utterances refer specially to the Supper: for the ordinance was not

[1] John vi. 52-58.

yet instituted ; and, besides, the whole strain of Christ's teaching shows that it was the communication of spiritual life that He had in view. He came to impart His own holy nature to those that believed in Him. To receive this inward grace and manifest it in constant obedience to the will of God is the supreme necessity of the Christian life. This is done by faith and not merely at the Lord's table.

iv. Yet again: the idea of such a change is opposed to the testimony of the senses. When the Lord Jesus performed a miracle, the result was such as men could take direct cognisance of through this channel. They saw and tasted the wine that was made out of water at Cana ; they saw and handled and tasted the food that was multiplied out of the loaves and fishes. But the Church of Rome demands that her members should believe in the fact of transubstantiation, while the senses of sight and touch and taste continue to inform them that no such change has taken place. Such a theory is thereby stamped as irrational and unworthy of acceptance by responsible minds.

These considerations are fully confirmed by what history tells us of the origin of the dogma. The germs of it probably began to appear in the fifth century, a period at which men were very prone to adopt exaggerated ideas about what they called "the Christian mysteries." This point is so far established by the fact that one of the Popes of that age strongly asserted that "the substance or nature of the bread and wine does not cease." But the doctrine itself was not mooted till the seventh century. It was not fully developed till the French abbot of Corbie openly adopted it in the ninth. The Church as a whole first promulgated it in the Lateran Council (1215). The doctrine is thus seen to be a mere traditional development of ideas for which not a single valid proof from Scripture can be adduced.

In the light of these facts the adoration of the host can only be regarded as an act of idolatry. To fall down before the transubstantiated elements either in the Christian assembly or when carried about from place to place, is as grave a sin on the part of the deluded people as it is on the part of the officiating priest to exhibit them.

Along with the dogma of Transubstantiation, the Reformers rejected the practice of communion in one kind. No candid apologist for Romanism has ever averred that the primitive Church did not invariably give both elements to the people. The denial of the cup to the laity was a direct result of the theory of transubstantiation. Möhler, for example, admits that it is a matter of notoriety that the usage arose first in the monasteries in the twelfth century and spread thence in ever wider circles through the Church and that the feeling that governed it was only "a very tender sense of propriety." "A pious dread of desecrating by spilling and the like, the form of the highest and holiest of which man can be counted worthy to partake, even in the most conscientious method of observance, swayed their minds." He even goes so far as to add : " For all that, we should rejoice, if it were set free to each one to determine whether or not he should drink of the consecrated cup ; and this might certainly be expected, if a universal desire for the enjoyment of this privilege were expressed with the same unanimity and love as from the twelfth century the opposite sentiment has been declared."[1] As the case stands, the Church has forbidden the granting of the cup to the laity and reserves to herself the right to decide whether it shall be granted again. Such a claim is unlawful. In view of Christ's own injunction to the twelve as simply His disciples, to take the cup and "drink all of it,"[2] the restriction practised by the Church of Rome can be set down only to the desire of elevating the priesthood above the laity and of surrounding the sacrament with a greater halo of mystery and awe.

As to the blessings imparted to the communicant in the Supper, it were unfair to deny that the Church of Rome rightly discerns the great aim of the ordinance to be the bestowal of spiritual nourishment. The Reformers could not tolerate the theory that the observance of it could have any effect on the forgiveness of even venial sins. But apart from the exaggerated and often materialised conceptions in which they indulged, the Fathers of Trent said not a little that is true on the value of the ordinance for the culture and advancement of the spiritual life. It is these elements of truth that have reconciled many of her adherents to tolerate the grievous errors with which the rite is identified in the Romish system. Protestantism accepts the truth and excludes the error by declaring that in the Supper, "The worthy receivers are not after a corporal and carnal manner, but by faith made partakers of His body and blood with all His benefits to their spiritual nourishment and grace."[3]

3. To the doctrine of the propitiatory sacrifice of the Mass, the Reformers offered the same uncompromising opposition as to that of Transubstantiation. Luther inveighed against it without ceasing, and Calvin seconded his efforts. The grounds on which they united are fully exhibited in their writings, and are accepted by the Reformed Churches to this day.

i. As before, we begin by saying that there is no trace of any such oblation in the words of institution, where, if at all, it ought to be found. No sophistry can impart a single sacrificial idea to the word there translated " do." The injunction, " Do this in remembrance of Me," must be interpreted in the light of the action it accompanied. This was simply the distribution of the bread and wine ; and all the Lord could have meant by it was that the disciples were to observe this same mutual participation of the elements for the future, in imitation of His example, in trustful recollection of His love, and especially with a view to a closer fellowship with Himself.

ii. Again : this view is opposed to Christ's own teaching on the

[1] *Symbolik*, s. 320.   [2] Matt. xxvi. 27.   [3] Sh. Cat. q. 96.

sacrifice He came to offer. This was to be accomplished only in His death on the cross. "I lay down My life for the sheep";[1] "The Son of Man came to give His life a ransom for many."[2] It was the life of Christ outpoured on the cross that purchased the forgiveness of sins. The victorious shout, "It is finished,"[3] was a public testimony that nothing more was needed to be done for the salvation of mankind. To judge from the analogy of other institutions, if the Supper had been a sacrifice representative or exhibitive of the cross, the Lord would have given specific instruction to that effect. Nothing of this sort is to be found.

iii. This theory of the Supper is no less contrary to the teaching of the apostles. The Lord's Table is not spoken of as an altar; nor did the apostles claim for themselves or give to others the title of "priests." Christ is never represented as a priest in the institution of the Supper. He fulfilled the function of an Aaronic priest in offering Himself up once for all on Calvary, and in presenting Himself before the Father as an ever-present sacrifice for sin. It is in heaven only that He is a High Priest after the order of Melchisedek, sitting as a royal priest on His throne. The writer to the Hebrews testifies that, after the death of Christ, "there remaineth no more sacrifice for sins,"[4] and never alludes to the Supper either as an indispensable representation of the sacrifice of Christ, or as a complement of its saving power.

iv. Still further: the doctrine of the Mass presupposes a function which the Church is nowhere in Scripture called on to fulfil. The Christian society is not in the Romish sense the living portraiture of Christ, reproducing His every act. The Church is indeed the body of Christ in vital union with Him, under His control and bound to manifest His spirit and carry on His work in the world. But to die an atoning death for sin was His sole prerogative. This commandment He received of the Father. No obligation to undergo this death in reality, or reproduce and continue it in figure, is laid on the Church. All that Christians owe to the cross is to receive the sacrifice by faith as it is now presented in the Lamb at God's right hand, to let its power tell on the soul, to manifest its spirit of self-surrender to God in a willing endurance of suffering for His cause, and, with all possible vividness, to preach it by the word of the truth of the gospel as the one source of salvation for the race. In spite of the sophistical protest of Trent, it is not possible for the Church of Rome to invite men to trust in the subordinate sacrifice for sin she professes to offer in the Mass, without thereby detracting from the glory due to Christ crucified alone. To pretend to offer this sacrifice in a bloodless manner is only an exaggeration of the offence: for "the blood is the life," and "without shedding of blood there is no remission of sins."[5]

It ought to set the force of these considerations beyond doubt, that

[1] John x. 15. [2] Matt. xx. 28. [3] John xix. 30.
[4] Heb. x. 26. [5] Heb. ix. 22.

we can point out the origin and progress of the erroneous opinions that culminated in the Mass. The term "oblation" was first applied to the gifts of food or wine that were brought by the members of the Church as a contribution to the *Agapæ* or love-feasts. Gradually the word was transferred to the elements of the Supper itself, and the clergy were regarded as priests. This change in turn rendered the idea of a sacrifice in the Supper more definite, till the simple rite Christ instituted as a channel of fellowship with Himself was made to occupy the place of His divine propitiation on Calvary.

With the rejection of this alleged function of the Supper, there falls to the ground the whole fabric of superstition and idolatry and fraud connected with Masses for the dead. These celebrations are made a matter of merchandise in the Church of Rome. The money that flows into her coffers from this source every year amounts to a vast sum. Like the Reformers in the sixteenth century, the Protestant Churches of to-day protest against this abuse as the grossest scandal in the life of Christendom.

CHAPTER VII

THE CONSTITUTION OF THE CHURCH — THE ROMAN PRIMACY

ALONG with provision for public worship and the use of the sacraments and other means of grace, the Christian Church requires arrangements for the due guidance and oversight of its congregations. No society can exist in a condition of order without some kind of constituted government. Disunion and confusion are the sure results where this is lacking. The Christian Church is no exception to this rule. Each separate congregation was intended by the apostles to have certain office-bearers who should undertake the responsibility of caring for the life and relations and comfort of its members.

Of the different forms of constitution to which this necessity has given rise, the Church of Rome from the earliest period adopted that which may be called Prelatic Episcopacy. Unlike Congregationalism in which, while a teaching pastor is appointed, the governing power remains in the hands of the members of each congregation; unlike Presbyterianism, which, while it regards the people as the ultimate source of power, devolves the exercise of it on a body of presbyters or ruling elders, occupying, with one set apart to the office of teacher, an equal footing as regards authority, and linked together by a series of ecclesiastical courts over a whole country, and which on this account may be called Presbyterial Episcopacy; Prelatic Episcopacy draws a distinction betwixt "bishops" and "elders," and commits the whole governing power to the bishops. The "bishop" is held to be a superior office-bearer to the elder or deacon. He is therefore appointed to the oversight of a larger or smaller number of congregations within a certain district called a "diocese." He alone can "confirm" or receive into the membership of the Church; he alone can suspend from membership; he alone can ordain presbyters or priests for the ordinary work of the ministry.[1]

In these respects, therefore, the Church of Rome only holds with the Greek and Anglican Churches. For in these also, at least in the High Church parties, the bishop is regarded as the sole fountain of ecclesiastical power. Christ, it is contended, committed all authority in the Church to the twelve disciples, as apostles. They appointed bishops to take their place and exercise the same jurisdiction. It is

[1] Council, Sess. XXIII. ch. iv.

only bishops who stand in the line of the apostolic succession that can be regarded as having the sanction of Christ for the government of the Church; they alone rule by divine right; they alone can ordain inferior clergy for the valid administration of the Christian ordinances. Without such "orders," there can be no true sacraments: without a "lord-bishop," there can be no true Church.

The Church of Rome, however, has never been content with simple Episcopacy even in its highest form. From a very early period after the imperial recognition of the Christian Church, especially from the beginning of the sixth century, the bishops of Rome began to claim pre-eminence over the Churches of other cities and provinces. Various influences helped to promote this ambition. The Roman prelates and those that surrounded them, were often distinguished for zeal, learning and administrative gifts. When controversies occurred, they were often appealed to as arbiters or judges of causes. Swift advantage was taken of every such occasion to establish a theory of inherited ascendency over other Churches. In the long run, though not till the fifteenth century, this claim was formally recognised. As it at present stands, the Church of Rome has not only diocesan bishops over all the world, but metropolitans or archbishops in the largest cities, a smaller number of cardinals above these, and, at the head of all, the Bishop of Rome as the Pope or Primate of the whole Church.

The first Council of the whole Church that gave full and formal sanction to this papal constitution was held at Florence in 1439. One of its definitions is devoted to the form of government under which the Church is placed, and it also indicates the grounds on which it is based. "Likewise we decree that the Holy Apostolic See and the Roman Pontiff hold a primacy over the whole world; and that the Roman Pontiff himself is the successor of blessed Peter, the Prince of the Apostles, and is the true Vicar of Christ and Head of the whole Church, and the father and teacher of all Christians; and that to him in the person of blessed Peter, the full power of feeding, ruling and governing the universal Church has been committed by our Lord Jesus Christ, even as it is contained in the transactions of œcumenical councils and the sacred canons."[1] The Council of Trent did not repeat this statement in its ordinary decrees. As has been indicated in a previous chapter, it insisted rather on the divine right of Prelacy, probably because it was the tenet which was opposed by the Reformers. Lest the declaration should be overlooked, it is supported by these two canons: "If anyone saith that in the Catholic Church there is not a hierarchy instituted by divine ordination, which consists of bishops, priests (presbyters), and ministers: let him," etc.;[2] "If anyone saith that bishops are not superior to priests (presbyters), or that they have not the power of confirming or ordaining, or that the power which they possess is common to them and to priests, or that orders conferred by them without the consent or vocation of the

[1] Mirbt, *Quellen z. Geschichte des Papsttums*, s. 100.   [2] *Ut sup.* canon 6.

people or of the secular power are invalid . . . let him," etc.[1] In the decrees on reformation, on the other hand, the position assigned to the Bishop of Rome by the Council of Florence is everywhere assumed. The Roman Pontiff is spoken of as "God's own Vicar on earth": he is "sovereign": his See is supreme: and its authority is always and in all things to be respected.[2]

These earlier declarations have in modern times been fully reproduced in the decree of the Vatican Council held at Rome in 1870. It first states that, "according to the testimony of the gospel, a primacy of jurisdiction over the whole Church was promised immediately and directly to the blessed Peter the apostle, and was conferred upon him." Then it adds: "What the chief Pastor and great Shepherd of the sheep, the Lord Jesus Christ, instituted in the person of blessed Peter the apostle, for the perpetual welfare and lasting good of the Church, this must, by the institution of Christ, last for ever in the Church, which, being founded on a rock, shall remain ever firm to the end of the world." A canon is attached to this effect: "If anyone shall say that it is not by the institution of Christ our Lord Himself, that is, by divine right, that blessed Peter has an unbroken line of successors in the Primacy over the whole Church, or that the Roman Pontiff is not the successor of blessed Peter in the same Primacy: let him," etc.[3]

Putting these statements together, we are able to summarise the positions on the topic which the Church of Rome contends for and undertakes to prove. They may be stated in these terms:—

First, that in the course of His earthly ministry, the Lord Jesus conferred on Simon Peter a primacy of jurisdiction and authority over the rest of the Twelve as well as over the whole Church, so that he was entitled to their obedience and submission;

Secondly, that this primacy was not to be confined to Peter, but was to be transmitted through him to an uninterrupted line of successors for all the later history of the Church;

Thirdly, that by the Lord's special guidance and under His divine sanction, the Apostle Peter became Bishop or chief ruler at Rome and died in the occupancy of that See; and

Fourthly, that by the authority of the Lord, Peter did actually entrust to all the future occupants of that bishopric the same jurisdiction over the whole Church of Christ that had been committed to him and that he himself had wielded.

If the Church of Rome cannot present us with a chain of valid evidence in support of these positions, her claims to the allegiance of men fall to pieces.[4] Her apologists realise this responsibility and undertake to give the proof that is craved.

[1] Canon 7.
[2] Sess. VI. Proëm. *Decree on Reformation*, ch. i. Sess. VII. *Decree on Reformation* (Preface).
[3] Cf. Hunter, *Outlines of Dog. Theol.* vol. i. p. 436.
[4] Cf. Cunningham, *Historical Theology*, vol. i. p. 213.

THE CONSTITUTION OF THE CHURCH—THE ROMAN PRIMACY 213

In behalf of the first two averments, the Romanists confidently appeal to the testimony of the Scriptures. Is there not, for example, "the position of eminence" which Peter is set forth in the Gospels as holding? On his first reception by Christ, it was intimated to him that his name was to be changed—a promise that is regarded as a token of special favour.[1] It is Peter too that pays the tribute for Christ and himself.[2] He was one of the three admitted to the Transfiguration, to the raising of Jairus' daughter, to the garden of Gethsemane.[3] Peter also acted as spokesman for the other disciples on several important occasions, and is singled out for a special message from the Lord, after He rose again.[4]

But there are also utterances of Christ addressed directly to Peter, which are held to set his primacy beyond doubt.

The first of these is the statement made to him after his avowal of the Messiahship and Sonship of Jesus. "And I also say unto thee that thou art Peter and upon this rock I will build My Church; and the gates of Hades shall not prevail against it. I will give unto thee the keys of the kingdom of heaven: and whatsoever thou shalt bind on earth shall be bound in heaven, and whatsoever thou shalt loose on earth shall be loosed in heaven."[5] Here, it is alleged, there is a dignity promised; and, when this is examined, it is found to be the primacy of jurisdiction in the Church. "For the foundation of a building is the most indispensable part of the building, being that on which the strength of the whole structure mainly depends. . . . The whole Church depends upon St. Peter, while he himself does not derive support from that which rests upon him."[6] In accordance with this dignity, Peter is granted possession of the keys of the whole Church as a token that he is constituted a ruler of it. "The connection is natural, for he that has the key is master."

Another statement of the Lord adduced here is His word to Peter at the last Supper: "Simon, Simon, behold, Satan asked to have you that he might sift you as wheat; but I made supplication for thee, that thy faith fail not: and do thou, when once thou hast turned again, stablish thy brethren."[7] Here, it is contended, Peter receives a promise of assistance in the primacy. He is assured that "the faith of others, especially of his brethren the apostles depends upon his support. . . . He has a divine commission to guide others in the faith, however eminent their station in the Church."[8]

Yet again: there are the repeated injunctions given to Peter by the risen Lord to take the oversight of His people. "Simon, son of John, lovest thou Me? Yea, Lord, Thou knowest that I love Thee. . . . Feed My lambs . . . Tend My sheep . . . Feed My sheep."[9] Here, it is said, the dignity which had been promised to

---

[1] John i. 42.
[2] Matt. xvii. 24–27.
[3] Luke viii. 51; Matt. xxvi. 37.
[4] Matt. xvi. 16; Mark xvi. 7.
[5] Matt. xvi. 18, 19.
[6] Hunter, *Outlines*, etc. vol. i. pp. 432, 433.
[7] Luke xxii. 31, 32.
[8] Hunter, *ut sup.* p. 434.
[9] John xxi. 15–17.

St. Peter and for the due hearing of which he was to receive special assistance, was actually conferred on him by Christ. For "it is the same office that is spoken of under the figures of the Foundation, the Bearer of the Keys, and the Shepherd." "The distinction of sheep and lambs for both of which St. Peter is to do the work of shepherd, emphasises the extent of his jurisdiction."[1]

In accordance with his reception of the primacy, Peter is held to occupy the most prominent position in the establishment and expansion of the Christian Church. It is he that guides the procedure of the one hundred and twenty disciples in choosing a successor to Judas. It is Peter that delivers the leading apology at Pentecost, and receives the first converts into the Church. He performs the first miracles, rebukes the traitor and the heretic and opens the door of faith to the Gentiles.[2]

In view of these facts it is maintained that the conclusion is inevitable that Christ appointed Peter to a primacy of authority over the other apostles and the whole Church, and intended that this jurisdiction should be continued in succession for the future. For the same needs that required such an appointment at the outset of the Church's history were to remain in still greater force in later centuries.

In behalf of the other two positions which the Church of Rome undertakes to establish, no candid apologist ever professes to adduce any direct evidence from Scripture. The only appearance of proof that can be detected is supposed to be found in a statement at the end of Peter's first Epistle: "She that is in Babylon elect together with you, saluteth you and so doth Mark my son."[3] The reference here is taken to be to the Church; and in accordance with the mystical interpretation of Babylon as the city of Rome in the Book of Revelation, Peter is regarded as sending this Epistle from his episcopal seat in Rome. For additional evidence, recourse is had to the voice of the Church, which is here of course held as of equal authority with Scripture. "That St. Peter was at his death Bishop of Rome is not a matter of divine revelation; but it is an historical truth so closely connected with dogma as to come within the range of the teaching authority of the Church: it is a dogmatic fact and we have it defined with infallible certainty by the Vatican Council."[4] On examining the available testimonies, we find them to consist of certain statements of some of the early Fathers which are supposed to lend some colour to the averments and which have accordingly been reproduced, amplified and confirmed in other decisions of the Pope and decrees of Councils.

To these proofs are added two other arguments: the first of which is that the primacy of Peter and his successors is only the natural and legitimate development of the prelatic constitution of the Church, and that it is absolutely necessary for securing and

[1] Hunter, *Outlines*, etc. p. 435.   [2] Acts i. 15, ii. 38, iii. 6, v. 1-11.
[3] 1 Pet. v. 13.   [4] Hunter, *ut sup.* pp. 408, 410.

manifesting that unity which is everywhere in Scripture predicted of the apostolic Church; the second being a supplementary negative contention to the effect that no Church save that of Rome has ever claimed to have been governed by St. Peter at his death. The claim is represented by a recent writer as "the most persuasive argument, both for the residence of St. Peter at Rome and for his Roman episcopate."[1]

The result of the whole argument as stated by the same theologian is held to be that the prerogatives conferred on St. Peter include among other things a primacy not of honour alone, but of jurisdiction over the whole Church, granted by God and not conferred by man : and that the monarchical constitution of the Church thus established was no merely temporary arrangement which died with the first monarch, but that it is an essential part of the constitution of the Church as now existing, and as it will continue till the end of time.[2]

In dealing with this argument, it is needless attempting to show in detail how unanimously the first Reformers set their face against the pretensions advanced in it. The primacy of Peter and the claims of the Church of Rome based on it, were regarded as the head and front of her offence. The same attitude is maintained by the Reformed Churches to this day. Nor is the resistance confined to Churches with a democratic constitution. Several dignitaries of the Anglican and Irish Episcopal Churches, for example, have rendered the highest service in the controversy with Romanism. We need mention only the names of Stillingfleet and Barrow, Usher, Jeremy Taylor and Salmon. Not a few defenders of Prelacy hold that episcopal rule has a divine right : many others are prepared to admit that the original words for "bishop" and "presbyter" are applied to the same class in the New Testament, and that Episcopacy has no higher sanction than that derived from its coming into vogue immediately after the death of the apostles : others will not go beyond contending that history has proved this form of constitution to be reasonable and beneficent and therefore admissible. Yet representatives of all these classes are to this day found standing loyally together in opposition to the aggressive policy of the Roman See. Instead therefore of entering into the controversy betwixt Prelacy and Presbyterianism or Independency, we shall simply pass in review the various links in the chain of evidence by which the apologists of Rome profess to support the positions here taken up.

In examining the Biblical evidence for the primacy of Peter, we have no interest in ignoring any prominence he may have had in the circle of the Twelve, when Jesus was with them. Peter had by nature the characteristics of decision, energy and courage. These were sure to bring him to the front in any society to which he belonged ; and the Lord could not but respect and admire him for them and suffer him to take the position which was his due. Hence

[1] Hunter, *Outlines*, etc. p. 411.   [2] Hunter, *ut sup.* p. 428.

he never objected to Peter's acting as the spokesman of the Twelve, but rather uttered words of commendation to him, when occasion required. But who can recall the Lord's intercourse with Peter without seeing that He was fully aware of the disciple's weakness, and that the last thing He contemplated was the appointment of Peter as Head of the apostolic college? The way in which He brought him to His feet ere he was finally called, His rebuke of him as ensnared by Satan, when the disciple ventured to direct his Lord, His warning to him against ambition, His prediction of failure and denial on the morning of the Trial, are overwhelming proofs that, while recognising and welcoming Peter's special gifts, the Lord never looked on him as occupying any position of superiority over the rest of the disciples.

This impression is only deepened, when we look into those special utterances of the Lord to Peter on which so much stress is laid.

The address at Cæsarea has been very differently interpreted. The Fathers, for example, on whose consent Romanists base their opinion, here adopt widely divergent views; some taking the rock to be Christ; others regarding it as the confession of the divine sonship; others as Peter's faith; others still as Peter himself. This diversity, so contrary as it is to the spirit of Romanism, is enough to strip their interpretation as a whole of all weight. For ourselves, we need not hesitate to give full force to the coincidence betwixt the original words for "Peter" and "rock," and frankly admit that the believing Peter is really the rock on which the Church was to be built. Only, as the whole situation manifestly demands, it is not Peter as a separate individual that the Lord has in view, but merely as a representative of the rest. It is the dramatic elevation of the Lord's language that gives Peter his apparent prominence. The promise of Christ is to the effect that it would be on such rock-like souls as Peter represented that He would rear the edifice of His Church. Peter would have his own place in founding and directing the Christian society, but it would be only as he was connected with others of the same spiritual type that its foundation could remain stable to the end. This view is confirmed by the fact that the same promise about "binding" and "loosing" which is given to Peter is with equal explicitness made afterwards to the Twelve as a whole. In no sense is Peter or are the rest thereby constituted masters of the Church militant. "Bind" and "loose" here mean simply "forbid" and "allow"; and all the power intrusted to them is that of deciding what was to be permitted or declared unlawful in the constitution and procedure of the Church. They held the keys simply as the stewards or servants of Christ.

The injunction given to Peter on the eve of Christ's arrest to strengthen his brethren is so utterly unsuitable as a proof of superiority that it is rather an indication of the Romanist argument's being in straits for evidence that it should be adduced at all in this connection. The command is attached to a warning to beware of the Evil one, coupled with a plain intimation that the disciple would be found wanting in the trial. All it can be legitimately held to include is the assurance that in answer to the prayer of Christ, Peter's faith would not utterly fail, and the duty of turning the failure and the subsequent restoration to the best account for the edification of his fellow-believers.

It is in the light of these facts that the commission given to Peter by the risen Lord yields its true meaning. The occasion on which he was instructed to feed the lambs and tend and feed the sheep was his restoration to the apostolate after his recent fall. Nothing but a studied blindness to all the circumstances of the case could extract from these injunctions given only after a humbling and thrice-repeated protestation of love to the Lord, any bestowal of an official dignity superior to that of the other ten disciples. The office of "shepherd" here spoken of is one which Peter himself[1] took delight in sharing with every other presbyter of the Church.

This view of Peter's relation to the other apostles is amply confirmed by his conduct as set forth by the historian of the Acts and in the Epistles. Peter did take a most prominent and honourable part in the founding and expansion of the Church. But there is not the slightest evidence that he acted as the recognised primate of the apostles.[2] John and James[3] had equal authority with him alike in the aggressive work of the Church and in its first general Assembly. Peter as the apostle of the Jews was on no higher platform than the later ordained Paul as the apostle of the Gentiles. All that he, along with his brethren, did for Paul was to give him the right hand of fellowship.[4] When at a subsequent crisis Peter seemed to swerve from a straightforward and consistent course of action in intercourse with the Gentiles and stood condemned by principles he himself had previously announced, Paul "resisted him to the face,"[5] and expostulated with him on the error he had committed. The whole attitude of Paul is such as could never have been taken up towards a superior official.

If the evidence adduced from the Scriptures in behalf of the primacy of Peter and its continuance in the Church thus breaks down, it is from the Protestant standpoint really a superfluous task to show at length that this jurisdiction was neither exercised by Peter at Rome nor transmitted by him with the authority of Christ to successors in that See. For, as we have seen, not even Romanists themselves pretend that this can be established from the Scriptures; and what has not the support of the written word cannot be regarded as binding on the conscience or as a matter of divine right. No exception can be made here in favour of the salutation at the close of Peter's first Epistle. Granting that the reference is to the Church and not to any eminent Christian woman, we cannot admit

[1] 1 Pet. v. 1.   [2] Acts iii. 4.   [3] Acts xv. 13.
[4] Gal. ii. 9.   [5] Gal. v. 11.

that in an Epistle devoid of figurative or symbolic presentments of truth, "Babylon" can be identified with Rome. There must have been a considerable Christian congregation of Hebrew origin in and around the site of old Babylon, and Peter evidently had authority to convey greetings from the brethren there to those dispersed in other provinces.

Our limits will not permit us to adduce and criticise the quotations from the Fathers and decrees of Councils that seem to support the residence and death of Peter at Rome. It must suffice to say that, tried by every fair test, the evidence is quite inadequate. Romanist apologists admit that it is necessary for them to prove that from the foundation of the Christian society, the Bishops of Rome as successors of Peter have claimed and exercised official primacy over the whole Church, or, at least, over all its branches. But when we examine the historical evidence of the first three centuries, we find that, while there is nothing of real value that can be adduced in support of the Romanist position, there is a great deal to indicate that the claim of subsequent Bishops of Rome was not then either acknowledged or known. Even the Fathers who, like Irenæus, Origen and Cyprian, use expressions that indicate a growing authority at Rome, make other statements which show that in their view all the apostles were on an equal footing and that this parity belonged to all the bishops of the Church since their time. Cyprian in particular not only announced these principles, but in his own controversy with his contemporary, Stephen, bishop of Rome, boldly acted on them.

As the additional arguments for the primacy of the Pope derived from its being necessary to the unity of the Church and its having been so long in fact claimed and enjoyed by Rome, have been already adverted to, and will fall to be noticed also in a later chapter, we need not dwell on them here. It is enough to say that it is one of the weaknesses of the prelatic constitution of the Church that it seems to demand such a consummation. The uniformity it obtains is not the spiritual unity which Christ desired. This is the outgrowth of inward spiritual fellowship only : that is imposed from without by the influence of human legislation. The continuance of a new departure in religious belief and action is no proof of its divine origin and sanction. If that were so, the claims of Mohammedanism might be thought to be not so much less strong than those of Romanism and yet it has no sterner foe.

CHAPTER VIII

THE TEACHING OF THE CHURCH—PAPAL INFALLIBILITY

THE third main function of the Christian ministry is to teach men the truth of God. The Lord Jesus charged the apostles to go into all the world and make disciples of all nations, teaching them to observe all things whatsoever He had commanded them. This has been taken as the ministerial commission for all time. The ministers are to preach the gospel, which the Spirit enables them to gather from the Scriptures as interpreted by the facts of the Christian redemption. Introducing the disciples thus won to the personal study of the Scriptures, they are to lead them into the whole counsel of God as therein set forth. Only thus can "pastors and teachers" expect the divine co-operation and blessing.

On the necessity of this work, all branches of the early Christian Church were agreed. It was only when the Church of Rome had acquired dominion over the minds of men, that the gospel was displaced by the sacraments and the study of the Bible by the teaching of manuals of worship. After the Reformation, as we have seen, ecclesiastical tradition took full and formal possession of the rights belonging to evangelical preaching and the exposition of the Scriptures. To add emphasis to her claims, the Church of Rome maintained that her teachers alone were entitled to say what was the true sense of the Scriptures, that her dogmatic statements as formulated by the Council of Trent alone represented what the members of the Church were to receive as truth, and that in all such public symbols, the Church was to be regarded as infallible or incapable of falling into error. So far from lowering her attitude on this point has the Roman Church been, that, during recent centuries she has only made the claim to this attribute the most prominent feature of her creed.

The question thus raised evidently demands careful discussion. It lies at the root of the whole controversy. If the Church of Rome can make good her claim to infallibility, the conflict with Protestantism must be regarded as settled in her favour. If she fails in the attempt to arrogate this feature, then every point of her teaching remains to be examined as in these pages on its own merits and in the light of the appropriate evidence.

On looking into the grounds for their position advanced by the Romanist theologians, we are met at the outset by the assumption that there must be in the world some supreme authority from which men may learn with absolute certitude what they are to receive as the truth of God. An accredited teacher of the Romish Church has recently said that "there is to be one faith, even as there is one Lord and one baptism; which oneness of belief cannot be received, unless there is a judge of controversies, who speaks intelligently and whom all may obey."[1] A very popular manual of instruction, approved by the highest authorities presents the same view in these terms: "To say that God has merely given to men forms of words which admit of different and contradictory interpretations and has left no authority on earth to decide which is the one true interpretation intended, amounts to a denial of Revelation altogether. A law which would admit of several inconsistent explanations would not have the nature of law, if there were not a court of justice to declare the true sense. The same might be said of a revelation capable of several discordant interpretations. . . . If there is an authority to declare the right sense of these passages, then all is simple enough; but without such an authority, it cannot be denied that, in the case supposed, Holy Scripture admits of contradictory interpretations, and consequently on such questions it would cease to be a revelation. There must therefore be some living authority on earth commissioned by God to decide the meaning of the revelation which God has given us. . . . Such an authority must be infallible. Its infallibility is contained in its very commission. We cannot conceive that God has appointed someone to teach us His Revelation and *commanded us to listen to it and believe it*, and yet that He would at the same time allow this guide to teach it incorrectly and lead us astray. God who is the very truth, *could not command us to believe false teaching*. Without such infallibility there could be no certainty of faith."[2]

This position once assumed to be unassailable, the next step of the Romanist argument is to indicate where this infallible authority is to be found. All the theologians claim that it must be the Christian Church herself. As the teacher already quoted further says, "This judge cannot be the reason of each man, which is weak and variable and has no binding force on the multitude; nor is it the Christian people at large, for we nowhere find that such power has been given to them as the apostles claimed for themselves; nor the head of the civil State, who has his own functions but is within the Church as a learner; nor, lastly, does it please God to settle controversies by revelations, except perhaps by private revelations that avail no one but the receiver. The Scripture is dead and cannot make its voice heard, and those who profess to be its expounders are at variance: there is no living

[1] Hunter, vol. i. p. 289. [2] Di Bruno, *Catholic Belief*, p. 35.

voice but that of the Church that can be the judge of whose existence we are assured."[1]

As to the grounds on which this view is based, there is first of all the contention of philosophical apologists like J. A. Möhler. This is connected with the special view of the Church suggested by the incarnation of the Word. The Church as a visible association is just the incarnation of the Son of God reproduced and continued in the world. "From the point of view just developed, the visible Church is the Son of God ever appearing in the midst of men in human form, eternally renewing and regenerating Himself: in short, His perpetual incarnation: just as in the Holy Scriptures the faithful are actually called 'the body of Christ.' Hence also it is manifest that the Church, though she consists of men, is yet not merely human. Rather, as in Christ Himself, the divine and the human are to be always distinguished, while both are still bound in unity, so is He perpetuated in the Church also in undivided entirety. The Church, His abiding manifestation, is at once divine and human : she is the unity of both. It is He that hidden beneath earthly and human forms works in her : and she has therefore a divine and human side in inseparable coexistence : so that the divine cannot be drawn apart from the human, nor the human from the divine. These two sides accordingly interchange their predicates. If the divine, the living Christ and His Spirit, is admittedly, the infallible, the eternally unerring element in her, then also must the human be infallible and unerring, simply because the divine has no existence for us without the human : though the human is not so in itself but merely as the organ and the manifestation of the divine. It is thus also that we come to understand how a function so great, so momentous and full of significance could be committed to men."[2]

Other Romanist theologians, however, while it may be not unwilling to accept this basis, prefer to rest their views of the infallibility of the Church on the express utterances of Scripture. With a great profession of candour, it is said : "We must not be supposed to maintain that because the Church claims infallibility, therefore she is infallible. None but the divine Founder could give this gift and we must look to His recorded words for the proof that He has given it."[3] The first passage adduced contains the words addressed by the Lord to Peter : "Upon this rock I will build My Church and the gates of hell shall not prevail against it."[4] This is held to imply the infallibility of the Church, because Satan who works by seducing into error, is in her case not to succeed. The next proof alleged is the final commission given to the apostles : "Lo ! I am with you always even unto the end of the world."[5] This promise is taken to mean that the apostles and their successors in the episcopate would succeed in the work of teaching and this

[1] Hunter, vol. i. p. 289.   [2] *Symbolik*, ss. 332, 333.
[3] Hunter, vol. i. p. 295.   [4] Matt. xvi. 18.   [5] Matt. xxviii. 20.

success is held to exclude the possibility of error. A third proof is found in the promise of Christ to the disciples at the Table: "I will pray the Father and He shall give you another Comforter that He may abide with you for ever, even the Spirit of truth. . . . He shall teach you all things."[1] It is claimed to follow, "that believers in Christ will be collectively preserved for ever from error as to His doctrine, or, in other words, that the Church is infallible in teaching."[2] Last of all comes Paul's description of the house of God as "the Church of the living God, the pillar and ground of truth."[3] "A body which taught falsehood could not be said to be the unshaken support of truth: so again we are led to the conclusion that the Church is infallible."[4]

On the question as to which Church is meant in these passages, Romanist theologians never entertain the slightest doubt: it is not supposed to admit of discussion. In their view there is but "one true Church, one holy, catholic and apostolic Church"; and that is the Church which, they claim, had the Apostle Peter as its first universal bishop, the Church that in all ages is in communion with the See of Rome. Hence the Catechism of Trent says: "But as this one Church, seeing it is governed by the Holy Ghost, cannot err in delivering the discipline of faith and morals, so all other societies which arrogate to themselves the name of Church, because guided by the spirit of the devil, are necessarily sunk in the most pernicious errors both of doctrine and morals."[5]

At this point, another question that has been much discussed in the Church of Rome comes into view. What is the precise seat of this infallibility? Granted that it belongs to the Church of Rome as a whole, through what special organs is it dispensed to the community? The answer returned to this question by theologians of the Church has varied much in different ages and in different countries. Some have been content to teach that this infallibility is vested in the Church as a whole. Others, like the French bishops, have contended that it belongs to the Councils of the Church. This was the view taken by the Council of Constance. Others still hold that it is attached to the Council and the Pope. The trend of opinion in the Italian Church has always been in favour of the view that infallibility belongs to the whole body of the episcopate connected with the See of Rome, but that it is specially concentrated in the chief Bishop of Rome, that is, the Pope.

To this last position, the whole Church of Rome is now irrevocably committed. At the last so-called Œcumenical Council held at the Vatican in Rome in 1870, the following decree on this topic was declared to set forth the mind of the assembled bishops: "The Roman Pontiff, when he speaks *ex cathedra*, that is to say, when in the exercise of his office of Pastor and Teacher of all Christians, he in virtue of his supreme apostolic authority defines

[1] John xiv. 16. [2] Hunter, vol. i. p. 299. [3] 1 Tim. iii. 15.
[4] Hunter, vol. i. p. 300. [5] Art. IX. q. 16.

that a doctrine in faith and morals is to be held by the whole Church, by the assistance promised to him in the person of blessed Peter, has that infallibility with which it was the will of our divine Redeemer that the Church should be furnished in defining a doctrine on faith or morals, and that therefore these definitions of the Roman Pontiff of themselves and not through the consent of the Church are irreformable." [1]

Romanist commentators on this Vatican decree have been very careful to point out its precise meaning and scope. In view of the intense reluctance to accept it which many bishops showed, this is a politic course. The dogma does not imply anything like personal infallibility in the Pontiff. Nor does it attribute infallibility to every utterance of his even as a teacher. It is only when " he teaches the whole Church on a point of faith or morals, and this in the exercise of his supreme apostolic authority," that this quality is held to attach to his statements.[2] Yet even as thus explained, this definition is seen to be the master dogma of the Church of Rome. Let this position be granted and every other claim she makes becomes paramount.

In support of this characteristic doctrine, the Vatican Council appealed both to Scripture and tradition. The three statements made by the Lord to the Apostle Peter that have been already adduced to establish the primacy of the Pope, are taken also to imply his infallibility. If Peter be the foundation of the Church ; if it is he who is always to confirm the faith of his brethren ; if it is his function to feed the sheep, then he and his successors in the Roman See, cannot but exercise the gift of teaching as well as of government without essential error ; and when they teach *ex cathedra*, their utterances must be heard and accepted by the whole Church. What then appears to be taught in Scripture is held to be confirmed by the testimony of history and tradition. A long array of instances is adduced in which the infallibility of the Bishop of Rome is said to be either assumed or expressly declared. The occupant of the Roman See did unquestionably often have the position of arbiter in doctrinal controversies ; and every such occasion is claimed as presenting another proof that his infallibility as the successor of Peter was acknowledged from the beginning.

How entirely this dogma is opposed to the principles of evangelical Protestantism is evident at a first glance. At the outset of the Reformation it was chiefly the alleged infallibility of Councils that had to be impugned. Dr. Eck tried to overthrow Luther's teaching by appealing to their decisions ; and the Reformer and his friends had no alternative but to assert the supremacy of Scripture, and the right of every Christian to judge of its meaning. Since the Reformation, it has been the infallibility claimed for the Pope that has gradually come into view. The decision of the Vatican Council

[1] Decrees of Vatican Council (1870), Sess. IV. ch. iv
[2] Hunter, vol. i. p. 444.

has now fixed attention on this dogma as the point of attack. Here we must be content to give a brief *résumé* of the way in which Protestantism repels the whole Roman claim.

The Romanist apologists start with the assumption that there must be some authority in the world by which conflicting interpretations of Scripture may be settled. The difficulties that seem to call for such interposition are always hugely exaggerated. The revelation that God has given of Himself in His word is really distinguished by perspicuity. But the assumption itself also is baseless. It is not for man to settle beforehand what is necessary or otherwise in the divine economy. God Himself is the sole judge of what is indispensable for the progress of His cause, and we must be wholly guided by what of this He has revealed to us in the Scriptures. What He gives we are bound to receive: when He withholds, we must be content with the resources we have. As a matter of fact, the *primâ facie* impression which a perusal of the Scriptures gives is entirely opposed to the Roman assumption. Instead of indicating any source of authoritative interpretation or declaring the necessity for it, they everywhere throw the responsibility for arriving at the truth on the individual believer. The word of God proclaims that it is a public revelation of what man is to believe concerning God and what duty God requires of man, and that it ought to be in the hands of all His creatures. The universal opportunity of study calls for individual and independent search. The very form in which the Scriptures are cast raises a barrier against the Roman claim.

For the position that it is the Church of Christ that is to be the infallible interpreter of Scripture and judge of controversies, the grounds adduced are a quite inadequate support. Möhler's contention that the Church is entitled to this function, because she is the representative of Christ on the earth will not bear examination. For in the sense he puts on the words, this is not the case. The Incarnation is the seed of the whole Christian redemption. The fact that Christ came in the flesh demands that the Church shall manifest her life and work visibly in the world. But this great event does not make the Church the full manifestation of the unseen Saviour. She is His "body," simply because, as vitally united to Him in heaven, she is sustained by His Spirit and kept under His control. The Church is not thereby entitled to exercise the prerogatives of Christ Himself. Moreover, a representative acts in behalf of one who is absent. If we think of Christ as absent in His own personality, then it is the Holy Spirit He sent that is His sole and all-sufficient representative. But in the highest view of His heavenly ministry, the Lord, though now unseen, is by His word and Spirit really present in the Church and at work in the world. The priestly, regal and prophetic functions with which the Church is intrusted belong to her only in subordination to Christ as now co-operating with her on earth in the superintendence of His own cause, and can be but imperfectly fulfilled by her at the best. It is a mere travesty of the apostolic doctrine to compare the unity of the indwelling Spirit with the Church with that which exists between the divine and human natures of the Son of God. The Church cannot receive prerogatives in forms that are really incommunicable. She has therefore no independent authority to decide on the meaning of Scripture. She cannot act as a mediator for herself. Under the guidance of the Spirit, the members and office-bearers of the Church are to study the word, and their authorised courts may express the results in symbols or formulas. But these are of value only as they approximate to the mind of Christ as exhibited in the word. Final or unquestionable authority can never be attached to them.

The view that thus cannot be established by general considerations is equally bereft of help from the more explicit statements of Scripture referred to. It is true that the gates of Hades shall not prevail against the Church; and this doubtless includes the promise that Satan's attempt to destroy her by error shall not succeed. But the utterance cannot be legitimately held to include the communication to the Church of infallibility or the gift of absolutely inerrable teaching. As has been shown, the promise is really one of indestructibility or, more specifically, indefectibility. In spite of the assaults of her enemies, and the tumult and conflict of the ages, there will always be a Church on the earth, loyal to the faith and service of her glorified Head. The promise of leading His disciples into all the truth was fulfilled by the Lord, when He enabled them to develop their gospel and write the New Testament. It is being gradually fulfilled to His ministers and His people still, as they study the Scriptures. But it cannot be held to imply that the Church as a whole shall never fall into error or teach it. The Church in Israel often fell into error, and, as history too distinctly shows, the Christian Church has been often for a time involved in the same snare. So also the Lord Jesus is to co-operate with His people in the evangelisation of the world, by the teaching of His truth; and, so far as they reflect His mind in their doctrine, they shall have His blessing. Yet even here there is no direct promise that they shall infallibly express His will. The Church is "the Ground and Pillar of the truth," not because she cannot err, but because she is the living manifest basis on which the truth as taught on earth rests, and because it is her supreme function to exhibit it to all the world. By the Church as a whole the truth of God will never be lost: rather shall she grow in the apprehension of it. More than this is not promised. Security against error depends solely on the presence and co-witness of the spirit of wisdom and revelation; and it will be enjoyed by the Church only as she receives His power and yields to His guidance.

To maintain in the face of such strong testimony that the Church of Rome in particular has this attribute of infallibility in teaching is still more hopeless. Even when she was acquiring dominion over the other Churches, there were many disciples in almost every country, and these amongst the noblest of their day, who dissented from her teaching as being contrary to the word of God. The Reformation itself was just a culmination of protest from every Church in Europe against the errors in doctrine and life into which the Roman Church had fallen. Since then, in order to obtain the merest pretext for a foundation of her teaching, she has had to erect her own tradition into a standard practically co-ordinate with the word of God. In truth, her claim to infallibility in the interpretation of Scripture has led the Church of Rome to abandon it altogether as the ultimate source of doctrine.

The attempt to fix more precisely the seat and source of authoritative teaching within her own pale, is equally futile. It cannot be the General Councils of the Church. For, as one of the Articles of the Anglican Church says of them, " When they be gathered together (forasmuch as they be an assembly of men, whereof all be not governed with the Spirit and word of God) they may err and sometime have erred, even in things pertaining to God."[1] The history of the Church of Rome often shows one Council contradicting its predecessor; as, for example, the Vatican Council contradicted the decisions of the Council of Constance. Nor can the whole body of the episcopate be the seat of infallibility. For, as we have seen, it cannot be proved that the so-called bishops of the Church of Rome, or indeed of any hierarchical Church, are in any exclusive sense the legitimate successors of the apostles. Promises of divine guidance made to the Twelve by the Lord are applicable to other ministers of the Church, only so far as they have received the commission and responsibilities of the Twelve. But the laying down of the truths of divine revelation for the perpetual guidance of men is not one of the functions that have been thus transmitted.

The claim of infallibility for the Pope, even in the sense to which it has been narrowed by the Vatican Council, is no less void. The three great "Petrine" texts that are adduced in support of the dogma are as worthless for establishing the infallibility of the Pope in teaching as they are for his primacy in government. Peter was not a "rock" in the capacity of a teacher beyond any of the other apostles. So many of the Fathers maintain; and apart from their unanimous testimony, the Church cannot uphold any view. The "faith" of Peter which was not to fail was not his doctrinal convictions, but his personal trust in the Lord, as a sinner needing to be saved by grace. The confirmation he was to impart to his brethren was simply the strength and encouragement which his experience of conversion and restoration would enable him to dispense to all amongst whom he was to live. The work of feeding the sheep to which he was called was nothing beyond the instruction which as an under-shepherd of Christ he was to give to the Churches he founded or visited.

The evidence from tradition in behalf of papal infallibility is

[1] Art. XXI.

almost too trivial to require examination. It was so unsatisfactory to the bishops assembled at the Vatican Council, that, rather than assent to its validity, many of them left the Council before the decree was promulgated. Several of the most learned theologians of the Church openly repudiated such an interpretation of the facts of history. These evidently had truth on their side. Not a few of the Popes of Rome openly embraced what were at the time considered heretical tenets ; and in their own position they did what they could to influence the opinions of others in the same direction. The plea that this is not *ex cathedra* teaching is a vain defence. In every doctrinal utterance, the Pope is the public functionary and mouthpiece of the Church. The Bishop of Rome who as a bishop adopts error cannot repudiate it in Council, without robbing his position of all claim to consistency and respect.

The conclusion to which this discussion points may now be briefly stated. It is the duty of every branch of the Church of Christ to engage in the study and interpretation of the Scriptures. They are also at liberty to present the results at which they arrive in doctrinal statements formulated so as to lead up to and elucidate the teaching of Scripture. But every member of each Church is called upon and is at liberty, not merely to receive these statements, but, so far as they are able, to examine them in the light of the evidence adduced in their behalf and then embrace or reject them as the proof seems to be adequate or not. Thus is due respect rendered to the Church, while any claim to infallibility is rightly repudiated. We deal with the Church on the same principle as we deal with lesser institutions. To use an illustration of Dr. Salmon's, "A town clock is of excellent use in publicly making known with authority the correct time—making it known to many, who perhaps at no time, and certainly not at all times, would find it convenient or even possible to verify its correctness for themselves. And yet it is clear, that one who maintained the great desirability of having such a clock, and believed it to be of great use to the neighbourhood, would not be in the least inconsistent, if he also maintained that it was possible for the clock to go astray, and if, on that account, he inculcated the necessity of frequently comparing it and regulating it by the dial which receives its light from heaven." [1]

There is but one "infallible teacher" in the Church of Christ, and He is the Holy Ghost sent down from heaven. The ascertainment of His mind is the ever-present work of the Church on earth as she studies the Scriptures. He is prepared to dispense the unerring truth to her ministers and people, while by personal search and prayer they show themselves desirous of it and prepared to receive it. In past ages, the blessed Advocate has given much that has greatly promoted the edification and comfort of Christ's people. He will give more all the days, even unto the end of the world.

[1] *Infallibility of the Church*, pp. 115, 116 (2nd ed. .

CHAPTER IX

THE AUTHORITY OF THE CHURCH—PAPAL SUPREMACY

THE constitution and teaching of the Church furnish a very ready transition to the authority which in virtue of these she wields. Every duly constituted branch of the Church that teaches her members and adherents is entitled to exercise a certain jurisdiction over them. The Church of Rome has gone beyond all others in magnifying this office. Governed by prelates claiming to rule by divine right and having at their head one chief bishop or Pope, dispensing also a doctrine that professes to be absolutely infallible, the Church of Rome asserts an authority that is practically unlimited. Since the preceding chapter exhibits only one of the spheres in which this authority is exercised, it will be fitting to examine somewhat more in detail the way in which it accrued to her, and therewith also the real scope of the province it aspires to govern and the forms it assumes.

After what has been said, it would be needless to dwell on the fact that it is over the whole Church of Christ that the Romish Church claims to exercise dominion. Thus much was, as we have seen, granted at the Council of Florence and in a general way at least has never been denied by any of the parties within her pale. The Gallican Church, it is true, fought hard against the idea that the Roman Primate could exercise jurisdiction over the whole Church as one body, the motive for this resistance being the fear lest the Pope should thereby be regarded as superior to all œcumenical Councils. Bossuet especially took up high ground on this point ; and at the Vatican Council (1870), there were not wanting indications that something of the same spirit still lingered in the hearts of eminent prelates of France. Yet even the defenders of the Gallican "liberties" would not have denied that in a real sense the Church of Rome through her pontifical head did have a certain jurisdiction over the Church of every country of the world. It is a distinct element in the creed of Pope Pius IV. that the Roman Church is "the mother and mistress of all Churches" ;[1] and to all that this implies every Romanist is bound solemnly to adhere.

In support of this sweeping claim, the Church of Rome, we have

[1] Art. X.

seen, appeals not only to the statements in Scripture that seem to teach the primacy of Peter but also to the history and tradition of the primitive Church. On the principles of Romanism, this latter kind of testimony ought to be specially clear and trustworthy. For if there be any one element of the Romish position more fundamental than another, it is the tenet that wherever the Scriptures do not give a certain sound, the lack can be supplied by historical tradition reaching up to the times of the apostles. Accordingly, not a few Romish apologists have at various times attempted, as some indeed attempt still, to show that from a very early period after Peter's primacy, the Church of Rome as the seat of the Apostolic See claimed to be regarded as the source of supreme jurisdiction over the whole Church and was in the person of her Bishop actually accorded that position. Every statement and action of the Bishops of Rome that seem to favour this view have been treasured. No less precious in this connection are any expressions of superior regard that letters or communications to these dignitaries may contain : while any references to the Roman bishops for decisions in matters of dispute amongst other Churches are also laid hold of for the same end. It is of such materials that the evidence from history in the first three centuries is admittedly composed. A favourable specimen is the well-known statement of Irenæus in which, speaking of the Church at Rome he says that "to this Church on account of its more powerful principality, it is necessary for every Church to have recourse."[1]

It is only fair, however, to say that some of the most distinguished Romish theologians are evidently not prepared to attach much weight to this kind of evidence. The chain seems too slender for the burden it has to carry. They prefer to accept the facts regarding papal supremacy presented by the history of the fourth and fifth centuries, and, believing that they represent an earlier tradition, to fall back on the authority of the Church as competent to define straight away what is to be regarded as rooted in apostolic teaching. Perron and Petavius may be taken as representatives of this class.

In more recent times the apologists of Rome have resorted to the Theory of Development as fitted, if not altogether to take the place of the argument from tradition, at least to supplement and buttress it. Cardinal Newman has shown how it may be utilised for this purpose. He frankly admits that the traces of Roman supremacy in the first age, various as they are, are faint and dim enough. But he contends that this state of the case is just what might have been expected. The idea of papal supremacy, derived from Scripture through the Apostle Peter, was present in the mind of his successors from the beginning as a doctrinal germ. There is every reason to believe that the principle of "a monarchical power in the Church" is an essential feature of the divine scheme ; simply because the Church needs it. But it was never promulgated in an express or formal way, because the outward circumstances of the Church were not

[1] Cf. Salmon, *Infallibility of the Church*, p. 381.

such as to require its publication. "St. Peter's prerogative would remain a mere letter, till the complication of ecclesiastical matters became the cause of ascertaining it. . . . The *regalia Petri* might sleep as the power of a chancellor has slept ; not as an absolute, for they had never been carried into effect, but as a mysterious privilege, which was not understood : as an unfulfilled prophecy. When the Church was thrown upon her own resources, first local disturbances gave rise to bishops, and next œcumenical disturbances gave exercise to Popes ; and whether communion with the Pope was necessary for catholicity would not and could not be debated till a suspension of that communion had actually occurred."[1] In the long-run a series of events did take place momentous enough to throw the Church of Rome back on her prerogatives and then they were elicited and exhibited in the fulness of their power.

The leading influences that tended to this result as well as the stages at which they took effect, "apart from the question of motive," the upholders of this theory have apparently no objection to state at length. The full presentation of them belongs to the historian. It may be simply said here that the paramount interest of the Roman Church in the smaller Churches she had founded ; the dignity of Rome as the capital of the empire ; the territorial division of the Church into prefectures, dioceses, and provinces in conformity with the divisions of the empire by Constantine, and the consequent appointment of patriarchs, exarchs, and metropolitans ; the decrees of successive emperors (some of them manifest forgeries) recognising the Bishop of Rome as exempt from human judgment and practically making him an arch-patriarch ; and finally the claim of that Bishop amidst the decay of the empire to be the successor of Peter as the Primate of the whole Church, are among the chief forces operating in this direction. By their dexterity and persistence in turning them to the best account, the Roman prelates in the long-run gained the sole right to the name and position of Pope and attained to undisputed supremacy over all the Churches of the West. As early as the Council of Chalcedon (451), Leo, archbishop of old Rome, claims to act with the authority of "St. Peter, who is the rock and foundation of the Church and the ground of faith." By the close of the sixth century, most of the Western Fathers fully acquiesced in the prerogative.

But the Bishops of Rome speedily showed that they had higher aims than that of ecclesiastical supremacy. The principle of the Pope's being the vicar of Christ contained the germ of a claim to exercise the supreme power on earth ; and they never rested till this summit was attained. Gaining first a certain range of territory for the Papacy, the Popes established the possession of temporal power. Within their own dominions they claimed temporal sovereignty. When they had once gained a footing amongst the monarchs of the world, they claimed to exercise complete temporal as well as

[1] *Development of Christian Doctrine*, pp. 150, 151.

ecclesiastical supremacy over all the nations and kings of earth. The influences and events by which this exalted position was reached and for a time held, lie patent on the surface of the history of Europe in the Middle Ages. Amongst these may be mentioned, the conversion of the barbarian kings of the north to Christianity and their willing acceptance of the long experience of Rome in everything pertaining to religion ; the large gifts of Lombard cities to the Pope by Pepin, his favourite in France ; the still greater donations of Charlemagne ; the claim of Pope Leo III. to confer the imperial crown ; the separation of the Italian provinces from the throne of Constantine and their virtual subjection to the Roman Pontiff ; the growing wealth of the bishops and clergy ; the deepening ignorance and superstition of the people by which they were more readily enslaved ; and above all the gradual exclusion of the emperor's right to interfere with or sanction the election of the Pope. By the use equally bold and stealthy of the opportunities thus afforded, the Popes gradually established the idea of their supreme temporal dominion in almost every country of Europe. Gregory VII., in spite of his later discomfiture, saw the victory won. His successor, Innocent III., may be said to have enjoyed all its fruits. In a letter of his, written at the close of the twelfth century, the pontifical and regal powers are compared to the sun and moon respectively. As the moon receives light from the sun, so the royal authority in each country is derived solely from the imperial source in the See of Rome.[1]

From the claim to this supreme ecclesiastical and temporal jurisdiction, the Church of Rome has never receded. The principles on which it was at first seized are bound up with her very existence. If Christ be the vicar of God and the Pope the vicar of Christ, she cannot dare to surrender what is really an essential right. For Christ is exalted as Head over all things for "His body, which is the Church." He is King of kings and Lord of lords. Since according to the theory of Rome, Christ's kingdom on earth is to be a counterpart of the heavenly reign, the Pope as His vicar must claim the lordship at once of the Church and every throne on the face of the earth.

The sphere in which the reality of this supremacy is most distinctly seen is of course the Church. As a living apologist has said, "The Church is at the present day governed as an absolute monarchy, the Bishop of Rome being the monarch."[2] The province over which he claims jurisdiction is technically defined as her "faith and morals." But this is a very comprehensive domain. Under "faith" falls every doctrine which the members of the Church are to believe and profess and therewith every form of worship and discipline they are to practise. Under "morals" come the whole outward life and relations and activities of the people. In short, nothing in human life would seem to be beyond the reach of papal legislation. The theologian just quoted says : "There are certain points of discipline

[1] Cf. Mirbt, *Quellen*, etc. s. 79.   [2] Hunter, i. p. 404.

which according to the common opinion are of divine and not of human institution : such is probably the religious observance of the weekly memory of the Resurrection of Christ: perhaps also the Spring Fast. The Pope, therefore, could not wholly abrogate these institutions, though he can modify the observance of them as he sees fit ; and his legislative power is subject to no other restriction ; every merely human law, though it may be ancient in the Church and even of apostolic origin, may be swept away by him who at the present day wields an authority equal, if not superior, to that of the apostles or other men by whom the law was enacted." [1]

This being so, it is easy to discern that the authority of the Roman See extends also to the whole political life and relations of the members of the Church, and so far as their influence can go, to the State of which they form a larger or smaller part. In the Romish theology, "politics are a part of morals." The present Pope, Leo XIII., has said that, "Politics are inseparably bound up with the laws of morality and religious duties." [2] As to the precise kind of jurisdiction which the Pope may legitimately claim to wield in the political life of a nation, there has been a difference of opinion. From the days of Gregory VII. to Pius V., the Popes assumed the right of universal temporal supremacy, on the ground that this had been assigned to them by divine right as the vicars of Christ. Cardinal Bellarmin, however, taught that, while entitled to exercise direct and immediate jurisdiction in the Church, the Pope had an authority in the State only of an indirect and mediate kind. The most common opinion of modern theologians is that the supremacy formerly exercised by the Popes was an accident of the age in which they lived ; and that, so far from possessing such jurisdiction in temporal matters are the Popes of modern times, that they have nothing but a privilege of "direction," which is due entirely to their spiritual position and authority. This is the view promoted by such writers as Cardinal Wiseman and Count de Maistre. Other prelates, however, no less eminent, evidently believe that within this power of direction slumbers all the temporal supremacy which by his very relation to Christ, the Pope is still entitled to claim. Of these the late Cardinal Manning may be taken as an example. For while he held that "the Church and the State should stand in relations of mutual recognition, amity and co-operation under the supreme direction of the Vicar of Jesus Christ, Pontiff and King," he also contended that "the right of deposing kings is inherent in the supreme sovereignty which the Popes as vicegerents of Christ exercise over all Christian nations." [3]

With such a hold on the ecclesiastical and civil relations of the people, the See of Rome may well assume that there is no department of human life that is exempt from its authority. Every movement for the progress and welfare of society must belong to its province. There is no enterprise by which social reform is carried

---

[1] Hunter, i. pp. 397, 398. [2] *Encyclical Letter*, 10th June 1890.
[3] *Essays on Religion*, etc. (1867), pp. 19, 20.

out that does not receive the most careful attention from Rome. The work of education is watched with sleepless solicitude. The Roman priesthood in every country is always agitating for extension or fresh endowments of her educational establishments. The family also must come more completely under the sway of the Church. Whatever is lacking in other channels can be supplied by the confessional. The life of every individual member of the Church indeed is really encompassed by her influence and authority on every side. It is an element of the Canon Law that it is "necessary to salvation that every human creature be subject to the Roman Pontiff."[1] When a man believes this, he has a motive for entire surrender of the most potent kind.

Thus the authority claimed by the Pope is intended to be at once cumulative and unlimited. Through the Church and the State, society and the family, it reaches the individual. Through the convictions of the individual, it returns with fresh energy to the family, the Church and the State, to influence, if it be possible, the whole world.

In dealing from the Protestant side with this vast array of pretensions, it would be quite legitimate to take up the position that, since they confessedly depend on the Roman primacy on the one hand and the infallibility of the Pope on the other, both of which have been shown to be null and void, the whole of this jurisdiction is left without any real basis. But for the sake of exhibiting the corresponding truth more fully, the foregoing chain of argument may be briefly passed in review.

The evidence for the jurisdiction of the See of Rome derived from the first three centuries is plainly of no value. The fact that the ablest Romanist apologists do not rely upon it testifies as much. Complimentary phrases used of the Roman Church do not imply an acknowledgment of authority. In that age the prelates of large cities were as ready to give adulation as they were eager to receive it. The phrase of Irenæus referred to is derived from a barbarous Latin translation of a lost work in Greek. At most, the reference is to the civil and social superiority of the city and not to ecclesiastical supremacy.

The proof supposed to be furnished by the fourth and fifth centuries is far from extensive or harmonious. The Eastern bishops never fully recognised the universal jurisdiction of Rome. The Sees of Antioch, Alexandria, and Constantinople claimed equal dignity. Several of the best Roman bishops expressly disclaimed the idea of lordship over other Churches. Gregory the Great, for example, declared that it was a sin to assume the title of universal Bishop and called himself "the Servant of servants." It was the Emperor Phocas, himself a murderer and a usurper, that first gave this title to the Roman bishops.

Even admitting that the Bishop of Rome did as a matter of fact

[1] Mirbt, *Quellen*, etc. s. 90.

attain the position of Pope and head of the whole Western Church, we cannot accept the explanation of the victory given in the Theory of Development. As we shall see presently, there is no antecedent probability that the Christian Church was to be one vast community under the government of a single monarch on earth. The earliest Christian literature yields no traces of the presence of this idea in the minds of men. The Bishops of Rome were animated in the struggle for supremacy by manifest ambition and lust of power and never hesitated to adopt any measures, however doubtful their character, that might be likely to further this aim. The claim to be the vicars of Christ was brought forward by the Popes at a comparatively late period of the conflict and was based on an interpretation of the words of Christ to Peter that cannot be said to have the unanimous consent of the Fathers. It was really an afterthought and was resorted to at all only because the imperial protection under which the Church had previously flourished, was beginning to pass away.

Besides, as we have seen, the Church has no power to pronounce on the legitimacy of any such development of doctrine. It lies outside the sphere of revelation and cannot possibly carry with it any divine right. The whole dogma of the papal authority is a mere human device, which, while it has not the least countenance in Scripture is further chargeable with being in direct contrariety to the great general principles concerning the Church, laid down there.

1. It is opposed, for example, to what the word of God teaches on *the real nature of the Church*. The Church of Rome proceeds on the idea that the whole Church in the world must have an outward corporate unity; and that the only way of securing this feature is to have one supreme ruler over it. De Maistre, who in this is followed by Newman, said: "If there be anything evident to reason as well as faith, it is that the universal Church is a monarchy. The idea of universality itself supposes this form of government, the absolute necessity of which reposes on the double ground of the number of subjects and the geographical extent of the empire."[1] But the unity that is to characterise the Church of Christ is everywhere set forth in Scripture as not outward, but inward, and corporate only as it is spiritual; and so far is the idea of an empire from determining her life and work in the world that the Lord Jesus expressly excludes it from the imitation of His people. "The kings of the Gentiles have lordship over them; and they that have authority over them are called benefactors. But ye shall not be so."[2] In view of this utterance, Dr. Julius Hare did not write too strongly, when he said: "In truth this Romish inability to recognise the unity of the Church without the help of a visible human centre is only another instance of that miserable incapacity for faith in spiritual realities which, we have repeatedly observed, is the pervading character of Romanism."[3]

2. For, in the second place, the doctrine of papal supremacy is

[1] *Du Pape* (Charpentier), p. 3. [2] Luke xxii. 25.
[3] *The Contest with Rome*, p. 237.

THE AUTHORITY OF THE CHURCH—PAPAL SUPREMACY 235

also opposed to the Scripture testimony on *the constitution of the Church*. It is true that the Church must have a head even as a spiritual society. But this head has been provided by God in His glorified Son. "Yet have I set My king upon My holy hill of Zion."[1] He "gave Him to be head over all things to the Church, which is His body, the fulness of Him that filleth all in all."[2] When the Lord Jesus withdrew from earth to heaven, He did indeed send a representative to take His place. But this was one who was in all things equal to Himself, "the Comforter, which is the Holy Ghost." He alone is the all-sufficient vicar of Christ on earth. The appointment of a human monarch over the Church is an affront alike to the sovereignty of Christ and the plenipotentiary dignity of the Holy Spirit.

3. The papal supremacy also involves a violation of *the real functions of the Church*. The Pope, as monarch of the Church, claims temporal sovereignty within his dominions and temporal supremacy over the kings of the earth. This is directly antagonistic to the mind of Christ. He has appointed a form of government for His Church; but it is intended to deal with men only in their spiritual and ecclesiastical relations. The exercise of civil authority is foreign to the province and aims of the Church. The will of the Lord is that the realm of the Church should be kept distinct from that of the State. Neither is to trench on the sphere or relations of the other: they are two separate and co-ordinate jurisdictions. The Church of Rome is right in so far as she maintains the independence of the Church in purely spiritual matters. In this respect, we are justified in following her example. But she errs in holding that the State is to be in any civil matters subject to the control of the Church. The teaching of Christ is as much opposed to spiritual despotism, as it is to Erastianism. "Render unto Cæsar the things that are Cæsar's: unto God the things that are God's."[3] "My kingdom is not of this world."[4] Any departure from these principles leads to tyranny and persecution.

4. Last of all, the papal supremacy is obviously *opposed to the scriptural delineation of human freedom*. By the constitution of the Church of Rome, the Pope is made the absolute lord of the individual mind and conscience. No member of the Church is at liberty to believe or teach or practise anything that is not in accordance with the dictates of the papal chair, however much it may seem to be sanctioned by the word of God. Speaking in the name of the Pope, Cardinal Manning said: "I acknowledge no civil superior; I am the subject of no prince; and I claim more than this: I claim to be the supreme judge on earth and director of the consciences of men: I am the last supreme judge of what is right and wrong."[5] In this utterance, he only summarised the teaching of the whole Canon Law. Every member of the Church of Rome is by his very hope of salva-

[1] Ps. ii. 6.   [2] Eph. i. 22.   [3] Matt. xxii. 21.
[4] John xviii. 36.   [5] Sermon, *Tablet*, Oct. 9, 1864.

tion bound hand and foot to the papal will. Not so taught the divine Head of the Church : "Thou shalt worship the Lord thy God and Him only shalt thou serve"; "We ought to obey God rather than man"; "The Head of every man is Christ."

It is no valid rejoinder to these objections to say that, as a matter of fact, the Popes of Rome did attain to this supremacy, exercised it for centuries, and, so far at least as the Church is concerned, maintain it up to this hour. We admit the historic fact: nay more, we grant that there is something very impressive in the way in which this Church has retained her strong dominion over so wide a field, while other empires have crumbled into ruins. But the argument from prescription is not sufficient to demonstrate that this sway has the divine approval, as the only exemplar of true ecclesiastical government. The Eastern Church in this view could easily be shown to have higher claims on the sympathy and respect of the world than that of Rome. The present religion of Thibet has endured for almost as long a period and swayed as large a multitude as the Church of Rome. The Llama or head of it is regarded as the vicegerent of God and the centre of all civil government. Yet as an eminent teacher of history and philosophy has described it, this religion of the Far East "is nearly, if not altogether, the most degrading and immoral and pitiless idolatry on the face of the earth."[1]

[1] Archer Butler, *Letters on Romanism*, p. 317.

CHAPTER X

THE CHURCH IN RELATION TO THE UNSEEN WORLD

THE life of the heavenly world has always been a subject of deep interest to mankind on earth. The pagan fancy peopled it with various orders at different stages of progress. The pious in Israel took advantage of every germ of truth or fact given in their sacred writings to expand their conceptions of its angelic inhabitants. When the hope of immortality was confirmed and illustrated by the gospel, the relations in which those who had passed within the veil stood to their brethren here on earth, became the subject of more engrossing thought and meditation.

By the Church of Rome this interest has been stimulated to the uttermost. During the course of many centuries, it has manifested itself in three different though closely related ways. In the first place, those that are thought or declared by the Church to have entered on the bliss of heaven, have become the objects of worship. Then any relics of their earthly life as well as pictures and images of them have received a similar veneration. In particular, the mother of our Lord has been exalted to the highest position of honour and authority; and every form in which the art of man can fittingly represent her glory has been declared worthy of full reverence. In this last chapter, we shall present and examine the teaching of Rome on these topics, stating first the forms in which the doctrine is held and then the grounds on which it is maintained.

1. On the honour or worship due to those who are regarded as having passed at once into perfect bliss, the Council of Trent has charged the priests to teach: "That the saints who reign together with Christ, offer up their own prayers to God for men; that it is good and useful suppliantly to invoke them and to have recourse to their prayers, aid and help for obtaining benefits from God, through His Son Jesus Christ our Lord, who is our alone Redeemer and Saviour."[1] The Catechism of Trent repeats essentially the same statement, including, however, with the saints in glory, the angelic spirits with whom they are now supposed to be united.[2]

In support of this doctrine, it is maintained that instances of the worship of angels and saints by men are given in the Scriptures;

[1] Sess. XXV. *Decree on Invocation of Saints*, etc.   [2] Pt. ii. ch. ii. q. 9.

and those from the Old Testament are adduced. Abraham and Lot bowed down before the angels that visited them.¹ Balaam fell flat on his face at the sight of the angel.² Joshua fell on his face and did worship before the angel who was Captain of the Lord's host.³ Saul stooped with his face to the ground and bowed himself before the spirit of Samuel.⁴ Obadiah fell on his face before Elijah.⁵ The sons of the prophets bowed themselves to the ground before Elisha.⁶ Nebuchadnezzar fell upon his face and worshipped Daniel.⁷ If men thus revered and worshipped saints on earth, why should they not also continue the same, if not greater homage to them, now that they are in heaven?

Similarly it is argued in behalf of the invocation of the saints in glory, that we are encouraged to ask the prayers of the righteous here on earth : "Brethren, pray for us" ;⁸ "Praying always with all prayer and supplication for all the saints and for me."⁹ Out of very love to us, the saints perfected in heaven will pray for their brethren on earth. Being in the presence of God, they will pray with greater power ; why should we not appeal to them in the like spirit to pray for us?

In anticipation of an obvious objection, the Romanist divines are careful to teach that the worship and invocation which we are thus to offer to saints, is not to be identified with that which is due to God. The latter must be of the highest kind (*latria*): the former is only the inferior worship that may be given to His creatures (*doulia*). Hence it is alleged there is in this practice, no infringement of the honour that is due to God alone.

The Church of Rome maintains that in support of this worship and invocation they have the testimony of the Church, if not from the earliest times, at least from a period sufficiently early to indicate what the practice of the primitive Church must have been. Special stress is laid on the example of Gregory Nazianzen, who towards the end of the fourth century made addresses to the souls of departed saints. Jerome is also claimed as testifying to the value of this kind of appeal to the spirits of the dead. They may be present everywhere like the Lamb whom they follow : they may also frequent the shrines where their relics are kept and where services in their honour are held.¹⁰ Through such influences, the practice became almost universal in the Churches over which Rome exercised the greatest sway.

One special means by which the Church of Rome has fostered the worship of the saints in heaven, has been her continual additions to the number of those who may be authoritatively regarded as saints of the Church. When it is proposed to add a departed member of her communion to the roll of saints, a formal debate on

---

¹ Gen. xviii. 2, xix. 1.   ² Num. xxii. 31.   ³ Josh. v. 15.
⁴ 1 Sam. xxviii. 20.   ⁵ 1 Kings xviii. 7.   ⁶ 2 Kings ii. 15.
⁷ Dan. ii. 46.   ⁸ 1 Thess. v. 25.   ⁹ Eph. vi. 18.
¹⁰ Cf. Browne, *Thirty-nine Articles*, pp. 511-519.

the subject of his claims to the honour is held in the presence of the supreme Pontiff. If he decides that the claims are valid, then the saint is canonised, that is, formally enrolled in the catalogue of the saints recognised by the Canon Law, in a public assembly. Thenceforward prayers may be addressed to him in public worship; masses may be performed in his honour; images and pictures of him may be placed in the churches; and even churches and altars erected to his reverential remembrance. Of such saints more or less well known and distinguished, the Church of Rome professes to have already many hundreds of thousands.

2. On the worship due to the relics and pictures or images of the saints, the Church of Rome at the Council of Trent made these statements : " The holy bodies of holy martyrs and of others now living with Christ . . . are to be venerated by the faithful; through which (bodies) many benefits are bestowed by God on men ; so that they who affirm that veneration and honour are not due to the relics of saints . . . are wholly to be condemned." "Moreover that the images of Christ, of the Virgin Mother of God, and of the other saints are to be had and retained particularly in temples and that due honour and veneration are to be given them." [1]

In behalf of the veneration of relics, Romanists adduce the facts that the pot of manna and the rod of Aaron were preserved in the temple; [2] and that miracles of healing were wrought by contact with the bones of Elisha, with the hem of Christ's robe, by the shadow of Peter passing by, by handkerchiefs and aprons that had touched the body of Paul.[3] The words of Isaiah are also quoted from the Vulgate : " In Him shall the Gentiles trust and His sepulchre shall be glorious." [4]

In support of the veneration of images they mention the facts that there were cherubim made of gold placed on the mercy-seat of the tabernacle ; [5] that Moses lifted up a brazen serpent before the people in the wilderness ; [6] that there were carved figures of cherubim in the temple.[7] The Vulgate version of a command in one of the psalms is also quoted : " Exalt ye the Lord our God and worship His footstool : for it is holy." [8]

Against the view that such practices savour of idolatry, the Church of Rome enters a strong protest. Speaking of the veneration of images, the Council of Trent said : " Not that any divinity or virtue is believed to be in them on account of which they are to be worshipped ; or that anything is to be asked of them ; or that trust is to be reposed in images as was of old done by the Gentiles who placed their hope in idols ; but because the honour which is shown them is referred to the prototypes which these images represent." [9]

Here also Rome claims the support of the ancient Church. The

---

[1] Sess. XXV. *ut sup.* [2] Ex. xvi. 33 ; Num. xvii. 8.
[3] 2 Kings xiii. 21 ; Matt. ix. 20–22 ; Acts v. 15, xix. 12.
[4] Isa. xi. 10.   [5] Ex. xxv. 18.   [6] Num. xxi. 8, 9.
[7] 1 Kings vi. 29.   [8] Ps. xcv. 9.   [9] *Ut sup.*

two Fathers already mentioned are held to give special sanction to the veneration of relics and images. Gregory Nazianzen ascribed miracles to the ashes of Cyprian. Jerome said : "We honour the relics of the martyrs that we may worship Him whose martyrs they are." Tertullian speaks of a picture of the Good Shepherd having been graven on a sacramental cup. Towards the close of the fourth century, pictures are introduced into churches. By the end of the sixth, many statues are also found there. A bitter and prolonged controversy on the worship of images was supposed by the Church of Rome to have been settled finally at the second General Council of Nice (787), which ordained that images were to be erected and honour paid them, though not the kind that was to be offered to God. It is on the teaching of this Council, that the Council of Trent professes to base its decrees.[1]

3. On the invocation of the mother of Jesus and the worship due to pictures or images of her, the Council of Trent issued no special decree. It was assumed that from her position as "the Virgin Mother of God," special honour would be paid to her amongst the saints of the Church, as had been done for centuries before. As a recent writer has said : "We hold that the privileges which she enjoys and the honour which is her due are decreed by God as 'convenient' sequels to the decree by which God willed that His Son should take upon Him human nature and be born of a woman."[2] One special privilege the Council did insist upon. In one of the canons attached to the decree on Justification it is distinctly indicated that "the Church holds of the blessed Virgin" that she was able during her whole life to avoid all sins "by a special privilege from God."[3]

The question as to whether she was free from original as well as actual sin was also raised. But it was found that on this topic there were grave differences of opinion amongst the Fathers ; and, to avoid an open conflict, it was agreed simply to leave the matter in the undecided state in which it had been left by the Constitutions of Pope Sixtus IV.[4] His decision was essentially a brief in favour of toleration : for he simply anathematised any who should declare the doctrine of the Immaculate Conception to be a heresy or the festival held in its honour to be illegal. Since that time, the growth of opinion in the Church, in spite of much controversy, has been on the whole so strong that, in response to what he regarded as a unanimous requisition of the bishops, Pope Pius IX. in 1854 issued a Bull in which, on his own responsibility, he finally settled all doubts by declaring that "the doctrine which holds that the blessed Virgin Mary was in the first instant of her conception by a singular privilege and grace of Almighty God, in virtue of the merits of Jesus Christ, the Saviour of mankind, preserved immaculate from all stain of original sin, has been revealed by God and should therefore be constantly and firmly believed by all the faithful."

[1] Cf. Browne, *ut sup.*
[2] Hunter, vol. ii. p. 545.
[3] Canon 23.
[4] Decrees, Sess. V. *ad fin.*

In recent times, there has also been a growingly favourable view of another opinion concerning the career of the mother of Jesus entertained by many writers amongst the Romanists. This is to the effect that, while the Virgin Mary was at her death taken at once to heaven, her body was buried in Gethsemane by the angels. There it was preserved from corruption and on the third day it was translated into heaven : so that she is now in a glorified body at the right hand of her Son. It is chiefly on the ground of this alleged ascension that the Virgin is addressed by such names as "Queen of the world," "Queen of the heavens." Hence also it is that the worship paid to her (*hyperdoulia*), though still short of what is due to God, is much higher than what may be lawfully rendered to the saints. Moreover it is thought only congruous with the whole career of "the Mother of God," that she should be regarded as having preserved her virginity throughout her whole mortal life.[1]

An adequate proof of all these privileges is thought by most Romanists to be found in the simple fact that Mary was the mother of the Son of God. But others do not hesitate to say that they are all, if not directly and explicitly taught, at least suggested and sustained in the written word. Much stress is laid on the parallel that appears to exist betwixt Eve and Mary. As the one was the mother of the natural race of mankind, so is the other, as the mother of the second Man, the Lord from heaven, the mother and mediator of all God's ransomed children. In this connection, the Vulgate version of the divine sentence on the serpent is quoted and referred directly to the Virgin Mary : "I will put enmities between thee and the woman and thy seed and her seed : *she* shall crush thy head and thou shalt lie in wait for her heel."[2] The seed is Christ; and the woman, it is held, must be Mary. Other proofs adduced are the salutation of the angel in which Mary is hailed as "full of grace,"[3] and the announcement of Elisabeth that she was "blessed among women."[4] When the dying Saviour said to His mother : "Woman, behold thy son,"[5] He really intrusted all the redeemed to her care. This position of guardianship is supposed to be indicated in the wonder appearing in heaven mentioned by the Apostle John, which was "a woman clothed with the sun, and the moon under her feet, and upon her head a crown of twelve stars."[6]

It is admitted by most Romanists, as, for example, by Cardinal Newman, "that there was no public and ecclesiastical recognition of the place which St. Mary holds in the economy of grace : this was reserved for the fifth century."[7] Evidence of its growth is found in the frequent use of the title "Theotokos" or "mother of God" by the Fathers in their writings. Towards the end of the fifth century, this title was used by some in the public prayers of the Church. In the

[1] Cf. Hunter, vol. ii. p. 581. [2] Gen. iii. 15.
[3] Luke i. 28 (Vulg.). [4] Luke v. 42.
[5] John xix. 26. [6] Rev. xii. 1.
[7] *Development of Christian Doctrine*, p. 145.

beginning of the seventh century, Gregory I. introduced the name of the Virgin into the Litanies. In the Council of Constantinople in 754, the refusal to invoke the Virgin Mary along with other saints was anathematised. Since that date her worship has become a constantly growing feature of the Roman service.

In dealing with this whole argument from the Protestant standpoint, we naturally turn in the first place to the proofs adduced from Scripture and the general inferences based on them. Almost every one of these is so irrelevant and inadequate that with the majority of readers, it might be sufficient simply to allude to them. But for the sake of others who may not be so familiar with their meaning, we may pass them briefly in review.

How futile it is, for example, to adduce the instances of personal veneration of angels or eminent men on earth. It cannot be shown that the acts recorded of Abraham, Lot, Joshua, Saul or others had any religious feeling in them. They were simply examples of the very respectful salutation of superiors in wisdom or position that was so common in the East. Who would be guided by the action of an idolatrous despot like Nebuchadnezzar? If Joshua really worshipped the Captain of the Lord's host, it must have been because he was inwardly persuaded that he was divine in origin and authority. The only angel that is mentioned as eager to receive the worship of men is the Prince of darkness; and the Lord Jesus said to him: "Thou shalt worship the Lord thy God, and Him only shalt thou serve."[1] It was on this principle that the angel whom John in his perturbation felt an impulse to worship, repelled the very appearance of such homage: "See thou do it not: I am thy fellow-servant."[2] Similarly Peter would not suffer Cornelius to fall before him: nor would Paul and Barnabas receive the sacrifice offered by the Lycaonians.[3]

As to the argument for invocation from the fact that we may ask intercession from saints on earth, it is enough to say that it is one thing to make such a request from those whom we know and who are placed in similar circumstances with ourselves: another to lift up petitions to others to whom we have no access that we can accept as valid. Why should we ask the prayers of spirits of men, concerning whom we have no certitude they can hear us? Why should we expect God to tell them to pray for us, while in Christ His Son we are spiritually as near to Him as they? Such a practice is distinctly idolatrous. No creature is entitled to any kind of religious worship whatever. Men may draw distinctions in the measure of honour due to God and His saints. The corrupt heart of man inevitably ignores them and sins by giving to the creature the honour that is due to God alone.

Equally worthless for the purpose are the texts quoted in support of the worship of relics and of the pictures and images of the saints. It is true that God did perform miracles of healing in connection

[1] Matt. iv. 10. [2] Rev. xix. 10, xxii. 9. [3] Acts x. 25, 26, xiv. 14, 15.

with the bones of Elisha; and the Lord Jesus by the hem of His robe and by contact with the physical life of His apostles. But the Scripture nowhere informs us that any relics of saints were ever to be retained by men as the channels of healing power. The body of Moses was buried out of sight, lest any idolatrous worship should be paid to it.[1] The pot of manna and Aaron's rod that budded were preserved simply as tokens of the divine interest in Israel and were never worshipped. When a desire to worship the brazen serpent was manifested, Hezekiah had it broken in pieces and was praised for his fidelity to the Lord in doing so.[2] The quotation from the Vulgate misrepresents the original Hebrew, which literally translated is: "Unto Him (Messiah) shall the nations seek and His resting-place (that is, His throne) shall be glorious."

As to the facts mentioned in support of the worship of images, it is not denied that there were emblematical figures in the tabernacle and temple. But Scripture gives not the slightest reason to believe that they were placed there to be worshipped or were ever in fact worshipped. The text from the Vulgate on which Bellarmin lays so much stress is another misrepresentation of the Hebrew. It really is: "Exalt ye the Lord our God and worship at His footstool: holy is He."

It is in vain that Romanists plead that their practice of image-worship is not idolatrous in the sense of the second commandment, because, unlike the heathen whose idol-worship it condemns, they do not rest in the idol itself, but look by means of it to the unseen personal spirit it represents. The intelligent heathen writers who defended the worship of images against the first apologists of Christianity can be proved to have taken up the very same position as the Romanists occupy now. They too contended that the image in itself was nothing to them: it was only a visible means of reaching the unseen prototype to which the homage offered was transferred. Yet the early Fathers of the Church, following the example and authority of the spokesmen of Jehovah, denounced their practice as idolatrous. Scripture condemns image-worship, not simply on the ground that those represented by the images are false gods and therefore not entitled to religious homage, but because "it is irrational, injurious and unlawful to introduce images or external visible representations into the worship of the invisible God"[3] for *any* purpose whatever.

No less inadequate are the proofs brought forward in behalf of the special privileges of the mother of Jesus. It is true that in having been chosen by God out of all the generations to be the mother of the Christ of God, Mary received one of the most honourable distinctions it is possible for the heart of man to imagine. But it is utterly unwarrantable to say that this fact alone, apart from other express statements of Scripture, entitles us to think of her

[1] Deut. xxxiv. 6.   [2] 2 Kings xviii. 4.
[3] Cunningham, *Hist. Theol.* vol. i. p. 374.

as having been preserved from all actual sin; or as having been kept immaculate in the first instant of her conception; or as having been always a virgin; or as having been translated to the right hand of her Son in heaven. The departure from the ordinary course of human life which was made in the conception of Jesus is stated in the most explicit way. Had Mary been the subject of any such moral or physical exceptions, it is only reasonable to expect that these too would have been indicated. Certain it is that the texts quoted furnish no basis for them. The verse taken from the Vulgate version of Genesis is an entire travesty of the original. On every fair interpretation of the prophetic sentence passed on the serpent, the woman is Eve and she alone; and it was not the woman but her seed—the children of God in the first instance and the Son of God in the long-run—that was to bruise the serpent's head. The Apostle Paul draws a parallel betwixt the first man and Christ the Lord.[1] The New Testament never compares Eve and Mary or regards the latter as playing any special part in "the economy of grace." She is not represented as being "full of grace," least of all in the sense of being sinless in conception or in conduct: she is only "highly favoured"; and if she is proclaimed to be "blessed among women," it is not that she is to be blessed by women, but only regarded as having been the subject of a unique and most honourable distinction. Mary herself accepted the function assigned to her but did not forget to acknowledge her personal need of salvation. Throughout the Gospels and the Acts of the Apostles, she retains her fitting place of subordination to the Lord Jesus. She is cared for by Him, but never commended as a source of help. She takes her place amongst the disciples at Pentecost, but receives no further mention in the New Testament.[2] The "woman clothed with the sun" in the Book of Revelation can only be a representation of the Church on earth. In a very real sense, Jesus was the only-begotten Son of the Church as well as the Son of God.

With these facts on the testimony of Scripture before us, it will only be necessary to make some general remarks on the evidence from the history of the Church.

The first is to the effect that it is vain for Romanists to appeal to apostolic tradition in behalf of the practices and doctrines now before us. The Church of the first four centuries, in spite of erratic tendencies in some quarters, set its face against the invocation of saints and the worship of relics and images, and gives not the slightest countenance to the worship of the mother of Jesus. From Justin Martyr to Origen and Origen to Epiphanius, the early writers testify that such practices were abhorrent to them. If Gregory Nazianzen and Jerome seem to favour them, it is still only in a guarded way: while their greater contemporary Augustine condemns them utterly. When the epithet Theotokos was applied to the Virgin, it was not as a title of honour to her, but as a mark of

---

[1] Rom. v. 12-19; 1 Cor. xv. 45-49. [2] Acts i. 14.

the divine dignity of her Son. The truth is that it was only when Christianity had practically gained the victory over paganism and became worldly enough to attempt conciliating the multitudes of heathen who under the influence of Constantine were willing to join the Christian Church, that the idea of invoking saints and worshipping images was tolerated. The heathen had been accustomed to invoke their gods many and lords many and to bow before the statues of their deified heroes. The Church simply substituted her saints for these pagan deities. The growing exaltation of the Virgin Mary will not be strange to those who remember the inveterate hold of the heathen mind in different ancient empires taken by the worship of the mother and her child.[1] The worship of the Virgin finds its prototype in the pagan adoration of Isis in Egypt, Ceres in Greece and Fortuna in Rome.

Moreover, the history of the early Church shows that, even when these practices and the doctrines associated with them had taken root in the Church, they were not always universally accepted. The Church of Rome, for example, regards the second Council of Nice held in 787 at the instance of the Empress Irene, as deciding finally the controversy about the lawfulness of worshipping images. But it is a matter of history that that Council was not regarded as œcumenical by the Eastern Church and that it was only within the sphere of Roman influence that its decisions were accepted. This is proved by the fact that, just as there had been a previous Council held at Constantinople in 754, which condemned the use and worship of images, so in 794 or seventeen years after the second Council of Nice, there was a most influential Synod held at Frankfort under Charlemagne which, in the name of three hundred bishops of the Western Church, formally rejected the Council of Nice and all its decrees. Similarly the so-called privileges of the Virgin Mary were a matter of dispute both before and after the Council of Trent.[2]

It is the force of these facts that has led so many Romanist theologians to regard the Theory of Development with such favour as a means of defending their system. Certain it is that the present topics are regarded as a very suitable field for the illustration and application of its powers. Cardinal Newman has shown at length how the idea of the devotion due to "the Blessed Virgin" took root in the Church and has now in spite of all opposition gained an overmastering hold of the popular mind. It is nothing to him that the idea itself should have no countenance in the Scriptures and that the result of its growth should be manifestly contrary to their spirit: it is enough that it has been developed and that its fruitage has approved itself to the taste of the Church. For reasons shown, this is a guide Protestantism cannot follow.

It is also very noteworthy that even within the circle of the infallible Church, there have been on these very points manifest

[1] Preuss, *Immaculate Conception* (Clark), p. 9.
[2] Cf. Preuss, *ut sup. passim.*

differences of opinion. Notwithstanding her boasted unity in belief and practice, the Church of Rome has here exhibited very remarkable variations. On the one hand, we have writers like Bonaventura who without interdict transferred to the Virgin the highest expressions of trust and self-surrender given in the Psalter to Jehovah and others like Alphonso Liguori who celebrate her glories in the most extravagant language possible to men. On the other hand, we have more candid philosophic theologians like Möhler who barely mention her name and, when they speak of the invocation of saints, are careful to say that the Council of Trent does not actually enjoin it as a duty but only reminds us that "it is useful and salutary."[1]

Yet it is very manifest that these practices and doctrines have at present a growing currency in the Church of Rome. The Jesuit professor of theology whom we have often quoted, gives a notable illustration. He himself evidently regards the historic basis of the idea of the Virgin's Assumption to heaven as a worthless legend. But he nevertheless says that "the belief in the bodily assumption of our Lady after her death has long been generally accepted in the Church and cannot be questioned without rashness."[2] "No one can prudently accept the story unless he believes that God's providence secures the Church from error; and no one who believes that the Church is our infallible guide can prudently doubt it."[3] He even ventures to add: "There is reason to think that had the sittings of the Vatican Council in 1870 been prolonged, the doctrine would have been defined as an article of faith." This consummation of the Romish system seems inevitable sooner or later. It needs no prophetic eye to see that, when it is reached, the Church will either have a victorious conflict for the first elements of Christian fact and evangelic truth or will sink farther back into the slough of a Christianised paganism.

[1] *Symbolik*, s. 449.
[2] Hunter, vol. ii. p. 586.
[3] Hunter, vol. ii. p. 587.

INDEXES

I. INDEX OF TEXTS

	PAGE		PAGE		PAGE
Gen. i. 26	15	Matt. xxvi. 27	207	1 Cor. iii. 15	88
,, i. 31	14	,, xxviii. 20	221	,, xi. 25	175
,, iii. 15	241, 244	Mark i. 15	42	2 Cor. v. 19	52
Deut. viii. 3	100	Luke xi. 32	131	Gal. i. 20	55, 69
,, xii. 32	181	,, xiii. 3–5	42	Eph. i. 23	165
Ps. xiv. 3	21	,, xvii. 7–10	81	,, ii. 18	64, 107
,, li. 10	59	,, xxii. 17	175	,, iv. 17–19	22
,, xcv. 9	239, 243	,, xxii. 25	234	Phil. ii. 10	88
Prov. xxx. 6	181	,, xxii. 31, 32	213, 216	2 Thess. ii. 15	142
Eccles. vii. 9	15	John i. 13	27	,, iii. 6	142
Isa. xi. 10	239, 243	,, iii. 6	21	1 Tim. iii. 15	101, 115, 165, 222, 225
Jer. xiii. 23	27	,, vi. 52–58	205		
,, xvii. 9	22	,, viii. 36	235	2 Tim. iii. 16	116
,, xxiii. 6	51	,, xx. 22, 23	64, 65, 172	Heb. iv. 12	99
,, xxxiii. 16	51	,, xxi. 15–17	213, 217	,, x. 26	208
Matt. iii. 1	42	Acts xvii. 28	15	Jas. i. 13	36
,, v. 29	87	,, xx. 28	165	,, iii. 2	78
,, vii. 17, 18	30	Rom. iii. 21–24	48	1 Pet. i. 2	72
,, xii. 32	87	,, iii. 26–28	52	,, i. 23	60
,, xv. 6	131	,, iii. 31	54	,, iii. 18–20	88
,, xvi. 18, 19	165, 213, 216, 221	,, iv. 5	52	2 Pet. i. 20	109
		,, iv. 25	51	1 John i. 8	62
,, xvii. 12	26	,, v. 19	52	,, v. 16	63
,, xviii. 18	64, 65	,, vi. 12	61	Jude 24	73
,, xxii. 21	235	,, vi. 23	81	Rev. xii. 1	241, 244
,, xxvi. 26	175	,, vii. 7, 18, 24	62	,, xxi. 27	88

II. INDEX OF SUBJECTS

ADOPTION, 68.
Assurance, 69–72.

BAPTISM, the entrance into the Church, 39; indispensable to salvation, 196; Romish rites, 195; effects claimed, 39, 40, 196; Baptism and Faith, 197.

INDEX OF SUBJECTS

CHURCH, as a saving institute, 39; *nature* of, 159; invisible Church, 165; notes of, 160, 168; *constitution* of, 200; different forms, 210; distinctive features of Romish Church, 211; the primacy of Peter, 212-215; Protestant objections, 215-218; *teaching of Church*, 219; necessity for infallible teacher, 220; the Church the divine instructress, 221; infallibility of Pope as defined at Vatican Council, 222; Protestant views, 224-226; the Spirit the only infallible teacher, 227; *authority of Church*, 228; grounds of Papal supremacy, 228; influences that promoted it, 230, 231; extent of Papal authority, 232; Protestant objections, 234-236; *worship* of Church, 178-186.
Confession, 64.
Consecration, 69.
Contrition, 64.
Counsels of perfection, 77.

DEATH, state after, 84; conquered by Christ, 89; of Christian, 90.
Development, theory of, 145; its origin in Kantian Rationalism, 148; first promulgated by Möhler, 149; defined by Newman, 150; arguments against it, 153-156.
Doctrine, its source in Scripture, 100; forms in which it is found in Scripture, 121; harmonious views of Protestant Churches, 145; Protestant method of development, 147.

ELECTION, 72.

FAITH, its nature, 43: its relation to justification, 52; its relation to Baptism, 197.
Forgiveness of sins, 46; Luther's experience, 47.

HEAVEN, entrance into, 90.

IMAGES, worship of, 239.

JUSTIFICATION, Romish view, 48, 49; Protestant view, 51; justification by faith, 52; objections to Protestant view, 54; counter-objections to Romish view, 55.

KINGDOM of God, as preached by the Lord, 41; its relation to Christ and the Church, 41.

MAN, as created, 11, 16; primitive condition, 14; made in the image of God, 15; as fallen, 17; total depravity, 21, 27; inability through sin, 24; works of natural man, 30.
Mass, Romish doctrine, 203; Protestant examination, 204.
Merit, *meritum de congruo*, 29; its relation to reward, 82; of good works, 82.
Ministry, 170; Romish views, 171, 172; Protestant views, 177.

PERSEVERANCE, 73.
Peter, primacy of, Romish views, 212; Protestant objections, 215.
Pope, infallibility of, 222; primacy, 212; supremacy, 228, 230.
Prayers for the dead, 186.
Priest, meaning of, 176; origin of priesthood, 173; Romish view of dignity, 172, 173; growth of priestly theory, 174.
Private judgment, 106.
Protest at Speier, terms of, 4; its significance, 5; its principles, 7.
Protestantism, different views of, 6; its real nature, 6; its three main principles, 7, 8.

REAL presence, 200; Protestant examination of, 205.
Reformation, causes of, 1.
Regeneration, Romish views of man's, 58; of instrument, 59; of effect, 60; of progress, 63; Protestant views of origin, 59; man passive in it, 59; real nature of, 61.
Religion, nature of, 1.
Repentance, its nature, 42, 43.
Reward, Protestant views of, 81.

SACRAMENTS, nature of, 187; elements, 188; number, 189; operation, 190; necessity, 191; Protestant views, 192-194.
Saints, worship of, 237.
Sanctification, 67.
Satisfaction, 64.
Scriptures, origin of the Latin translation, 95; their authority and use in Middle Ages, 30, 96; mediæval method of interpretation, 97; new view of meaning and contents before and at Reformation, 98; Protestant use of, 99, 109; *Responsibility of Christian towards*, 102; this respon-

sibility defined, 106; the grounds of it stated, 107; *Authority of Scripture*, 111; differences on authority defined, 113; Romish views of source of authority, 113; Protestant view, 115; *Perspicuity of Scripture*, 119; Romish views, 120; preliminary objection to them, 120; grounds on which it is held, 123; claimed in Scripture itself, 124; perfection of Scripture, 127; Romish views, 128; objections to Romish views, 129-131; grounds of Protestant view, 135-137.

Sin, in relation to divine providence, 32; sense of sin, 45; guilt of sin, 51; venial and mortal sin, 62; post-baptismal sin, 63.

Speier, first diet of, 2; second diet, 3.

Supper, Lord's, Romish rites, 200; real presence, 201; transubstantiation, 201; worship of elements, 201; communion in one kind, 202; the Supper as a sacrifice, 203; Protestant views of, 204, 209.

TRADITION, origin of, 138; three classes of tradition, 128; written and un-written, 128; objections to nature and use, 129-131, 135-137; erection of tradition into standard, 139; Romish pleas for tradition examined, 141-144.

Transubstantiation, 201; Protestant examination of, 205.

VIRGIN MARY, worship of, 240-242; Protestant objections, 243-244.

WORKS, good, of natural man, 30; obligation of, 74; sense of the term good, 75; Romish views of possibility, 76; of their merit, 79; of their influence on others, 82; Protestant views, 77, 80; works of supererogation, 77, 79.

Worms, diet of, 2.

Worship, Romish changes on, 179; Protestant objections to innovations, 181; additional pleas of Romanists examined, 183; practice of the Free Churches, 184; Anglican views, 185; prayers for the dead, 186; worship of saints, 237; of images, 239; of Virgin Mary, 240; Protestant objections, 242-246.

III. INDEX OF WRITERS

AQUINAS, on authority of Scripture, 96; on number of sacraments, 190.
Augustine, on bondage of will, 33.

BANNERMAN, D., on nature of Church, 182.
Bannerman, J., on mode of worship, 182.
Bellarmin, on primitive condition, 13; on assurance, 70.
Butler, Archer, on duration of the Papacy, 236.

CALVIN, on inability of man, 24; on sin of Judas, 35; on order of repentance, 43; on testimony of spirit with the word, 116; on tradition, 133; on mode of worship, 181.
Candlish, R. S., on adoption, 169.
Cunningham, on inability of man as inherited, 28; on nature of faith, 52; on assurance, 71; on authority of Scripture, 112; on development of doctrine, 154; on primacy of Peter, 212; on worship of images, 243.

DALE, R. W., on private judgment, 106.
D'Aubigné, on diet of Speier, 3.
Delitzsch, Fr., on effect of death on spiritual life, 91.
De Maistre, on theory of development, 149; on supremacy of Pope, 234.
Di Bruno, on mortal and venial sin, 63; on infallibility of Church, 220.
Dorner, J. A., on principles of Protestantism, 8; on Luther's view of Scripture, 111.

GILLESPIE, G., on mode of worship, 185.
Gladstone, W. E., on intervention of the Church, 162.

HALLAM, on origin of Reformation, 2.
Hodge, C., on origin of Purgatory, 86; on tradition, 143.
Hunter, S. J., on condition of man as fallen, 20; on justification, 51; on praying for the dead, 186; on offering of Eucharist, 202; on primacy of

INDEX OF WRITERS

Peter, 212, 213; on Papal infallibility, 220-223; on Papal supremacy, 231, 232; on immaculate conception of virgin, 240; on assumption of virgin, 246.

Jacob, G. A., on Christian ministry, 175.

Keble, on tradition, 144.
Kurtz, on Lutheran mode of worship, 180, 185.

Laud, on authority of Scripture, 141.
Lewis, Taylor, on total depravity, 22.
Lightfoot, J. B., on Christian ministry, 174, 177.
Litton, on nature of Church, 162, 163.
Luther, statement at diet of Worms, 2; on diet of Speier, 5; on justification by faith, 48; on good works, 75; on word of God, 100; on study of Scripture, 102, 104; on worship, 180; on ceremonies, 183.

Manning, Cardinal, on effects of baptism, 41; on supremacy of Pope, 232, 235.
Möhler, J. A., on primitive condition of man, 11; on man as fallen, 19; on sin in relation to Providence, 33; on assurance, 72; on good works, 75, 76; on Protestant view of Christian's death, 90; on infallibility of Church, 113; on priority of Scripture, 142; on development of doctrine, 149; on visible Church, 162, 166; on number of sacraments, 191; on the Church's right to offer sacrifice, 203; on communion in one kind, 207; on infallibility of Church, 221.

Mozley, on perspicuity of Scripture, 125.

Newman, on Protestantism, 104; on private judgment, 108; on perspicuity of Scripture, 120; on development of doctrine, 150-153; on baptism, 191; on papal supremacy, 230; on dignity of virgin, 241.
Nitzsch, C. I., on priority of Scripture, 134.

Preuss, on immaculate conception of Virgin, 245.

Rainy, R., on primitive condition of man, 16; on development of doctrine, 148.
Ritschl, on social principle of Protestantism, 8.

Schaff, on social principle of Protestantism, 8.
Smith, W. R., on what history teaches us to find in Bible, 99.

Taylor, Jeremy, on invisible Church, 167.
Turretin, on divine government of sin, 37.

Vilmar, on faith, 44.

Wiseman, Cardinal, on authority of Church and Scripture, 113; on perspicuity of Scripture, 119; on authority of Church, 129.

Zwingli, on image of God, 106.

www.ingramcontent.com/pod-product-compliance
Lightning Source LLC
Chambersburg PA
CBHW021354230426
43666CB00006B/523